# BETWEEN TWO WATERS

# BETWEEN TWO ≈ WATERS

## Narratives of Transculturation in Latin America

Silvia Spitta

Rice University Press
Houston, TX

Requests for permission to reproduce material from this work should be addressed to
    Rice University Press
    Post Office Box 1892
    Rice University
    Houston, Texas 77251


LIBRARY OF CONGRESS CATALOGING-IN-PUBLICATION DATA

Spitta, Silvia, 1956–
    Between two waters : narratives of transculturation in Latin America /
Silvia Spitta.
        p.        cm.
    Includes bibliographical references and index.
    ISBN 0-89263-321-2
    1. Latin American literature—History and criticism.
2. Intercultural communication.   3. Acculturation.   I. Title.
PQ7081.S72   1993
860.9'98—dc20                                        93-11346
                                                     CIP

## Tamalitos de Cambray

(receta para 5,000,000 de tamalitos)
—a Eduardo y Helena que me pidieron
una receta salvadoreña

Dos libras de masa de mestizo
media libra de lomo gachupín
cocido y bien picado
una cajita de pasas beata
dos cucharadas de leche de Malinche
una taza de agua bien rabiosa
un sofrito con cascos de conquistadores
tres cebollas jesuitas
una bolsita de oro multinacional
dos dientes de dragón
una zanahoria presidencial
dos cucharadas de alcahuetes
manteca de indios de Panchimalco
dos tomates ministeriales
media taza de azúcar televisora
dos gotas de lava del volcán
siete hojas de pito
(no seas malpensado es somnífero)
lo pones todo a cocer
a fuego lento
por quinientos años
y verás qué sabor.

## Little Cambray Tamales

(makes 5,000,000 little tamales)
—for Eduardo and Helena, who asked me
for a Salvadoran recipe

Two pounds of mestizo cornmeal
half a pound of loin of *gachupin*
cooked and finely chopped
a box of pious raisins
two tablespoons of Malinche milk
one cup of enraged water
a fry of conquistador helmets
three Jesuit onions
a small bag of multinational gold
two dragon's teeth
one presidential carrot
two tablespoons of pimps
lard of Panchimalco Indians
two ministerial tomatoes
a half cup of television sugar
two drops of volcanic lava
seven leaves of *pito*
(don't be dirty-minded, it's a soporific)
put everything to boil
over a slow fire
for five hundred years
and you'll see how tasty it is.

CLARIBEL ALEGRÍA, *Women of the River.*
Transl. D. J. Flakoll

# CONTENTS

# ACKNOWLEDGMENTS

Like all texts, this book could be read for its autobiographical elements, but it should also be read for the traces so many friends have left in it—sometimes unwittingly—over the years.

It all began as a dissertation at the University of Oregon, and although it became an altogether different book, my advisors Juan Epple and Steven Rendall are responsible for its early conceptualization. Many discussions over the years with my dear friends Linda Kintz, Karla Schultz, Maria De Priest, and Jane Todd have shaped my thinking in more ways than they will ever know.

At Dartmouth, Raúl Bueno has read everything I put on his desk, always commenting with kindness and insight; Diana Taylor's reflections on performance have taught me many things, including how not to get bored in academia; Susanne Zantop, a critical, yet patient reader has somehow managed to unravel my transcultural syntax and, amidst cafecitos and dinners with 1/2, has kept me going. Carol Bardenstein and Hani Azzam, very necessary friends, have helped me tackle (and survive) the intricacies of New England rural life.

Throughout the years, Alberto Sandoval, with his immense intellectual and personal courage, has been a steady source of inspiration and laughter.

This book also owes a great deal to all the people who helped me gather materials from near and afar. Talking about pigs and politics, Patsy Carter and Marianne Hraibi at Baker Library have consistently made every effort to locate materials from all too-often arcane sources. Barbara Reed has passed on everything regarding the Cuzco School that crossed her path. My colleagues Patricia Greene and José Colmeiro photographed the archangels in Salamanca; in Lima, Leonor and Tomás Unger tracked down books on Peruvian colonial art.

Lois Parkinson Zamora is ultimately responsible for the publication of this book. Susan Bielstein, my editor at Rice Press, has been a pleasure to work with.

And most importantly, of course, my family: My mother Mayvor, with her endless supply of stories about Peruvian artisans and artists, taught me to see things I would have never seen. My brother Martin has always lent me a helping hand and an open house and, although so far away, has managed to live as if next door. And always, I have to thank Gerd for rushing me through my life (while I only manage to slow down his) and for sharing the practice of the everyday. I dedicate this book to Lou and Sean who know little yet about transculturation but wonder how one can spend so much time with it.

# BETWEEN TWO WATERS

# 1 ≈
# TRANSCULTURATION AND
# THE AMBIGUITY OF SIGNS
# IN LATIN AMERICA

*Throughout the world indigenous populations have had to reckon with the forces
of "progress" and "national" unification. The results have been both destructive
and inventive. Many traditions, languages, cosmologies, and values are lost,
some literally murdered; but much has simultaneously been invented and revived
in complex, oppositional contexts. If the victims of progress and empire are weak,
they are seldom passive.*

— JAMES CLIFFORD

In his speech "Yo no soy un aculturado" [I am not acculturated],
delivered in 1968, one year before his death, José María Arguedas explained
that all his literary, ethnographic, and personal efforts had been motivated
by the desire to live as a happy demon the life of the Andes and the cities, of
Quechua and Spanish, of magic and socialism, of animism and Christianity.
Arguedas attempted to expand the borders of the national, which had until
then excluded all but a small literate minority—what Ángel Rama referred
to as "la ciudad letrada" [the lettered city] [1]—to include all the heterogeneous cultures, languages, races, and bodies in that impossibility called "Perú."
Arguedas managed, to the extent possible for his time, to achieve this in his
work, but his incomplete final novel, *El zorro de arriba y el zorro de abajo,*
reveals the anguish and despair that resulted from the ultimate failure of his
attempt. This book is written in the wake of Arguedas's desire to live between two waters.

The same opposition that informed the life and work of Arguedas also
informs this book. On one side is acculturation, the sheer and irredeemable

loss of one's culture, language, history, tradition—even the body and its rhythms; on the other side is transculturation, the overcoming of loss by giving new shape to one's life and culture after the catastrophes of Conquest, colonization, and modernization.[2] Transculturation can thus be understood as the complex processes of adjustment and re-creation—cultural, literary, linguistic, and personal—that allow for new, vital, and viable configurations to arise out of the clash of cultures and the violence of colonial and neo-colonial appropriations. Crucial here is the Arguedian understanding of the intercultural dynamics that have arisen because of the Conquest. As Arguedas and others have pointed out, cultural influences, even if not equivalent in force, nevertheless do not flow unidirectionally. It is this point that theories of assimilation tend to overlook. The difference between describing an event such as the Conquest as an "encounter" and describing it as a "catastrophe" not only brings to the fore ideological questions implicit in our use of language, but also puts into evidence the fact that if both the colonized and the colonizer are asserted to change in a colonial situation, they nevertheless change at a different rate and with a different sense of urgency. The issue here, as for Arguedas, is that of explaining how indigenous cultures such as the Andean, threatened with extinction, have managed not only to survive, but even in some cases to thrive, despite such destruction. This question has acquired renewed urgency in light of that event staged as "1992," during which so many indigenous groups from North and South America, all independently of one another, stated with both sadness and amazement: "We are still here after five hundred years." That Rigoberta Menchú won the Nobel Prize for Peace can be attributed not only to the fact that the Swedish Academy finally did something right, but also to the fact that this phrase was repeated so many times during that year and that it was perhaps heard by many.

The extreme difficulty of pinpointing or understanding what actually occurred with the Conquest explains the profusion of terms that have been used to attempt an approximation of this catastrophe: acculturation, adaptation, assimilation, melting pot, Manifest Destiny, degradation, "bad" or literal translation on the one hand; and transculturation, miscegenation, métissage, hybridization, syncretism, resemanticization, de- and re-territorialization, heterogeneity, displacement, and "good" or creative translation on the other. It is no accident that there is such a proliferation of terms, nor that these terms are such a mouthful, for the dynamics they attempt to describe are truly complex. They are terms with long histories. The first group was mobilized in the interests of the colonizers to justify domination, and the latter, more recently, in the interests of the colonized and of decolonization. And it is no accident that I, writing in the mid 1990s, deploy them here in the interests of a more inclusive form of literary criticism. However, since many of these terms are so often used interchangeably or in different and contradictory contexts, it will be necessary to explain why I have chosen to favor one—transculturation—over the others, and how I deploy and redefine the term.

### Transculturation: A Cuban Theory

In the 1940s Fernando Ortiz, a Cuban anthropologist, coined the term "transculturation." His was a specifically Latin American reading—or a culturally motivated misreading—of the ideological metatext of the term "acculturation," which was coming into vogue among North American anthropologists at that time. Whereas the theorists of acculturation had envisioned that process as one of interaction and mutual influence between cultures, Ortiz understood it from a Latin American perspective as a theory that described the one-way imposition of the culture of the colonizers. In fact, "acculturation" was first defined systematically by Redfield, Linton, and Kerskovits in the 1930s as follows: "Acculturation comprehends those phenomena which result when groups of individuals having different cultures come into continuous firsthand contact, with subsequent changes in the original cultural patterns of either or both groups."[3] However, Ortiz's suspicions of the term have been proven right. Even if "acculturation" initially was used to refer to the process of mutual interaction and change in cultures that come into contact with one another, it has nevertheless been used mostly to stress the one-way imposition of the dominant culture, since anthropologists generally study the impact of acculturation on the colonized. Given this anthropological praxis, acculturation has often been used synonymously with assimilation to signify the loss of culture of the subordinate group.[4] Bronislaw Malinowski, who in the preface to Ortiz's *Contrapunteo cubano del tabaco y el azúcar* enthusiastically endorsed Ortiz's use of the term, never made use of the concept in his own publications.[5] Even a general Spanish dictionary corroborates Ortiz's critique. Acculturation is defined as "s. civilización, instrucción, educación, transmisión de cultura" [civilization, instruction, education, transmission of culture].[6]

Ortiz created the neologism "transculturation" to undermine the homogenizing impact implicit in the term "acculturation," which in his view obfuscated the true dynamics at work in colonial situations. Instead, Ortiz insisted on understanding intercultural dynamics as a two-way *toma y daca* (give and take). Like Arguedas, who declared "yo no soy un aculturado," Ortiz countered the one-way imposition of culture implicit in the term acculturation, which would attribute all the losses only to the subjected side, and defined transculturation in Cuba as a three-fold process: the partial loss of culture by each immigrant group (he included African slaves in this group of "immigrants"), the concomitant assimilation of elements from other cultures (European, African, and Asian), and finally, the creation of a new, Cuban, culture.[7] Since foreign influences were invariably present, and continue to be so, the "new" culture, however, is never achieved: it is forever in the making, inevitably deferred. The "new" could be said to refer to the distance that mediates between an African in Africa and a Cuban of African-European-Asian descent. It is in this sense an explanation of *difference from* the originary cultures rather than a descriptive term. As Ortiz explains, employing the biological terms so prevalent at the time, "la criatura siempre tiene algo de ambos progenitores, pero también siempre es distinta de cada uno de los dos" [the child always inherits something from both parents, but is also always different from each one of them].[8]

Ortiz's *Contrapunteo* situates the discussion of transculturation within the social and economic dynamics that arise out of the production of tobacco and sugar in Cuba. Tobacco—indigenous, dark, and gendered male by Ortiz—is a labor-intensive crop traditionally grown on small farms along the banks of rivers and tended by individual families. Sugar—imported, white, and gendered female—is a product grown on immense *latifundios* (plantations) and requires a large labor force at peak times. An exogenous product, a white product—literally and figuratively—sugar was the reason why African slaves were brought to Cuba and why African culture became preponderant in Cuba. The two crops, according to Ortiz, give rise to two very different types of social and economic conditions on the island: tobacco is grown on a small scale, usually by one family, using few or no machines, and requiring continual care year round. The production of sugar, on the other hand, is highly centralized, mechanized, and depersonalized. Tobacco is one of the few vestiges of the original island culture, whereas sugar is imported and stands for foreignness; it is the "agricultural equivalent of empire."[9] The tension between them gives rise to and at the same time characterizes

Cuban culture. At a more general level, the history of each product is also the history of transculturation: sugar, a white import, has changed the landscape of Cuba while tobacco, a native Cuban crop, has changed the leisure habits of the rest of the world.[10] Together with alcohol (rum), sugar and tobacco form the holy trinity of Cuban exports, commodities of pleasure and indulgence.[11]

It is no accident that Ortiz used the term "counterpoint" as a synonym for transculturation, since he was interested in showing that African and European elements are of equal importance in the shaping of "Cuba." Because the term counterpoint "comes from the Latin *contrapunctus,* properly *punctus contra punctum,* meaning 'note against note' or, by extension, 'melody against melody,'" it was a fitting symbol for the process Ortiz wanted to underline.[12] Critics have followed Ortiz in using music as a referent for the intercultural dynamics of Latin America, perhaps because the processes of transculturation are so clearly exemplified in music. Furthermore, the difference between cultures is often most readily seen in the distinctive ways that they shape bodies and their rhythms.

The use of "counterpoint," no matter how well it may serve Ortiz's project, is, however, deeply problematic. For the musicologist, counterpoint pertains specifically to Western polyphonic music, particularly, for example, the compositions of Palestrina and Bach. In this sense, Ortiz's discussion of polyrhythmic Afro-Cuban music in terms of counterpoint hardly seems apt. But more importantly, perhaps, counterpoint in music theory refers to a distinctive characteristic of the notes or melodies that through their tension fuse into a musical composition: their equality. Counterpoint then would seem to be a singularly inadequate metaphor through which to explore transculturation, since it inevitably precludes attention to unequal relations of power.

Using the term more loosely, however, to refer to the subtextual tension of any musical composition and, by extension, to the cultural configuration of Cuba, counterpoint suggests not so much the note-against-note structure of contrapuntal musical compositions, but an African subtext and rhythm in a more general contrapuntal relationship to European music and culture. As Stuart Hall points out,

Africa, the signified which could not be represented directly in slavery, remained and remains the unspoken, unspeakable "presence" in Caribbean culture. It is "hiding" behind every verbal inflection, every narrative twist of Caribbean cultural life. It is the secret code with which every Western text was "re-read." It is the ground-bass of every rhythm and bodily movement. *This* was—is—the "Africa" that "is alive and well in the Diaspora."[13]

In the end, it is this expanded, transculturated, metaphorical notion of counterpoint that operates in Ortiz's texts.

However, in his concern to counter the image of colonized peoples as passive recipients of a dominant colonizing culture, Ortiz repeatedly tends to overlook imbalances of power. Just as his musical metaphor suggests equal power relations, Ortiz follows this tendency in his deployment of gendered metaphors that also assume equality. In his appeal to the family and to relations between the sexes as a model for transculturation, women and men, mothers and fathers, although physiologically different, are assumed to be equal. Women and men, however, are never equal when it comes to power—particularly in a colonial context based on the violence of one race over another and one gender over another. Modern Latin America is not—as Ortiz seems to assume—the product of a happy marriage of differences.

Although Ortiz proposed that his theory could explain any encounter between two cultures,[14] therefore making claims for its universal validity, we need to understand it as a specifically Cuban theory. In fact, Cuba, and the Antilles more generally, are a special phenomenon within Latin America, not only because of their insularity but also because their indigenous populations were completely wiped out in the early years of the Conquest. Their inhabitants now consist almost exclusively of immigrants: Europeans, descendants of African slaves, Asians, and North Americans.[15] It is in this context that Ortiz's theory of transculturation has to be situated. This is a significant point that needs to be stressed, because even though the term "transculturation" can be useful in describing the dynamics of cultural contact very generally, it must continually be redefined for specific contexts. The Andean nations, for example, where the population is still mainly indigenous, provide a context very different from that of Cuba, as do marginalized cultures in the United States today, such as those of African-Americans, Native Americans, Latinos, and Asian-Americans.

Ortiz's reinterpretation and reconstruction of Cuba went against a long tradition of the "whitening" of Latin American culture.[16] In his endeavor to bring to light precisely those roots and cultural elements—the African—that were, and to a great extent still are, erased and repressed in Cuba, his work has served as a precursor to much contemporary revisionist Latin American scholarship, as my analysis of Arguedas's work will show.

## Transculturation: An Andean Theory

Although Arguedas adopted Ortiz's term "transculturation," he redefined the word to make it applicable to Perú. In that country, unlike in Cuba, the indigenous population, although ravaged, managed to survive—and in some cases to thrive—even under such harsh conditions as those imposed by the colonizers. As I mentioned above and as I will discuss further in chapter 5, Arguedas devoted his life to explaining how and why certain groups had managed to persist while others had not, as well as to tracing the transformations, many of them very violent, that were taking place in Perú during his lifetime.

In his comparative studies of Andean communities, Arguedas found that in those regions that thrived, natives and Spaniards had intermarried and worked together as a group—that is, had transculturated. In these places, the stark confrontations between master and slave, Spaniard and Andean, oppressor and oppressed, the written and the oral, and the city and the rural areas had not, for one reason or another, been instituted. Areas that had remained accessible since the Conquest to influences from the West developed what he called "antibodies" to modernization, whereas isolated regions where Andean and Spaniard had remained opposed over the centuries disintegrated with the advent of new technologies. That is, communities that had been vital and that had transculturated were strong and actually benefited economically from the building of the Central Highway and the improvement of communications in the 1930s. In isolated areas, on the other hand, indigenous communities could not resist the impact of modernization and were forced to leave in search of a livelihood in the metropolitan centers of the coast.[17]

Shattering the elite's perception of the popular classes as a homogeneous, indistinguishable mass, Arguedas's ethnographic studies of the shantytowns that emerged as a result of this migration showed that Andean immigrants tended to regroup there according to origin. They thereby managed to continue the life of their communities in a transplanted space that merges both easily and uneasily with the space of mass culture.[18] The phenomenon of *chicha* exemplifies the new cultural configurations that arise out of the confluence of mass and traditional Andean cultures. Chicha, the most popular music in Perú in the last decade, is a fusion of Andean and tropical (Afro-Hispanic) elements. "It reflects mass Andean immigration to the coastal cities and resignifies both traditions. [The] fusion of the Andean and the modern urban occurs at every level." [19]

Andean migrations to the cities of the coast not only brought with them a change in musical compositions and musical taste, but also changed the urban landscape of metropolitan centers such as Lima, which since the 1970s has become increasingly "Andeanized." Before these migrations, the center of the city coincided with the center of power—the "ciudad letrada." Today, the centers of power have been displaced to the suburbs, and the center of the city has been largely taken over by Andean immigrants whose commercial activities take place on the sidewalks next to the big banks, yet operate at their margins. The place of power and the place from which a Peruvian intellectual speaks have also ceased to coincide [20]—which means that the formerly taken-for-granted idea of the nation defined by and for a minority is now, literally, under siege. Furthermore, Arguedas's ethnographic studies show that he went against a long Western tradition in which the gaze of the folklorist or the searcher for the exotic tended to petrify "primitive" cultures in space and time. He discards the nineteenth-century ideal of the "primitive" as the place where the West would find its own childhood.

Arguedas's findings and the increasing complexity of his fiction (from the stark master/slave opposition in his early collection of stories *Agua,* to the convoluted world of *El zorro de arriba y el zorro de abajo,* in which he depicts the lives of migrants in a booming coastal town) necessarily give rise to new conceptions of culture and literature. The first, crucial to this book, is the notion of cultures as being always in flux. In fact, Arguedas believed that a culture that becomes static is doomed. Likewise, a rigid imperial power, a power unwilling or unable to absorb foreign elements, is not viable. Vital cultures invariably and necessarily transform themselves over time and under the impact of foreign influences. The second conception is that since cultures are not static, subjectivity and identity—particularly for Latin America and other colonial contexts—must be understood as historical and cultural constructs that are always in flux, split between two or more worlds, cultures, and languages. And finally, if the characters depicted in novels and if the subjectivities of writers are assumed to be split and in flux, then one also must call for the creation of new types of readers. That is, readers who are capable of reading at least biculturally and bilingually and who thus do not read Latin American novels and narratives monologically.

Arguedas's ethnographic and novelistic project was monumental in that he tried to depict a Perú in all its diversity and with all of its contradictions, and to do so without marginalizing or excluding any one group. An impossible project to be sure, but one that in all its open-endedness and final dissolution (witness *El zorro de arriba y el zorro de abajo*) has nevertheless given rise to numerous reflections on contemporary Latin American literature, literary history, ethnography, and culture. The most important of these is Ángel Rama's *Transculturación narrativa en América Latina,* which takes as its point of departure Arguedas's ethnographic and novelistic portrayal of the split and bicultural world of Perú. Rama attempts to redefine "transculturation" in order to analyze the processes at work in a Latin American literature that consciously situates itself at a cultural intersection: between different ethnicities and linguistic traditions (Quechua, Guaraní, indigenous Mexican, and Afro-Brazilian on the one side and creole/Spanish and Portuguese on the other); between different geographic areas ("retrograde" rural areas and "modern," rapidly acculturating metropolitan centers); between different literary movements (avant-garde and diverse and unsuccessful regionalisms and *indigenismos*[21]); and between different conceptions of the literary (written and oral). All of these processes came to the fore in the period between the two world wars, which saw the greatest modernizing impact in Latin America. Authors such as Guimarães Rosa, Rulfo, García Márquez, Roa Bastos, and Arguedas, whom Rama calls "los transculturadores," again creating a neologism, take on the task of *mediating* between the different fields of tension created by the diverse cultures, languages, and worlds that coexist in different relations of power in their countries. Their project—like that of their well-known predecessor Guamán Poma[22]—is truly radical, since they appropriate the nineteenth-century European realist novel in order to write about a world exterior to that novel.

The impact of industrialization between the two world wars presented Latin Americans with the drastic choice of either modernizing—that is, acculturating and renouncing their traditions (the ridiculous adoption of Santa Claus—snow, sled, and all—in the tropics is but one example)—or becoming culturally obsolete. In light of this, the transculturating impulse is one in which writers, echoing what was taking place at the level of general culture, take what they can use from Western literary forms in order to save what they can from the traditional, rural, and oral cultures of their countries. That is, they produce an engaged literature, one that opts for the poor and that attempts to mediate between the "first" and the "third" worlds—globally as well as within their own countries. Hence these writers appropriate the novel in order to write about an indigenous mythic, ritual, and oral culture. Under the impact of these "new" worlds, the form of the nineteenth-century European realist and naturalist novels begins to give way and change radically. That is, in the process of appropriating a form and forcing it to conform to an alien referent, these writers fundamentally alter the form of the novel.

The transculturators also take Spanish and Portuguese as signs of the erudite from which they want to distance themselves, and in the most successful cases they invent a new literary language marked by the impact of indigenous languages such as Quechua and Guaraní. That is, they overcome the limitations of the regionalist and indigenista movements by diminishing the distance between the language of the narrator and that of the characters. Where once the narrators had expressed themselves in "good" Spanish and the indigenous characters in "bad" Spanish, thereby affirming those very same class differences that indigenista writers claimed to undermine novelistically, the narrators now speak in much the same way as do the Peruvian-Indian or mestizo characters in the novel. The difference then is that between a novelistic point of view that situates itself as superior and distant to the world it describes—a folklorist position—and a more interior vision that is closer to the referent. The former had been the perspective of indigenista and regionalist writings of little sophistication. These were destined for European and North American readers who expected and got an exotic view of Latin America, as well as for Latin American elites whose hegemony was justified by such works. The latter produced a literature for internal consumption and for readers who, like the authors themselves, positioned themselves between two or more worlds and were interested in literature as a potential mechanism of vindication.

Furthermore, previous indigenistas had focused on idealized versions of the Incas—all situated in the glorious and safely distant and archival past—and therefore had much too easily overlooked the misery that characterized Andean life at that time. The transculturators, by contrast, focus on the present and on current problems.[23] However, given the problems of literacy in Latin America, the works of the transculturators are once again located in some intermediate space between what José Carlos Mariátegui called "indigenista literature" (a literature about the Indians) and a literature by and for the Indians—a project of the future and a literature still to come.[24]

As I will argue throughout this book, the texts of the transculturators, as well as Rama's analysis of their works, open the door to a radical rewriting of the Latin American literary tradition. It no longer can be read according to the codes of one culture alone, because the signifier is split between two or more cultures and becomes unstable. In the novels of transculturation, one can see the coexistence of at least two different cosmologies and systems of logic operating in parallel within the very narration and—as I will argue—within the narrators themselves. They no longer posit themselves as the unifying bourgeois conscience of the nineteenth-century novel, but rather as subjects irredeemably divided at least between two worlds, two languages, and two cultures. The narrative then becomes the representation of that original division of the bicultural Latin American subject.

The Peruvian critic Antonio Cornejo Polar, thinking along lines very similar to Rama's but avoiding that writer's culturalist approach, extends his argument to encompass all of Latin American literature. Arguedas, he notes, is the springboard for his reflections, since to study Arguedas's work is "una manera de definir cómo trabajar sobre nuestra literature" [a way of defining how to study our literature].[25] Unlike Rama, who focused his discussion of transculturation on the period of modernization between the two world wars and who favored a few novelistic transculturators, Cornejo Polar expands the margins of the discussion. He argues that Latin American literature, given the continent's history of conquest and colonization, cannot be any less heterogeneous than the disjointed cultures that gave rise to it. He characterizes such intrinsically heterogeneous literatures in the following way:

Caracteriza a las literaturas heterogéneas, pues, la duplicidad o pluralidad de los signos socio-culturales de su proceso productivo. Obedecen, en síntesis, a un proceso de producción en el que hay por lo menos un elemento que no coincide con la filiación de los otros . . . esta disparidad crea una zona de conflicto . . . [que] corresponde muy estrechamente al conflicto de sociedades no uniformes, partidas y bimembradas por la acción de una catástrofe histórica como puede ser la Conquista.

[Heterogeneous literatures are characterized by the duplicity or plurality of the socio-cultural signs of their productive process. In synthesis, they obey a process of production in which there is at least one element that does not coincide with the filiation of the others . . . this disparity creates a zone of conflict . . . [which] corresponds very closely to the conflict of nonuniform societies, societies split and torn asunder by the effects of a historical catastrophe of the magnitude of the Conquest.][26]

Important, as Cornejo Polar points out, is the fact that until very recently, the essentially heterogeneous character of Latin American literature was obscured. This obfuscation can be attributed primarily to the elite and erudite constitution of a critical apparatus that tended to examine only those texts that validated its own perspective. Whatever did not conform to its narrow parameters—conflated into definitions of "the national"—was marginalized. By positing the essentially heterogeneous character of Latin American literature, Cornejo Polar also opens up the very concept of what constitutes "the literary" and criticizes the elitist and racist underpinnings of those definitions.[27] "The national" and "the literary" are shown to have been the dream of a certain class and of the "white" minority in Latin America. By accepting the heterogeneity of Latin American literature, the critic not only must question the limited and limiting concept of "the national," but also must include into the domain of the literary elements from the indigenous cultures that had previously been excluded. Returning to Mariátegui's assertion that a truly indigenous literature in Perú is still to come, we could argue that critics such as Cornejo Polar and Rama, by opening up our conception of the literary, are preparing the ground for including manifestations from previously marginalized oral, Andean cultures.[28] Of course, these critics owe much to redefinitions of the literary in Mesoamerica, where a rich literary tradition inherited from pre-Columbian days does exist.[29]

As I indicated above and as the focus on the Andean regions has shown, Ortiz's theory of transculturation needs to be redefined for specific cultural contexts and geopolitical situations. Transculturation is one thing for Cuba and it is quite another for Perú. My aim here is to analyze what happens to the theory of transculturation when it is appropriated by Cuban-American critics as they write both about Cuba and the Caribbean and about the newly emerging Cuban-American ethnicity. The route is circuitous: departing from Fernando Ortiz's 1940s Latin American response to North American theories, transculturation is today being redefined from the perspective of the United States. Cuban-American critics such as Gustavo Pérez Firmat and Antonio Benítez Rojo read Cuba as a nostalgic "there." They see it through the eyes/I's of a "here" that is only now being accepted as a place of residence and no longer as utopia; that is, no place of exile.[30] They are, on the one hand, returning to Ortiz, yet reinscribing transculturation with precisely those very connotations of assimilation that the theory was meant to combat. As a result, they replace "transculturation" with terms such as "translation" and "chaos." On the other hand, they take transculturation further than did Ortiz by creating a theory of the bicultural U.S. minority subject.

## Cuban Blues: Cuba and Ortiz Viewed from "Here"

As the title suggests, Gustavo Pérez Firmat's *The Cuban Condition: Translation and Identity in Modern Cuban Literature* is the elucidation of what he calls the "translational rather than foundational" nature of Cuban literature and culture—particularly that of the criollist/creole writers of the 1940s.[31] Antonio Benítez Rojo's *La isla que se repite: El Caribe y la perspectiva posmoderna,* dedicated to his "distant master" Fernando Ortiz, is in turn an attempt to postulate the overarching identity of the whole Caribbean using Cuba—or what he calls the "plantation machine"—as a paradigm. Both works, even though very different in nature, are similar in their theorization of a Cuban—and in the case of Benítez Rojo, a Caribbean—literature and in their use of Ortiz's theory of transculturation.

For Pérez Firmat, transculturation is translation. Etymologically, translation implies the carrying over, displacing, and transferring of meaning from one language into another. The term is therefore particularly appropriate with regard to geographical, cultural, and linguistic displacements. As Pérez Firmat writes, "translation [is] displacement. The intralingual translator is someone who knows that in order to pick his words, he has to keep his distance."[32] In *The Cuban Condition,* translation figures as a positive, creative endeavor. It is the process whereby Cubans take the language of the colonizer—Spanish—and infuse it with African and Asian elements, creating "cubanismos" or a vernacular Cuban different from peninsular Spanish. Ortiz himself insisted on speaking and writing in his own "Cuban" Spanish. Even such neologisms as "transculturation" and *ajiaco* (Cuban stew—Ortiz's specifically Cuban image for transculturation) are reactions to and transculturations of specifically North American theories such as those of acculturation and the melting pot.[33] As Pérez Firmat insists, Cuban writers use language to stake out their distance from the mother tongue and the motherland ("la Madre Patria") and thus inscribe "Cuban Spanish" as a national language. They do the same at the literary level: while they gain their inspiration from Spanish literature, they re-create it, or—what amounts to the same thing—they creatively translate and displace it into what becomes Cuban literature.

The most visible example of this process is Nicolás Guillén, who is known for his radical use of the vernacular in poetry. The titles of some of his poems (for example, "Sensemayá") and of his seminal collection of Afro-Cuban poems, *Sóngoro cosongo,* signal this move. As Pérez Firmat points out, however, Guillén also uses "learned" forms such as the sonnet and the madrigal and "translates" them into mulatto madrigals and mestizo sonnets.[34] In the poem "El abuelo," he addresses a woman in true courtly fashion, "¡Ah, mi señora!," and follows the European tradition dictated by classical rhetoric of directing the male gaze from the woman's head downward to her torso. But Guillén "blackens" the content of the poem by referring to the woman's African blood—embodied in her long-gone African grandfather—which underlies her European appearance. In this sense her grandfather, "el que te rizó por siempre tu cabeza amarilla" [the one who puts the curls in your golden head], is the grandfather of most Cubans.[35]

For Pérez Firmat then, translation—both linguistic and literary—is always intralingual (from Spanish to Cuban and from the Spanish literary tradition to a Cuban literary tradition). It is never passive or literal, but creative. To avoid too great a closeness to the source, a collapsing of the "copy" with the "original," the translator must deviate from the original "in perceptible ways."[36] It is in this sense that Pérez Firmat asserts that Cuban culture is characterized by a "translation sensibility." Skirting a discussion of loaded terms such as "original," "copy," and "intertextuality," he concludes that Cuban literature is translational rather than foundational.[37]

Pérez Firmat's choice of "translation" over "transculturation" is unfortunate, given the negative associations invariably elicited by the term "translation." As Willis Barnstone recently wrote in his *The Poetics of Translation: History, Theory, Practice,* in which he tries to valorize and redeem translation as a creative endeavor, "the shame of translation is real, alas, universal, even though superficial and absurd, more real and more traumatic than Harold Bloom's related 'anxiety of influence' (a similar dialogical battle between authors in a tradition)."[38] Not only is translation a negatively loaded term, but within the parameters Pérez Firmat establishes in *The Cuban Condition,* Spanish literature implicitly functions as foundational and nontranslational, whereas Cuban literature is considered derivative. As Barnstone points out, all literatures are translational, and to argue that one text is a translation whereas another is an original is to "obey a feudal principle of originality."[39] Furthermore, given that questions of authenticity, originality, derivativeness, and imitation-as-degeneration are all issues that have plagued Latin American literary and artistic histories, I think it is in our interest—as Latin American critics—to use Ortiz's "transculturation" to signify the two-way, multi-leveled cultural interchanges, borrowings, displacements, and recreations characteristic of both Latin American and European literatures, languages, and cultures.

Although Pérez Firmat insists that Cuban literature is receptively creative, his favoring of the term "translation" over "transculturation" is also problematic in that translation, like language, has served as the handmaiden of empire. Translations of the Bible into Quechua were used to evangelize indigenous populations in the Andean nations, and priests learned Quechua in order to gather information that was used in the attempt to eradicate the native religion. Moreover, translations of European literary texts in Latin America served to acculturate the literate elite to a European tradition. For the monocultural and monolingual reader, translation tends to reduce the Other to the familiar and effaces the text's difference, moving it into the domain of the reader.[40] When understood in these terms, translation loses its implied innocence and pretensions of equality, since the displacement and the transfer of meanings must then be situated within a context of inequality, exploitation, and violence. Moreover, in claiming an always-epigonic position for the Cuban writer—given in the translational rather than foundational status of Cuban literature—Pérez Firmat's argument undoes Ortiz's claim that culture contact is never unidirectional. "Transculturation," then, is a term we should keep, since it avoids these problems of translation and describes the dynamics of the colony from the position and the perspective of the colonized.

As I will show throughout this book, translation (if understood as both intra- and interlingual) is an important component of any transculturation. However, it is but one aspect of a series of very complex processes. To consider the whole issue of transculturation in terms of intralingual translation is to impoverish what is a very diverse and multilayered process. The transfer or translation, as we saw above, is seldom only intralingual. Usually it is accompanied by interlingual as well as transcultural processes that in Latin America, and particularly in the Andean nations, involve a transfer from an oral, Quechua-mestizo popular culture (as in *cultura popular*)[41] to a modernist, Western-shaped, and Western-oriented literary tradition. That is, the transfer of languages, meanings, and literary traditions takes place not only within one country (and within groups that stand in very different relations of power to one another), but also between two countries, one of which is in a relation of power and domination over the other. "Cuba" is therefore constituted out of imposed and chosen Spanish and European elements (which, as Ángel Rama pointed out, tend to be picked not from the mainstream but from the margins of those cultures), as well as elements from Africa, Asia, and other Latin American countries.

Antonio Benítez Rojo, in *La isla que se repite,* expands the margins of the discussion. Using Cuba as an example, he attempts to delimit "the Caribbean" as an entity with a singular identity. Although colonized by different powers (Spain, Holland, Britain, France, and Portugal), and therefore not only culturally but also linguistically divided, the Caribbean, he argues, is nevertheless a metaarchipelago of sorts—not only because it functions as a way station between North and South, but also because it shares an African inheritance and the socioeconomic structures of the plantation (in the form of sugar plantations). Benítez Rojo argues that although the plantation serves as a common denominator, regional differences must be attributed to the different rates by which plantations in the Caribbean have been institutionalized. Thus Spain, because its rate of industrialization was slower than that of the rest of Europe, did not institute a system of sugar plantations in Cuba until well into the eighteenth century. African slaves and freed Africans were by that time better integrated into Cuban society and therefore were an active presence in the Africanization of Cuba. However, in British colonies such as Barbados and Jamaica, where the plantation was instituted very early on, the islands were far less Africanized, even though, paradoxically, most of the population (more than 90%) were African slaves. On these islands the slaves were isolated on the plantations, and because the islands served the sole purpose of exporting sugar, they were organized accordingly. Cities in their own right, such as Havana, did not come into being until recently.[42]

Benítez Rojo derives the impetus for his study from a postmodern reading of—or from a search for the postmodern elements in—Ortiz's *Contrapunteo.* He argues that Ortiz's counterpoint between tobacco and sugar not only refers to these products, but also sets in motion a much larger metaphorical field: between myth and history, blacks and whites, slaves and plantation owners, art and machines, small rural landholdings with labor intensive crops and huge plantations, quality and quantity, national and foreign capital, independence and dependence, sovereignty and intervention, desire and repression, the discourse of power and that of resistance, the revolutionary and the reactionary.[43] But for Benítez Rojo, Ortiz's whole scheme ultimately can be reduced to the counterpoint between "las fábulas de legitimación propias de los Pueblos del Mar y de Occidente" [the fables of legitimation set forth respectively by the Peoples of the Sea (the Caribbean) and by the West]; that is, to the coexistence and interplay between premodern and modern elements in the Caribbean.[44] And it is this counterpoint that in turn takes precedence throughout *La isla que se repite* and that is used to affirm the identity of the Caribbean. The institutionalization of sugar planta- tions—what Benítez Rojo calls the plantation machine—is the single most important economic factor in the shaping of the Caribbean. The counter- point between tobacco and sugar is turned by Benítez Rojo into the coun- terpoint between the master narratives of Western modernity (particularly the discourse of scientific legitimation) and the praxis of premodern orality and immanence in Cuba.[45] The dichotomy between the modern and the primitive, the cooked and the raw, the West and the rest, is re-elaborated within a postmodern context—not of binary oppositions but of counter- points—in which fragmentation, instability, lack, noise, and chaos are em- phasized over totality, synthesis, acculturation, and miscegenation.[46]

However, for Benítez Rojo the counterpoint between modernity's nar- ratives of legitimation and those of premodern, oral cultures ultimately re- volves around two different conceptions and functions of rhythm. For the West, rhythm has become the one-two, one-two of imperialism, militarism, and scientific knowledge.[47] For premodern, oral cultures such as those that persist in Cuba, rhythm is carnivalesque, polyrhythmic (and resistant to no- tation), and intimately tied to a religion/cosmology that pervades every as- pect of life and endows the Word with the effectiveness and power it pos- sesses in oral cultures. It is this typically Caribbean rhythm that for Benítez Rojo creates a regional unity across the diversity of languages, cultures, races, histories, and economies prevailing in the area. Under the impact of that rhythm, the imperialism of rock or of big-band music, for example, is transformed into the mambo, cha-cha-cha, the bossa nova, the bolero, salsa, or reggae; which is to say that "la música del Caribe no se hizo anglosajona sino que ésta se hizo caribeña dentro de un juego de diferencias" [Caribbean music did not become Anglo-Saxon, but rather the latter became Caribbean within a play of differences].[48] To avoid the pitfalls of binary oppositions, Benítez Rojo always insists on the "play of differences" or the counter- point—in Ortiz's terms—between elements that are usually seen as opposed. Therefore, if something as elusive as rhythm can be seen as an underlying common thread that could be used to affirm a Caribbean identity—albeit tenuously—it is nevertheless operative in a field that is always in danger of being torn asunder by its cultural and linguistic differences. For Benítez

Rojo, it is the tension between one and the other, between centripetal and centrifugal forces, between modernity and premodernity, that could be said to define the Caribbean. That same tension also creates the undefinability of the Caribbean, which is embodied in a rhythm that defies notation and that ultimately eludes Benítez Rojo's own attempt to define it.

For Benítez Rojo there is neither synthesis nor syncretism; there is only an ill-defined "supersyncretism." It is a supersyncretism created by a process whereby

el significante de *allá*—el del Otro—es consumido (leído) conforme a códigos lo-cales, ya preexistentes; esto es, códigos de *acá*. Por eso podemos convenir en la conocida frase de que la China no se hizo budista sino que el budismo se hizo chino. En el caso del Caribe, es fácil ver que lo que llamamos cultura traditional se refiere a un *interplay* de significantes supersincréticos cuyos "centros" principales se locali-zan en la Europa preindustrial, en el subsuelo aborígen, en las regiones subsaharianas de Africa y en ciertas zonas insulares y costeras de Asia meridional.

[the signifier of *there*—of the Other—is consumed (read) according to local codes that are already in existence; that is, codes from *here*. Therefore we can agree on the well-known phrase that China did not become Buddhist but rather Buddhism be-came Chinese. In the case of the Caribbean, it is easy to see that what we call traditional culture refers to an *interplay* of supersyncretic signifiers whose principal "centers" are located in preindustrial Europe, in the sub-Saharan regions of Africa, and in certain island and coastal zones of southern Asia.] [49]

This "supersyncretism" refers to all the extraterritorial, cultural significa-tions embodied in one Cuban symbol or sign. Thus, la Virgen de la Caridad del Cobre, patroness of Cuba (Benítez's Rojo's primary example), has her origins in three cultures: European (as Virgin of Illescas, a Spanish virgin with Byzantine origins), indigenous American (containing elements of the *taíno* deity Atabey or Atabex), and African (deriving from Ochún, a Yoruba deity).[50] Yet only someone with a vast knowledge of the flow of intercultural influences would know this. For the great majority of people, she is a Cuban virgin. But here the term "Cuban" erases the long trajectory of intercultural signification that she embodies.

What we see taking place in Benítez Rojo's argument is the inversion of what took place in most Latin American nations during and after inde-pendence and the era of nationalism. Then, words such as "Cuban" had the effect of reducing nationality to one factor: creole consciousness and desire. Their definition tended to exclude the disenfranchised majority. Here, we see the opposite move at work: that is, the term "Cuban" is being opened up to all its different roots and possible significations. It becomes an inclusive term—a term that breaks down national boundaries and that situates the native in the exogenous, and vice versa. It is in this context that we must understand Benítez Rojo's assertion that la Virgen del Cobre, "Virgen cubana," is an impoverishing terms because it erases all the different elements that constituted her. It is in this sense too that the Caribbean is a region unified by a common plantation machine and an underlying rhythm, and at the same time it is a region of differences, discontinuities, and unstable identities.

Benítez Rojo's analysis, with its emphasis on chaos, discontinuities, fragmentation, counterpoint, and diversity, could be seen as a postmodern reading of Ortiz and the Caribbean. He is, however, very adamant in disclaiming any continuity with postmodernism precisely because it has excluded Latin American and Caribbean forms of knowledge and therefore must be seen as embodying specifically North American and European perspectives. For Benítez Rojo, there is a postmodernism implicit in Ortiz and in all Caribbean ways of life that is very different from, and unrelated to, Eurocentric theories of postmodernism. He writes:

me interesa el *Contrapunteo* porque pienso que es uno de los libros más consecuentes con las dinámicas de lo caribeño que se han escrito alguna vez—lo cual hago extensivo a Ortiz y al resto de su des-ordenada obra—, y también, sobre todo, porque provee el método para conducir una lectura del Caribe que resulta diferente a las de la modernidad y posmodernidad, al fin y al cabo perspectivas estrictas de Occidente, lecturas estrictas de Occidente.

[I am interested in the *Contrapunteo* because I think that it's one of the most revealing books ever written about the dynamics of the Caribbean—a judgement that I extend to Ortiz himself and the rest of his (dis)ordered work—and also, especially, because it offers a method by which one can conduct a reading of the Caribbean that has an outcome different from any that might have been done from the perspectives either of modernity or of postmodernity, which are, finally, strictly Western perspectives and Western readings.] [51]

In other words, he discovers in the Caribbean a postmodernism *avant la lettre*. Jean Franco similarly argues that the postmodern is a European and North American phenomenon and that while much Latin American fiction may appear postmodern, it has a very different genesis: "Hybrid genres," she writes,

have always abounded in Latin America. Thus, both "national allegory" and postmodern imply an impoverishment for they overlook an entire culture history in which essay, chronicle, and historical document have been grafted onto novels, a history of rereadings and rewritings which give rise to voluminous compendia . . . that defy categorization. Such texts may seem "postmodern" because of a sum of characteristics—pastiche, nostalgia, and the like—and because they reflect the dissolution of any universal system of meaning or master discourse.

However, Franco continues, postmodernism "cannot adequately describe those texts that use pastiche and citation not simply as style but as correlatives of the continent's uneasy and unfinished relationship to modernity."[52]

Even if Benítez Rojo distances himself from a Eurocentric postmodernism, and even if he implicitly posits the concept "transculturation-as-counterpoint" as a Latin American alternative to postmodernism, he nevertheless cannot quite stake out his terrain without having his discourse be taken over by postmodern elements. This problem confronts not only Benítez Rojo, but all Latin American critics today. For if postmodern elements in Latin American literature and culture can be traced all the way to the colony, then what is postmodernism when studied in a Latin American context? Is it something that has always been there—and in every other culture, including North America and Europe—and that we are only now identifying because postmodernism itself provides us with the language to see and name these processes? Or does postmodernism bear no relation to Latin America other than an uneasy and equivocal overlapping? Or—and this is the option I favor—is postmodernism yet another unacknowledged Western cannibalization of the "third world"? And if I insist on the third option, where does that leave Benítez Rojo's argument, indebted as it is to postmodernism and coming as it does from a very specifically Cuban context *in* the United States?

It is not my intent here to attempt to resolve the issue of the relationship between postmodernism and Latin America, but it is a problem that needs to be discussed in connection with the question of transculturation and popular culture. Many of the processes of transculturation that will be discussed at length in the chapters that follow also entail negotiations very similar to those seen in popular culture and its precarious balance—and tension—between some sort of integrity, ethnic resistance, creative reception, and passive consumption. If, to take an example elaborated above, the Virgen de la Caridad del Cobre, patroness of Cuba, is a Virgin who has her origins in at least three very different cultures and systems of signification, and if she is nevertheless considered Cuban, she is still and always will be, in Benítez Rojo's words, an "uneasy composite of differences." Thus, anyone with an interest in the matter will be able to detect in the color of her skin or in her attributes the different cultures and elements from which she derives. Since a label such as "Cuban" tends to stress unity over diversity, it becomes the trace of a long history of erasure of the different—particularly African—roots of Cuban culture.

Finally, one should consider the significance of the fact that Ortiz's theory has been bypassed for more than forty years and, aside from certain Latin American exceptions discussed above, is only now being mobilized by Cuban literary critics residing in the United States. For, even if Pérez Firmat and Benítez Rojo invoke Ortiz, they nevertheless displace transculturation into translation or chaos. Africa, even though written in as vestige or desire, remains absent as both signifier and diaspora. With his choice of "chaos" and privileging of rhythm, Benítez Rojo constructs an ever-vanishing Caribbean, a nostalgic mirage of everything that the United State is not and never can be for a Cuban academic living here and now.[53] For, to quote Stuart Hall again:

Who can ever forget, when once seen rising up out of that blue-green Caribbean, those islands of enchantment. Who has not known, at this moment, the surge of an overwhelming nostalgia for lost origins, for 'times past'? And yet, this 'return to the beginning' is like the imaginary in Lacan—it can neither be fulfilled nor requited, and hence is the beginning of the symbolic, of representation, the infinitely renewable source of desire, memory, myth, search, discovery.[54]

With migration to the United States, the Caribbean is lost for the enunciating "I" of *La isla que se repite*. It is reconstructed as a disappearing and elusive entity, forever the object of yearning and desire, forever the repository of all that is experienced as absent and lacking in the "here" of the enunciation. This brings us to the deeply ambivalent yet unproblematized assumption of the "here" of *La isla*. Where is the "here" for a displaced Cuban in the United States? To complicate the issue even further, and to use Benítez Rojo's own words, is the Caribbean of chaos and rhythm, "the Other" that is "there," being read with the codes of an ambivalently experienced "here"?

For Pérez Firmat, the ambivalence of the "here" of the enunciation is manifested in the desire to trace a continuity of "hyphenated thinking" between himself and Ortiz. He situates Ortiz as an "ethnic" writer and argues that the "trans" in Ortiz's "transculturation" is first and foremost the "trans" of the transitory nature of Cuban identity. "Mr. Cuba [Ortiz] also thinks in hyphens," Pérez Firmat asserts.[55] In a very general sense this is true of every one of us. Nonetheless, to think in hyphens for a Cuban and to think in hyphens for a Cuban-American are two different things. For Pérez Firmat, to think in hyphens means to claim descent from Ortiz as well as from Desi Arnaz. It is to situate himself in a here and there that informs his interpretation of Cuba and that is informed by a reaction to a certain North American stereotyping or tropicalization of Latin men that circumscribes the possibility of Latino self-definition and self-representation in this country.

What divides Ortiz's theorization of transculturation from contemporary reworkings of the term like those of Benítez Rojo and Pérez Firmat is, then, not only the distance of forty or more years, but also the gap that separates an anthropologist situated in Cuba from literary critics situated in the United States who begin to theorize from the hyphen that both separates and links the Cuban and the American. The attempt to theorize transculturation from the United States has today become an attempt to expand the borders of the national to include the Cuban living in the United States, as in Pérez Firmat's most recent study of the latinization (read Cubanization) of the United States,[56] or to expand the margins of the Caribbean, as in Benítez Rojo's studies, to include cities as far north as New Orleans and as far south as Montevideo.[57] Despite their differences, these two critics share the realization that borders are conventions, subject to change. Both argue that the Caribbean has come to the United States, that this country is increasingly becoming tropicalized, and that, as Gloria Estefan sings, "the rhythm is going to get you."

## The Transculturated Subject

In the above discussion I have insisted on situating the theory of transculturation within specific contexts in order to avoid diluting and displacing transculturation into meaninglessness. I have also tried to show the sorts of adjustments that need to be made for different cultural contexts. Further, I propose both a reduction and an amplification of the concept of transculturation as it has variously been articulated by its key theorists, Arguedas, Rama, and Ortiz, who have for the most part limited their analyses to processes taking place in Latin America from the 1930s to the 1970s, the periods of "modernization." A reduction because as a literary critic I focus only on Latin American narratives, whether they be chronicles, religious handbooks, paintings, novels, stories, or autobiographies; an amplification not only because I expand the margins of the discussion to the five hundred years of colonial and neocolonial rule, but also because I address the issue of European transculturations in early Spanish colonial texts.

Chronicles such as Cabeza de Vaca's *Naufragios* (see chapter 2) evidence an incipient transculturation and show how Spanish conquistadors adapted to and were transformed by the New World. Cabeza de Vaca's is perhaps the most stunning transformation of which we have an account. Likewise, in the writings of the extirpators of idolatries (see chapter 3), we see how priests, intent on evangelizing in the Andes, soon realized that they lacked the knowledge about Andean beliefs that would allow them to detect, much less eliminate, idolatrous practices. Hence, many began to learn Quechua and other indigenous languages and to study Andean cosmology. The result of their immersion into the culture of the Other, exacerbated by their isolation over many years in Andean villages, was that they became Andeanized and often ineffective evangelizers. I begin my study with these two early examples of Spanish transculturations because although most theorists of transculturation insist that culture contact is a two-way process, they nevertheless neglect to write about how Spain changed with the Conquest and colonization of America. Hence, they—like most ethnographers who study only subordinate cultural groups—inadvertently create the impression that acculturation has been and remains the primary intercultural process at work in Latin America.

In chapter 4 I analyze Andean artistic transculturations that took place in painting between the seventeenth and nineteenth centuries. The works of art of mestizo and Andean artists are clear visual narratives of transculturation. Just as Cabeza de Vaca's *Naufragios* and the writings of the extirpators of idolatries can be read in two very different ways, so too the paintings of the Cuzco School can be read according to two different, and at times religiously incompatible, codes.

The discursive and visual representations discussed in these chapters evidence the multiple readings that the heterogeneity of Latin American cultures gives rise to. Given that two codes, at least, are operative in any one text, it follows that the Latin American subject is also split: bilingual and bi-, if not multi-, cultural. Since the different processes of transculturation have been at work since the Conquest, the Latin American subject is always "in process" and situated along what I have called a "continuum of mestizaje." The ethnographic and novelistic writings of José María Arguedas witness the transcultural subjectivity of the mestizo, who must negotiate a tenuous path between two worlds (see chapter 5).

In chapters 6 and 7 I discuss transculturation from a feminist perspective in the work of the Mexican writer Elena Garro and the Chicana Gloria Anzaldúa. Rama's positioning of transculturators in the role of mediators—however much it may coincide with those writers' self-definition—becomes problematic here. Although women are considered the social mediators par excellence—witness la Malinche's alleged role in the Conquest—they remain entirely absent from Rama's analysis. When seen from this perspective, however, we must conclude that the position of the transculturators in Rama's discourse is feminized, for they refuse to inhabit the space of the ruling class and choose to align themselves with the poor and disenfranchised. If Octavio Paz's crass distinction that the option for the Mexican male is either that of assuming the passive role and being *chingado* (raped) or of taking the active role and being the *chingón* (rapist) is appropriate here, then the transculturators, by their option for social justice, choose the former. Mexican and Chicana women writers, on the other hand, have no option. They write in the shadow of Malinche/Eve's betrayal of male culture and are forever condemned to rewrite the Conquest, and Malinche's role therein, as a sort of unavoidable initiation into writing.

Three main concerns inform my analyses throughout. The first of these is to understand transculturation as a process that starts with the Conquest and carries on into the present. The second is to examine it not as a single process, but rather as many different processes of assimilation, adaptation, rejection, parody, resistance, loss, and ultimately transformation of Spanish *and* indigenous cultures. Instead of using "translation" or "miscegenation" or "mestizaje" to describe these processes, I will use "transculturation" as both a transitive and intransitive verb ("to transculturate"), for, in the continual give and take of culture contact, individuals are changed and change themselves as well as the surrounding world.[58] The transculturated subject, then, is someone who, like Arguedas, is consciously or unconsciously situated between at least two worlds, two cultures, two languages, and two definitions of subjectivity, and who constantly mediates between them all—or, to put it another way, whose "here" is problematic and perhaps undefinable. The third concern, and the one that perhaps carries most weight throughout, is to see the colony as a space that has given rise to an extreme ambiguity of signs and symbols. It is thus a semiotic space imbued with different, often contradictory—in any case, polyphonic—and incommensurable meanings that carry into the dynamics of contemporary Latin America. For as well as allowing for very divergent readings of the same signs and symbols, the colonial, I argue, also gives rise to subjectivities and subjects—and hence narrators—that are living in a borderland, defining themselves according to and being defined by two or more different cultural systems. They are therefore split and in flux in a much more complicated way than that allowed for by modern European psychoanalytic theories of subjectivity and traditional monocultural understandings of culture. If "identity" means that a person "belongs to a place"[59] and has a sense of belonging, how is that affected by the increasing migratory patterns that characterize the world today? Where is the "here" from which the enunciating "I" narrates? Who is that "I"? And can one still speak of a coherent identity?

Questions of identity become especially complicated in a Latin American context such as that of the Andean nations. It is extremely difficult to know and to understand two cultures so well that the transculturations both described by and effected in different narratives and by different narrators become apparent. The increasing preoccupation with issues of transculturation today may result not only from migratory patterns of displacement and the resurgence of new "identities" that challenge old concepts of identity, but also from the breaking down of the former isolation of the disciplines from one another. The increased interdisciplinary dialogue allows us to read and decipher a novel such as Arguedas's *Todas las sangres* in light of his ethnographic studies, or a colonial text such as *Naufragios* within the context of modern Native American studies, or Anzaldúa's *Borderlands* as a transculturated bildungsroman that posits a new type of subjectivity.

NOTES

All translations are by the author, unless otherwise stated. In every case, I have opted for literal renderings at the expense of elegance. Wherever possible, I have used the term "Andean" instead of the problematic "Indian" or "Amerindian." However, I have kept the term "Indian" wherever the point is a "racial" classification (as in "Indians" and "mestizos").

1. See Ángel Rama, *La ciudad letrada,* and also his *Transculturación narrativa en América Latina,* 65.

2. For Arguedas, with modernization and the building of the Central Highway leading into the Andes in the 1930s, the isolation—which had actually preserved indigenous culture—began to break down. Thus, modernization violently threatened that world. See chapter 5.

3. *International Dictionary of Regional European Ethnology and Folklore,* 19.

4. See David Hunter, ed., *Encyclopedia of Anthropology,* 1.

5. Bronislaw Malinowski's endorsement of the term "transculturation" and his critique of "acculturation" read as follows: "Aparte de su ingrata fonética (suena como si arrancara de un hipo combinado con un regüeldo), la voz *acculturation* contiene todo un conjunto de determinadas e inconvenientes implicaciones etimológicas. Es un vocablo etnocéntrico con una significación moral. El inmigrante tiene que "aculturarse" *(to acculturate);* así han de hacer también los indígenas, paganos e infieles, bárbaros o salvajes, que gozan del "beneficio" de estar sometidos a nuestra Gran Cultura Occidental" [Aside from its harsh phonetics (it sounds as if it started off from a hiccup combined with a belch), the term *acculturation* implies a whole set of specific and inconvenient etymological implications. It is an ethnocentric word

with a moral signification. The immigrant has to "acculturate"; as well as the natives, the pagans and infidels, the barbarians and savages, that enjoy the "privilege" of being subjected to our Great Western Culture] (emphasis in original). Bronislaw Malinowski, "Introducción," in Fernando Ortiz, *Contrapunteo cubano del tabaco y el azúcar*, xii.

6. Emilio M. Martínez Amador, *Standard English-Spanish and Spanish-English Dictionary*.

7. Ortiz's definition of transculturation reads as follows: "Entendemos que el vocablo *transculturación* expresa mejor las diferentes fases del proceso transitivo de una cultura a otra, porque éste no consiste solamente en adquirir una cultura, que es lo que en rigor indica la voz anglo-americana *aculturación*, sino que el proceso implica también necesariamente la pérdida o desarraigo de una cultura precedente, lo que pudiera decirse una parcial desculturación, y, además, significa la consiguiente creación de nuevos fenó- menos culturales que pudieran denominarse *neoculturación*" [We think that the term *transculturation* better expresses the different phases in the process of transition between one culture and another, because this process does not consist exclusively in acquiring a culture, which is what the Anglo-American term *acculturation* really means; rather, the process also necessarily implies the loss or uprooting of an originary culture, which could be termed a partial deculturation, as well as the consequent creation of new cultural phenomena which could be described in terms of a *neoculturation*]. See Ortiz, *Contrapunteo*, 103, and also its translation, *Cuban Counterpoint: Tobacco and Sugar*.

8. Ortiz, *Contrapunteo*, 103.

9. Gustavo Pérez Firmat, *The Cuban Condition: Translation and Identity in Modern Cuban Literature*, 56. I thank Lois Parkinson Zamora for bringing this book to my attention.

10. For an interesting historical study of the transculturation of agricultural products, see Herman J. Viola and Carolyn Margolis, eds., *Seeds of Change: Five Hundred Years Since Columbus*.

11. Ortiz, *Contrapunteo*, 88.

12. Willi Apel and Ralph T. Daniel, *The Harvard Brief Dictionary of Music*, 72.

13. Stuart Hall, "Cultural Identity and Diaspora," 23.

14. Ortiz himself emphasized the African over the Asian in his studies of Cuba.

15. Françoise Lionnet, apparently unaware of Ortiz's work, uses the term "métissage" in much the same way as Ortiz uses "transculturation." She bases her study on the history of the island of Mauritius, which was uninhabited and—like Cuba—settled by successive waves of immigrants. See Françoise Lion- net, *Autobiographical Voices: Race, Gender, Self-Portraiture*.

16. See Thomas E. Skidmore, "Racial Issues and Social Policy in Brazil, 1870–1940," 7–36. For an account of the transformation that Ortiz's studies of Afro-Cuban culture underwent during his lifetime, see Roberto González Echevarría, *Alejo Carpentier: The Pilgrim at Home*, 44–51.

17. José María Arguedas, *Formación de una cultura nacional indoamericana*.

18. For an excellent study on this point, see William Rowe and Vivian Schelling, *Memory and Mo- dernity: Popular Culture in Latin America*. See also Néstor García Canclini, *Las culturas populares en el capitalismo*.

19. Rowe and Schelling, *Memory and Modernity*, 121–2.

20. Guido A. Podestá, "La deconstrucción de Lima," 349–69. As Julia Kristeva points out, in the Judeo-Christian tradition, those who were admitted into the temple were the ones who were permitted to speak. Concomitantly, exclusion from that space condemned a person to silence. See Julia Kristeva, *The Powers of Horror: An Essay on Abjection*, 93.

21. *Indigenismo* is the literary movement whereby writers, located in the capital cities of Latin America, took an idealized version of "the Indian" in order to address issues of social injustice and inequity that directly affected not the people about whom they were writing, but themselves. They therefore assumed "el desvalido indio, el castigado negro—para usarlos retóricamente en el memorial de agravios contra los colonizadores, pretextando en ellos las reivindicaciones propias" [the helpless Indian, the punished black—to use them rhetorically in their list of grievances against the colonizers, using them as pretexts to address their own revindications]. Rama, *Transculturación*, 12.

22. See Rolena Adorno, *Guamán Poma: Writing and Resistance in Colonial Peru*.

23. For an excellent discussion on indigenismo, see Antonio Cornejo Polar, *Literatura y sociedad en el Perú: La novela indigenista*.

24. As Mariátegui wrote: "La literatura indigenista no puede darnos una versión rigurosamente ve- rista del indio. Tiene que idealizarlo y estilizarlo. Tampoco puede darnos su propia ánima. Es todavía una literatura de mestizos. Por eso se llama indigenista y no indígena. Una literatura indígena, si debe venir,

vendrá a su propio tiempo. Cuando los propios indios indios estén en grado de producirla" [Indigenista literature cannot render a rigorously true account of the Indian. It has to idealize and stylize him. It also cannot give us his soul. It is still a mestizo literature. That is why it is called indigenista and not Indian. An Indian literature, if it is to come, will come in due time. It will come when the Indians themselves start producing it]. José Carlos Mariátegui, *7 ensayos de interpretación de la realidad peruana*, 335.

25. Cornejo Polar, *Vigencia y universalidad de José María Arguedas*, 29.

26. Cornejo Polar, *Literatura y sociedad en el Perú*, 63.

27. As Cornejo Polar argues: "No está demás subrayar que al ganarse para la crítica y la historia literarias la categoría de pluralidad, se cancelan para siempre todas las opciones que a nombre de una falsa unidad cercenaban el proceso y el *corpus* de nuestra literature" [It isn't superfluous to underline that the gaining of the category of plurality for criticism and literary history cancels out all those other options which in the name of a false unity reduced the process and corpus of our literature]. Furthermore, this process of inclusion forces the critic to "desenmascarar la ideología discriminadora, de base clasista y étnica, que obtiene la homogeneidad mediante la supresión de toda manifestación literaria que no pertenezca o no pueda ser asumida con comodidad por el grupo que norma lo que es o no es nacional y lo que es o no es literatura" [unmask the discriminatory nature of ideology based on class and ethnic prejudices that claims homogeneity by suppressing all literary manifestations that do not belong to nor can be assumed comfortably by those who establish the norms of what is or isn't the national and what is or isn't the literary]. Cornejo Polar, *Sobre literatura y crítica latinoamericanas*, 23–4.

28. Important examples of such revisions of the canon are César Toro Montalvo's recently published *Historia de la literatura peruana*, which begins with a discussion of Inca and Quechua literature. See also Edmundo Bendezú Aybar, *Literatura Quechua*.

29. See Miguel León Portilla, *Literaturas de Mesoamerica*; Serge Gruzinski, *L'Amérique de la conquête: Peinté par les Indiens du Méxique*; and Joaquín Galarza, *Lienzos de Chiepetlán*.

30. See Pérez Firmat, "Transcending Exile: Cuban-American Literature Today," and Antonio Benítez Rojo, *La isla que se repite: El Caribe y la perspectiva postmoderna*.

31. Pérez Firmat, *Cuban Condition*, 8.

32. Pérez Firmat, *Cuban Condition*, 5.

33. Ortiz justified the use of ajiaco on the grounds that the stew is made by combining a variety of meats and vegetables—whichever ones are in season or available—and therefore conveys the ethnic diversity of Cuba. Secondly, as Pérez Firmat points out, the ajiaco "is agglutinative but not synthetic; even if the diverse ingredients form part of a new culinary entity, they do not lose their original flavor and identity." However, even this very Cuban term is a displaced, localized translation of the "melting pot." With its metallurgical and homogenizing connotations, the "melting pot" is doubly inappropriate to describe Cuba, not only because in the melting pot everything is synthesized, but also because Cuba became the way station that it was precisely because of its lack of minerals. See Pérez Firmat, *Cuban Condition*, 24, 27–8.

34. Nicolás Guillén, *Sóngoro Cosongo. Motivos de son. West Indies ltd. España, poema en cuatro angustias y una esperanza*, and Pérez Firmat, *Cuban Condition*, 68.

35. Pérez Firmat, *Cuban Condition*, 71.

36. Pérez Firmat, *Cuban Condition*, 5.

37. Pérez Firmat, *Cuban Condition*, 4.

38. Willis Barnstone, *The Poetics of Translation: History, Theory, Practice*, 9.

39. Barnstone, *Poetics of Translation*, 13.

40. See Susana Jákfalvi-Leiva, *Traducción, escritura y violencia colonizadora: Un estudio de la obra del Inca Garcilaso*.

41. I use the term in Spanish because in the English expression "popular culture," the Latin American intersection of class, ethnicity, and folklore is absent. See Rowe and Schelling, *Memory and Modernity*, 2. See also García Canclini, *Las culturas populares en el capitalismo*.

42. Benítez Rojo, *Isla que se repite*, and its translation, *The Repeating Island: The Caribbean and the Postmodern Perspective*.

43. Benítez Rojo, *Isla que se repite*, 178.

44. Benítez Rojo, *Isla que se repite*, 178. *Repeating Island*, 171. This same counterpoint is at work in Ortiz's text, where African beliefs appear alongside Western ones and are given an equal explanatory power and validity as scientific theories. It is for this reason that Ortiz's work has been so easily dismissed

by modern anthropologists and critics who see it as unorthodox and unscientific. Ortiz himself situated his work as always unfinished, always in process, just like a fugue that could go on endlessly.

45. As Benítez Rojo writes: "la práctica narrativa de los Pueblos del Mar es muy distinta a la del relato de legitimación de Occidente, pues en ésta el problema de la legitimidad es el referente de un dilatado proceso de indagación, verificación y comentario, mientras que en aquélla el relato provee su propia legitimidad de manera instantánea, al ser emitido en presente por la voz rítmica del narrador, cuya competencia reside sólo en el hecho de haber escuchado el mito o la fábula de boca de alguien." *La isla que se repite,* 175. [The narrative practice of the peoples of the sea is very different from the West's narrative of legitimation, since in the latter the problem of legitimacy is the subject of an extended process of inquiry, verification, and comment, while in the former the story itself instantly provides its own legitimacy whenever it is spoken in the present moment in the narrative's rhythmic voice, whose competence lies only in the speaker's having listened to the myth or the fable issuing from someone's mouth. *Repeating Island,* 168.]

46. Benítez Rojo, *Isla que se repite,* xxxv.

47. Benítez Rojo, *Isla que se repite,* xxxiii.

48. Benítez Rojo, *Isla que se repite,* xxvii. *Repeating Island,* 21.

49. Benítez Rojo, *Isla que se repite,* xxxiv. *Repeating Island,* 21.

50. For a complete tracing of her origins, see Benítez Rojo, *Isla que se repite,* xviii.

51. Benítez Rojo, *Isla que se repite,* 158. *Repeating Island,* 156–7.

52. Jean Franco, "The Nation as Imagined Community," 210–1.

53. This critique is indebted to a discussion I had with Alberto Sandoval after hearing a talk delivered by Benítez Rojo at Dartmouth College, Hanover in May 1992.

54. Hall, "Cultural Identity and Diaspora," 236.

55. Pérez Firmat, "From Ajiaco to Tropical Soup: Fernando Ortiz and the Definition of Cuban Culture," 13.

56. Pérez Firmat, "Life on the Hyphen." See also Pérez Firmat's "Introduction: Cheek to Cheek" in his *Do the Americas Have a Common Literature?*

57. Benítez Rojo, Dartmouth lecture, May 1992.

58. Françoise Lionnet justifies her choice of "miscegenation" in the following way: "This is why a word like *métis* or *mestizo* is most useful: it derives etymologically from the Latin *mixtus,* 'mixed,' and its primary meaning refers to cloth made of two different fibers, usually cotton for the warp and flax for the woof: it is a neutral term." I disagree with her here, finding that in most cultures today racial mixture is viewed ambivalently, if not negatively. As I argue throughout, for Latin America, mestizaje, or miscegenation, often used synonymously with transculturation and/or translation, carries precisely those sexual connotations absent in the latter terms and yet crucial to explain the dynamics of cultural and sexual "encounters." See Lionnet, *Autobiographical Voices,* 14.

59. As Néstor García Canclini writes: "Hubo una época en que las identidades de los grupos se formaban a través de dos movimientos: ocupar un territorio y constituir colecciones—de objetos, de monumentos, de rituales—mediante los cuales se afirmaban y celebraban los signos que distinguían a cada grupo. Tener una *identidad* era, ante todo, tener un país, una ciudad o un barrio, una *entidad* donde todo lo compartido por quienes habitaban ese lugar se volvía idéntico o intercambiable. . . . ¿Para qué sirve seguir pensando la cultura en la dirección etimológica, como "cultivo" de un territorio, cuando las fronteras nacionales se vuelven porosas . . . ?" [There was a time when group identities were constituted by two movements: by inhabiting a territory and by collections of things, monuments, rituals, by means of which the signs that distinguished each group were affirmed and celebrated. To have an *identity* was, before all, to have a country, a city, or a neighborhood; an *entity* where everything that was shared by those who inhabited that space became identical and interchangeable. . . . Why continue thinking of identity in its etymological sense as "cultivation" of a territory, when national borders have become porous . . . ?]. García Canclini, "Escenas sin territorio: Estética de las migraciones e identidades en transición," 9.

## 2 ≈
# SHAMANISM AND CHRISTIANITY: The Transcultural Semiotics of Cabeza de Vaca's *Naufragios*

Álvar Núñez Cabeza de Vaca, along with Alonso del Castillo, Andrés Dorantes, and Estebanico (a Moroccan slave), was one of the few to survive the ill-fated expedition of Pánfilo de Narváez, which set out from Spain on June 17, 1527 to explore and conquer Florida.[1] From the outset, the expedition was plagued by a series of misjudgments that culminated in the separation of most of the men from the main fleet, their shipwreck, and the death of all but the above-mentioned four. As a consequence, Cabeza de Vaca and those who accompanied him lived among Native American tribes for six years and then wandered across what is today the Southwestern United States, arriving in New Spain (Mexico) in 1536. Because the expedition was a complete failure, the down-to-earth account of this fabulous adventure, originally titled *Relación que dio Álvar Núñez Cabeza de Vaca de lo acaescido en las Indias en el armada donde yva por governador Pánfilo de Narváez* but now better known as *Naufragios*, lets us glimpse a different side of the Conquest.[2] Cabeza de Vaca and his men were totally out of control and at the mercy of the elements and of various Native American tribes.[3] In order to survive, they were forced to adapt to the New World and incorporate its "alterity" to an unprecedented degree. Their assimilation to the indigenous tribes among which they lived for many years radically altered their conception of the world.

Cabeza de Vaca's narrative deployment of both Native American and Spanish cultural codes is one of the earliest examples we have of a Spanish transculturation. Two different, and at times mutually exclusive, cultural systems structure *Naufragios,* indicating the degree to which Cabeza de Vaca adapted to the indigenous way of life and showing how one sign or symbol can be read equally well according to quite different cultural logics. The book demonstrates this most powerfully, perhaps, in its narrative of how Cabeza de Vaca became a Native American shaman of great success. While relating this achievement, Cabeza de Vaca seeks to obfuscate his shamanic "idolatrous" practices, framing them in biblical terms. At the narrative level he therefore creates a conceptual impasse in which the coherence of the Christian discourse to which he appeals is undermined by the shamanic practices he describes.

Because it is also a testimony of transculturation, *Naufragios* is a singular text in that body of accounts known as "chronicles of the New World." Given Rama's observation that "los transculturadores" conceive of themselves as mediators between cultures, Cabeza de Vaca can be considered a transculturator. Not only does *Naufragios* negotiate a tenuous path between Spanish and Native American cultures, but Cabeza de Vaca reports that, at the end of his journey, he tried to negotiate between "bad" Spaniards and the indigenous population. In fact, he was a mediator in more ways than one, since as a Native American shaman his role was to reconcile the here and now with the beyond: to take the hyphen out of dis-ease, so to speak.

If Cabeza de Vaca'a assimilation into the New World were to be situated along a continuum, it would be located somewhere between Columbus's refusal to acknowledge the alterity of the New World and, at the other extreme, the position of shipwrecked Spaniards who adapted so well to the tribes among which they lived that, when found and "saved," they refused to return to Spain. In the chronicles we find many such cases. In Pero Vaz de Caminha's account of his arrival in Brazil, two ship's boys steal a skiff and escape at night before the Portuguese set sail to Calcutta. Such occurrences were frequent during the Conquest and can be seen already in the diaries of Columbus, who writes that many of his men had repeatedly asked him to let them stay on islands in the Caribbean. They also appear later, as in Bernal Díaz's history of the conquest of Mexico, which tells of sailors who had been shipwrecked and were later found. The sailors had adopted Native American dress and customs, married, and had children; they refused to leave their new families to go with the Spaniards. These men, of whom we have no primary written record, point to the other side of the accounts given in the chronicles. If Columbus's voyages can be schematized in literary terms as the trajectory from Paradise to Paradise Lost, or from discovery to destruction, the men who willingly stayed behind can be said to have remained in the stage of Paradise. In other words, they participated in the *ideal* vision of the New World and not in its instrumentalization and destruction.[4]

Since Cabeza de Vaca's account both belongs to and yet deviates considerably from the New World chronicles, it will be necessary to situate *Naufragios* more precisely within that family of texts before undertaking an analysis of this transcultural narrative.

## The Chronicles of the New World

The term "chronicles" does not denote a specific genre or form; chronicles can be letters, diaries, accounts, or *relaciones,* as well as histories.[5] Even if they have different generic forms, they have one thing in common: their referent is the New World. It is in this sense that they form a "textual family." [6] With few exceptions, the chronicles are official documents written for the Portuguese and Spanish Crowns as a direct response to the royal request for information, which was usually worded as "hacer relación" (to give an account). The main function of the chronicles is therefore not literary but documentary.[7] By 1574, the Spanish Crown's desire for information had been formulated in an official questionnaire, which the chroniclers were ordered to answer point by point and which asked innumerable questions about the new discoveries. Before that year, however, no official format had been established and the accounts were structured according to the need for information most pressing at the moment of their writing.[8]

The political climate in which the chronicles were written and the writers' goals in composing them were often more important in determining their nature and content than was the New World that they attempted to describe. For example, Columbus insisted that there was much gold in the New World, when in fact he found hardly any; his aim was both to convince the Crown of the viability of his enterprise and to keep his many creditors at bay. Many of these accounts, especially during the period of the Conquest (which is generally considered to have begun in 1519 with the entry of Cortés into Tenochtitlán, the center of the Aztec empire), were written for the *Consejo de Indias,* a body of government set up to administer the new Spanish colonies. The chronicles, then, are often a brilliant "hoja de servicios"— a record of services rendered—and are dominated by the chroniclers' desire for fame and power.[9]

Since the administrators of the *Consejo de Indias* seldom had any experience in the New World, their decisions were based on the often-slanderous reports of the chroniclers. These reports served to sustain the *Consejo* practice of maintaining situations of strife between the conquistadors in order to maintain its own position of superiority in relation to the individual.[10] Since the Crown perceived the individual's drive for self-aggrandizement as potentially harmful to the collective good, it used, glorified, and ultimately ruined distinguished conquistadors and colonial administrators in its attempt to control and maintain its own power. In these texts, the chronicler was thus obliged to justify, negotiate, praise his allies, and denigrate his enemies in order to obtain recognition from the Crown.[11]

The chronicles must be understood in relation to a center of power that the writers attempt to manipulate and turn in their favor by identifying their own private interests with those of that power.[12] In other words, they reflect and echo the Crown's imperial, monolithic, and monologic "I/eye" in the New World. Far from being the free observations of the chroniclers, these texts were the official vehicle of religious and cultural power.[13] Beatriz González argues that, because the official version was the only one allowed throughout the colonial period, the effect has been to create an image of apparent stability, where colonial texts—instead of revealing the conflictive complexity of the time—actually construct a noncontradictory image of European culture both in and for America.[14] The perceived imperial need to present itself as a totality, in turn, had the effect of organizing the discourse about the invasion and Conquest along epic lines.[15]

Although split among themselves, the chroniclers nevertheless become the representatives of empire. They confront the alterity of the New World from an identification with that imperial "I/eye." In the beginning, they never question the superiority of their own culture and do not hesitate to insist on the necessity of imposing it in the New World. This is true even when, like Álvar Núñez Cabeza de Vaca and the Dominican Bartolomé de Las Casas, they disagree with the political methods of subordination and exploitation and attempt to criticize the genocide of indigenous populations and to curb imperial power.

In most cases the chronicles were written by merchants, sailors, soldiers, and priests—generally men of little learning who wrote because they had to and who often were directly involved in the events that they described. In most cases they were the history makers as well as the history writers, creating in their narratives a collapse between the narrative "I" and the "I" of the protagonist whose experiences are being related.[16] The chroniclers assume a position similar to that of the narrators of testimonial literature, and this establishes a further coincidence between history and experience.[17] The fact of having witnessed the events described often serves as the only guarantee of their veracity.

The chroniclers thus equated historical veracity with personal testimony, and they did not distinguish fact very clearly from fiction. As was often the case in Renaissance historiography, literature shaped the perception of reality to a great degree. Myths of giants, sirens, Amazons, paradise, and the fountain of eternal youth, as well as the medieval bestiary, biblical stories, romances, and novels of chivalry, interfered with perceptions of reality. The chronicles therefore contain a curious mixture of reality and fiction—with no distinction made between them—that is akin to what we now would call the fantastic.[18]

Because the chronicles are texts that cross an ocean and mediate for the first time between two worlds, they effect a tenuous passage between cultures. At their very core is the ethnographic impulse to give an account of one culture to another. Then as now, however, no equality is implied: a literate culture, which sees itself from the vantage point of civilization, gives an account of a "primitive," oral culture. Since, in accounting for the "new," we are invariably "coming home," James Clifford's observations on contemporary ethnography apply equally well to the fifteenth century: "One no longer leaves home confident of finding something radically new, another time or space . . . the familiar turns up at the ends of the earth."[19] Thus Columbus, who stumbled on a new world, was unable to account for his discovery. He lacked both the concept of a fourth world (one that was not Europe, Africa, or Asia) and the words with which to describe it.[20] Instead, he imposed on the New World paradigms with which he was familiar and insisted that he found only what he already knew, namely the East as described by Marco Polo and others. There are, however, many ruptures and inconsistencies in Columbus's texts—particularly in the difference between his first and fourth diaries—that point to a less coherent and consistent vision than is generally attributed to him. Pero Vaz de Caminha, exploring the coast of Brazil, was aware that he was in a new continent and tried to give as accurate and as precise an image of it as he could. But although a careful observer, he was locked within the paradigms of his own time and, in the end, was also incapable of accounting for new and different cultures. As Rolena Adorno has pointed out, Renaissance thought, traditionally praised in the European history of ideas for the invention of a so-phisticated classificatory system and for its acknowledgment of difference, proves to be inadequate when analyzed from the point of view of the study of non-European phenomena.[21]

The chronicles point not only to the shortcomings of sixteenth-century thought, but also to the basic impossibility of any attempt to understand a different culture. Western thought is bound to find in the new what is already known. It is perhaps only those who stay long enough, and who, in the process, begin to change and to question the imperialist "I/eye," who can hope to approximate the new. We see such ideological dislocations in the account Cabeza de Vaca gives of the nine years he spent as a white shaman, wandering among different tribes in what is today the Southwestern United States and down into Mexico. In fact, his *Naufragios* can be considered an anti-epic, since he could only report a major shipwreck and failed conquest. Critics have argued that in the address to the Crown with which his narrative begins, Cabeza de Vaca attempts to substitute an *account* for *action,* which as a royal subject was expected of him; that is, to substitute words and information about the inhabitants' customs for the acquisition of bounty and the conquest of lands.[22] True as this may be, I think Cabeza de Vaca went further than that. Having become a conquered conquistador and thus unable to assume an epic stance, he claimed instead that he had been successful as an evangelizer. Thus, in his narrative we see the progressive transformation of the man of war into the Shamano-Christian conqueror of souls.

## The Discourse of the Borderlands

In the opening address of *Naufragios,* Cabeza de Vaca tries to convince the Crown that the information in his account has as much value as gold or conquest. He was proven right, because with its detailed descriptions of the customs, child-rearing methods, mourning rituals, and means of subsistence of the various Native American tribes, *Naufragios* is the only ethnographic account we have of the indigenous tribes of Southwest Texas. In fact, the Smithsonian *Handbook of North American Indians* relies on Cabeza de Vaca's account for information about the Native American tribes around Galveston Bay, among which he spent six years before proceeding across the continent. These eight or nine tribes, now generically named after one of them, the Karankawas, were later annihilated by Spanish and French incursions, and therefore very little is known about them.[23]

Cabeza de Vaca's account is important not only as ethnography, but also as the first account of a Spanish transculturation in America. Because it narrates the development of a group of men over a nine-year period, *Naufragios* shows a progression in their thinking in relation to the new lands, a progression that is otherwise absent in the chronicles. Cabeza de Vaca and the three others who survive the shipwreck begin to understand Native American customs. In the process of adapting to a different way of life in order to survive, their conception of life, the body, culture, medicine, and religion changes radically. Several things begin to happen that alter the Spaniards' self-understanding. First, the horses and gunpowder, which had previously been efficient in subjugating Native American tribes, prove ineffective in the marshes and everglades of Florida.[24] Second, the extreme hunger that the Spaniards experience turns them into cannibals. This circumstance horrifies the Native Americans and turns on its head the dichotomy upon which the Conquest had depended for its ideological validation: now it is the Spaniards, not the Native Americans, who are uncivilized and barbarous. The sense of the Spaniards as barbarians is further accentuated when they lose all vestiges of what had qualified them in their own eyes as civilized: their clothes. Third, and perhaps most important, solidarity among the Spaniards—the "us" that had always been so monolithically opposed to "them"/ Native Americans—disintegrates. Pánfilo de Narváez refuses to take charge of the situation, arguing that "cada uno hiciese lo que mejor le paresciese que era para salvar la vida, que él ansí entendía de hacer" [each one should do what he deemed best in order to save his life, which was what he intended to do].[25] In other words, it is every man for himself and Native Americans and American nature against them. Now the Spaniards no longer confront the New World as the monolithic civilized "I/eye" of Empire, but as helpless, naked, and cannibalistic individuals.

The vaccuum left by the breakdown of solidarity among the Spaniards is filled by a new and different intercultural code that forces Cabeza de Vaca's men to redefine and resituate themselves at the juncture of two cultures— in the borderlands, so to speak.[26] Thus, after many years spent wandering across the continent and living among different Native American tribes, they reach other Spaniards and there is a split between the imperial "I/eye" and Cabeza de Vaca's "I/eye," with the result that these two will never again quite see eye to eye.

The process of Spanish transculturation begins to take place on the Island of Malhado, which is surmised to have been Galveston Island or Follet's Island, now attached to the mainland, where Cabeza de Vaca suffers great hardship at the hands of Native Americans. He soon realizes that although he is a burden to the island's inhabitants, he is also their slave, and that his survival depends on his usefulness.[27] He learns to be valuable to the community by going from one tribe to another, providing each community with whatever it needs. In learning to trade among different tribes, Cabeza de Vaca must learn not only different Native American languages, but also the various cultural uses and values attached to objects. He no longer exchanges beads and trinkets of little value for gold, as did all the Spaniards before him, but instead trades seashells from the coast for objects from the inland areas—skins, flint stones, and cane for bows and arrows. This is perhaps the first time in the chronicles that we find an equal exchange between Spaniards and Native Americans. Beginning with Columbus, it is always the Native Americans who give everything in exchange for nothing.[28] The most salient proof of his learning about culturally defined value is that Cabeza de Vaca no longer regards gold as the paradigm of the desirable or the valuable. Its place has been taken by food, which will allow him to survive. As he writes, "me hacían buen tratamiento y me daban de comer, por respecto de mis mercaderías . . . y entre ellos era muy conoscido; holgaban mucho cuando me vían y les traía lo que habían menester" [they treated me well and gave me food, because of my merchandise . . . and I was well known among them; they were very happy when I arrived and brought them whatever they needed].[29] Although he trades—an activity that so far had been used to characterize Western civilization—he trades according to non-Western values. In learning the different value of objects, he also learns that value is culturally determined, a convention, and not intrinsic and universal as understood by imperial Spain. It is therefore interesting to note that all mention of gold and precious stones is absent from *Naufragios* until Cabeza de Vaca and his group reach New Spain and begin to hear rumors of the presence of other Spaniards.

Cabeza de Vaca finally achieves a degree of independence when Native Americans initiate him into the arts of shamanism. In this way he becomes indispensable to the tribes along Galveston Bay. In fact, the tribe that had enslaved him on the Island of Malhado forces him to heal in exchange for food. When he protests, true to Western logic, that he has no degree nor knowledge of medicine, his food is taken away. He then quickly overcomes cultural constraints and observes that Native Americans have no such thing as titles and that they heal according to traditional practices:

Curan las enfermedades soplando al enfermo y con aquel soplo y las manos echan dél la enfermedad . . . Lo que el médico hace es dalle unas sajas adonde tiene el dolor y chúpanles alrededor dellas. Dan cauterios de fuego, que es cosa entre ellos tenida por muy provechosa . . . y después desto soplan aquel lugar que les duele y con esto creen ellos se les quita el mal.

[They heal illnesses by blowing on the patient and with that breath and with the hands they expel the disease . . . The healer cuts where they have the pain and he sucks around the cuts. They cauterize with fire, a procedure that is held in high regard among them . . . and after this they blow where the pain is and with this they believe that the disease is gone.] [30]

Cabeza de Vaca learns to heal by blowing, cutting, sucking, and the laying on of hands, as well as by using special plants and medicinal herbs and stones. He is taught that "las piedras y otras cosas que se crían por los campos tienen virtud" [stones and other things that grow in the fields have virtue] and that he can cure and diminish pain by rubbing a hot stone over the sick part of the body. [31] Like a Native American shaman, he learns to pray for rain and to influence the weather; that is, he begins to see the world in animistic terms. But he does not manage to relinquish his Christian upbringing altogether. When he begins to heal, he does so using the shamanic method taught him while also making the sign of the cross and praying an Our Father and a Hail Mary.

## The Transculturator as Shaman

Cabeza de Vaca's method—additive and syncretic—seems to have worked remarkably well. Those who were so treated "decían a los otros que estaban sanos y buenos" [told the others that they were healthy and well]. [32] His healing prowess reached "miraculous" proportions when he resuscitated a man believed to be dead by blowing on him and saying his customary prayer. This event, which created a great stir, is described in terms that parallel the biblical rising from the dead of Lazarus. That is, even though Cabeza de Vaca became a shaman of great renown and even though he operated well within Native American culture, he had to resort to biblical discourse to render his experiences. In a sense, he could not have done otherwise, for, just as Columbus had been forced to frame his discourse in the epic and heroic mode with which he was familiar, so too Cabeza de Vaca had no words other than biblical ones with which to describe his shamanic experiences. It is, of course, also possible that he was afraid of being persecuted by the Inquisition for "idolatrous" practices, and was thus forced—as happened in the Andean region of Perú, which I will discuss in the next chapter—to disguise his shamanism in Christian terms.

Whatever the reasons may be, Cabeza de Vaca writes of his captivity, trials, and tribulations in terms reminiscent of Christ's passion:

y la tierra es tan áspera y tan cerrada que muchas veces hacíamos leña en montes, que cuando la acabábamos de sacar nos corría por muchas partes sangre, de las espinas y matas con que topábamos . . . A las veces me acontesció hacer leña donde después de haberme costado mucha sangre no la podía sacar, a cuestas, ni arrastrando. No tenía, cuando en esos trabajos me vía, otro remedio ni consuelo sino pensar en la pasión de nuestro redentor Jesucristo y en la sangre que por mí derramó, y considerar cuánto más sería el tormento que de las espinas El padesció, que no aquél que yo entonces sufría.

[and the land was so rough and so closed and sometimes we went to the forests to cut wood, and when we were done taking it out we were bleeding all over because of the thorns and bushes in our path . . . I didn't have another alternative or consolation than to think in the passion of our redeemer, Jesus Christ, and in the blood he spilled for me and to consider how much worse His torment might have been from the thorns than the one I was suffering.] [33]

The initial parallel that Cabeza de Vaca draws beween Christ's and his own sufferings is further emphasized by the miraculous healings and by the increasingly large crowds that come out to welcome him and receive his blessing as he travels from village to village and from tribe to tribe down into New Spain. As with Christ, all the people came out "para que los tocásemos y santiguásemos como habíamos hecho a los otros con quien habíamos estado" [so that we should touch and bless them as we had been doing with the people with whom we had been previously].[34] Eventually, in another biblical echo, Cabeza de Vaca writes that he must bless the food of three or four thousand people before the latter dare eat.[35]

However, even if Cabeza de Vaca frames his experiences in Judeo-Christian terms, his healings are nevertheless the first example we have of an "idolatrous practice" carried out by a Spaniard—which could partially explain his insistence on diminishing the importance and extent of his shamanic practices. In his narrative, the closer he gets to the other Spaniards in New Spain and to the end of his journey, the more he emphasizes the miraculous, Christian, and evangelizing function of his healings and the more he minimizes the importance of his shamanic practices. At the beginning of *Naufragios,* he describes his method of healing as a combination of "blowing" and "blessing/making the sign of the Cross" (that is, both shamanism and Christianity), but towards the end of his journey and the end of his narrative, he mentions only Christian practices and his great success at evangelizing and resettling native populations.

It is therefore not surprising that critics have tended to read *Naufragios* either as Christian or as fantastic literature, overlooking the bicultural, Native American elements that enter the narrative and disrupt the coherence of Cabeza de Vaca's discourse. Enrique Pupo-Walker, for example, situates *Naufragios* within a fertile European, medieval, popular, hagiographic tradition of wandering saints and martyrs.[36] And Beatriz Pastor reads some episodes in *Naufragios* as examples of fantastic literature, pure fabrication, or both.[37] Analyses such as these, illuminating as they are, cannot account for Cabeza de Vaca's success among the various Native American tribes. By reading *Naufragios* as fabrication or literary convention, they disregard its Native American and testimonial elements. For if Cabeza de Vaca had been operating solely within a European tradition, he could not have had any success among the tribes he encountered, given that his actions (blowing and making the sign of the Cross) would have had no resonance in a world that did not share the Christian tradition. The large crowds that come out to greet him would remain unaccounted for. If the reader is not to dismiss it as fabrication, Cabeza de Vaca's acceptance within the Native American world had to stem from his mobilization of indigenous belief systems as well as Christian ones.[38]

The parallels that Cabeza de Vaca draws between himself and Christ are only one aspect of a larger phenomenon of incipient transculturation by a Spaniard. They are also a literary effect that points to the gap between text and referent that characterizes the chronicles.[39] However, if in the chronicles there is a disjunction between the chroniclers' discourse about the New World and the New World as referent, in Cabeza de Vaca's narrative we find yet another and greater disjunction: that between his practices as a Native American shaman and his use of a biblical discourse to frame these experiences. The biblical model serves to render Cabeza de Vaca's otherwise incomprehensible experiences in America comprehensible to a European reader. At the same time, it obfuscates the shamanic practices and the American reality that he relates. Furthermore, the collapse between a narrative and an experiential "I," as evidenced in so many chronicles, becomes doubly problematic in *Naufragios* because Cabeza de Vaca's shamano-Christian experiences cannot be encompassed by a European narrative "I."

That Cabeza de Vaca could and did appeal to Christian rhetoric in his chronicle was only natural given that he himself was a Christian. However, it was also facilitated by the coincidence between some of the American Indians' shamanic practices and Christianity. In fact, in most tribes the world over, a man or woman is initiated into shamanism by means of his or her ritual death, dismemberment, journey to the beyond, and ultimate resurrection.[40] The superior abilities of the shaman derive from his or her capacity to heal by mediating between patients and the supernatural, which in turn comes about through long periods of fasting, altered states due to the use of drugs, or both. Many of these elements coincide with the life of Christ: his fasting in the desert; his illumination; his ability to communicate with God, to cure the sick, and to raise the dead; and his death and final resurrection. Cabeza de Vaca seems to play with the indeterminacy created by the overlapping of these two very different religious traditions and belief systems. On the one hand, he insists on his Christ-like evangelizing journey, which, as Pupo-Walker points out, is a medieval hagiographic topos. On the other hand, he insistently points to his shamanic practices and his assimilation into Native American culture.

In order to understand why and how Cabeza de Vaca was so successful as a shaman, it is important to attempt, in so far as is possible, to approximate the times, the customs, and the beliefs of the tribes among which he operated. This is no easy task, since the Karankawas were annihilated by their contact first with the Spaniards and then, a century later, with the French. Much of the information we have about the tribes among which Cabeza de Vaca spent his first six years in North America is based on his own account. In fact, W. W. Newcomb, Jr., in his study of the Karankawas, simply repeats what Cabeza de Vaca had observed in *Naufragios*.[41] We have no data about the religious beliefs of the Karankawas. Thus, to understand what Cabeza de Vaca was doing and what cultural codes he had to mobilize in order to have had such a resonance in the Southwest, we must rely on data recently gathered by anthropologists about other tribes the world over. This endeavor is simplified by the fact that shamanism is and was a generalized phenomenon among different tribes in the Americas with minor, regional variations. Mircea Eliade finds "the broad outlines of one and the same shamanic complex from Alaska to Tierra del Fuego."[42] He also argues that "it appears that in the past, at least among some tribes, the shamans' magical power was . . . greater and more spectacular" than it is today.[43]

An important consideration in the case of Cabeza de Vaca is the fact that the shaman is generally chosen in that capacity because he or she is in some way different from the rest of the community. In most cases, twins, breach babies, albinos, and other such individuals are chosen by the community to fulfill the role of shaman, which would point to shamanism as a community's way of negotiating internal difference. In Cabeza de Vaca's case, his difference would have been evident in his skin color, beard, language, and eccentric behavior. His initiation into shamanism, then, would point to the Native Americans' acceptance of him into their community—but into an indeterminate space both inside and outside it.

As I shall argue below, it is this ambivalent and indeterminate space— inside and outside Native American and Spanish culture—that Cabeza de Vaca will inhabit during his years of traveling in the Southwest. This indeterminate space, the space of the hyphen—as it has been theorized for Chicano literature—is the trademark of all narratives of transculturation situated as they are between cultures (see chapter 7).

The position of the shaman as both inside and outside the community was and is so important because shamans mediate between the world of the living and that of the dead, between matter and the spirits, the sacred and the profane, the natural and the supernatural. Their mediation is so crucial because disease is actually dis-ease: the violation of taboos, disorder in the sacred, the rupture of wholeness between the community and the world. Therefore, "sickness is invisible since most sickness was thought spiritual in nature and its cure could only be effected by a superior supernatural power."[44] Disease was, and continues to be, understood to take two different forms at the level of the body: that "due to the introduction of a pathogenic object, and that resulting from 'soul loss.' The treatment in the two cases is essentially different. In the first the effort is directed to expelling the cause of the trouble; in the second to finding and restoring the patient's fugitive soul."[45]

Shamanic diagnoses consist of finding the reasons for a person's disease by means of divination and the shaman's superior ability, dreams, and visions, which are induced either by fasting and deprivation or by drugs and hallucinogenics.[46] The healings consist of a ritual that restores order and balance into the world. They do not take place in isolation and are not an affair exclusively between the shaman and the patient. Rather, the whole community contributes by participating in ritual dancing and singing. This would explain Cabeza de Vaca's continual mention of the dancing and celebrating that take place as he heals. In *Naufragios* he writes "nos trajeron sus enfermos, que santiguándolos decían que estaban sanos . . . y con lo que los otros que curábamos les decían, hacían tantas alegrías y bailes que no nos dejaban dormir" [and they brought us their sick, who, after we blessed them, said they were cured . . . and with what those who were cured told the others, they danced and celebrated so much that they did not let us sleep].[47]

In most cases, Cabeza de Vaca describes this process as one of cause and effect and does not specify that the whole celebration—the healing as well as the ritual dancing and celebrating—was part of one and the same ritual. He usually writes: I healed and everyone celebrated for the next three days. We therefore cannot ascertain whether he was not fully aware of how the process of healing worked, or whether he simply chose not to mention it in his narrative. However, there is one incident in which he describes the celebration as beginning upon their arrival to a new settlement:

Nos metimos en las casas que nos tenían hechas, y nosotros no consentimos en ninguna manera que aquella noche hiciesen más fiesta con nosotros. Toda aquella noche pasaron entre sí en areitos y bailes, y otro día de mañana nos trajeron toda la gente de aquel pueblo para que los tocásemos y santiguásemos como habíamos hecho a los otros con quien habíamos estado.

[We entered the houses they had reserved for us and we absolutely forbade them from celebrating any further with us that night. They spent that whole night celebrating and dancing and on the next morning they brought us everyone so that we would touch them and bless them, as we had done with those with whom we had been.][48]

Once the ritual healing in which the shaman and the community participate has taken place, the sick person can get better. Perhaps more important than the herbal and medical healings themselves is the ritualistic part of the shaman's ceremony, where order and balance are restored to an unbalanced world. Therefore, when Cabeza de Vaca raises his hands to bless the people and makes the sign of the cross, Native Americans read his gestures as part of the shamanic healing ritual. Making the sign of the cross particularly lends itself to such a reading, since by pointing to the four corners of the world, he restores unity and order. The sign of the cross is a sign that can be read equally well by these two different cultures, who give it two very different symbolic meanings. The problem for us, however, is that of determining the extent to which Cabeza de Vaca consciously manipulated two overlapping religious codes.

Cabeza de Vaca's description of one healing that he performs reveals more than any other the extent of his involvement in actual shamanic healing practices, as well as his knowledge of Native American medicine. He describes this case in great detail and I will quote it at length because it is the clearest example of his shamanism:

me trajeron un hombre e me dijeron que había mucho tiempo que le habían herido con una flecha por el espalda derecha, y tenía la punta de la flecha sobre el corazón; decía que le daba mucha pena e que por aquella causa siempre estaba enfermo. Yo le toqué y sentí la punta de la flecha y ví que la tenía atravesada por la ternilla, y con un cuchillo que tenía le abrí el pecho hasta aquel lugar y vi que tenía la punta atravesada y estaba muy mala de sacar; torné a cortar más y metí la punta del cuchillo y con gran trabajo en fin la saqué. Era muy larga y con un hueso de venado; usando de mi oficio de medicina le dí dos puntos, y dados se me desangraba, y con raspa de un cuero le estanqué la sangre e cuando hube sacado la punta pidiéronmela y yo se la di y el pueblo todo vino a verla y la enviaron por la tierra adentro para que la viesen los que allá estaban, y por esto hicieron muchos bailes y fiestas como ellos suelen hacer. Y otro le corté los dos puntos al indio y estaba sano y no parescía la herida que le había hecho sino como una raya de la palma de la mano, y dijo que no sentía dolor ni pena alguna. Y esta cura nos dió entre ellos tanto crédito por toda la vida cuanto ellos podían y sabían estimar y encarescer.

[they brought me a man and they told me that he had been wounded a long time ago with the tip of an arrow, which had gone in through his right shoulder and nested over his heart. He said that it gave him much unhappiness and that he was therefore always sick. I touched him and felt the tip of the arrow and saw that it had gotten in through the cartilage. And with a knife I opened his chest until I reached that place and saw that the arrow was in a bad place and difficult to remove, so I cut more deeply and with the tip of my knife and a great deal of effort, I finally managed to take it out. The tip of the arrow was very long and made of deer bone. Making use of my knowledge of medicine, I gave him two stitches, and since he was bleeding profusely, with the shavings of a hide, I stopped the bleeding. And the Indians asked me for the tip that I had taken out and I gave it to them and the whole village came to see it and they sent it inland so that those who lived there could see it. And because of this they danced and celebrated much as is their wont. And soon thereafter I took the two stitches out and the Indian was healthy and only a thin line, like the lines in the palm of the hand, remained of the wound. And he said he felt no pain or unhappiness whatsoever. And this cure gave us a great reputation among them.] [49]

This account describes an operation of remarkable sophistication. Not only does Cabeza de Vaca extract the tip of an arrow from the vicinity of the heart, but he sews and cauterizes the wound, leaving only a thin scar. Even more important, the patient survives his treatment and is cured. An operation of this magnitude could only have been the work of someone who had learned a great deal about indigenous medicine, and not the work of a man who insists that he cures merely by the grace of God. This description, as well as other incidents, situates Cabeza de Vaca within a Native American cultural, religious, and medical context and undermines the coherence of his Christian discourse.

Although Cabeza de Vaca draws upon the Bible to explain his experiences, particularly by paralleling Christ's sufferings and his own, there is one aspect of his relationship with the Native Americans that is absent in biblical accounts of the life of Christ. Cabeza de Vaca repeatedly writes that the Native Americans fear him, and fear was never a component of Christ's life. Cabeza de Vaca's manipulation of fear must be understood within a Native American conception of shamanism. As Willard E. Park points out: "No doubt the shaman's status among many peoples is due almost as much to the fear of his powers as to respect and awe felt for his powers."[50] That is, the shaman's capacity to heal was accompanied by an equal capacity to hurt.

Within the narrative, what Cabeza de Vaca codes as his Christ-like healing power stands in counterpoint to the destructive forces embodied by one evil shaman. This shaman had been greatly feared and dreaded by Native American tribes some fifteen years before the arrival of the Spaniards. He was called Mala Cosa (Bad Thing) and he literally tortured different tribes with his treatments. His exploits reached fabulous proportions and were probably greatly exaggerated over time. Mala Cosa was described to Cabeza de Vaca as a very small, bearded man whose face was never seen clearly, and who when asked where he came from, would point to the earth. This shaman instilled great terror and horror with his treatments and operations, brutally slashing the sick, cutting out sections of their intestines, and then healing the wound by the laying on of hands. Cabeza de Vaca and his group laughed in disbelief when they were told about Mala Cosa—until they saw the scars that his treatments had left.

Critics have explained Mala Cosa's presence in *Naufragios* as the narrative's element of the fantastic.[51] However, Mala Cosa can be readily understood if situated within a Native American shamanic context. Shamans are chosen in that capacity as a way of negotiating "difference" within Native American communities. Thus, the only difference between Mala Cosa and most other shamans is the fact that he is doubly eccentric because he belongs to no one community but travels from tribe to tribe—or, as he tells the Native Americans, comes from the ground. Interestingly, once Cabeza de Vaca undertakes his journey from the Southwest down into Mexico, he too takes on Mala Cosa's doubly eccentric position with regard to the Native American world.

Cabeza de Vaca plays with the double-sided powers of the shaman by invoking the good, Christ-like side of his own power while also threatening the Native Americans with his potential for evil when they do not do his bidding. He thus situates himself as heir to two different traditions: the good Christ on the one hand, and the evil shaman on the other. The Native Americans who accompany the Spaniards from one tribe to the next tell the others that, if displeased, Cabeza de Vaca has the power to make them all die. Because of this, when they first reach any new village, the Native Americans were "temblando, e sin osar hablar, ni alzar los ojos al cielo" [trembling, not daring to speak nor to raise their eyes], just as they had acted when Mala Cosa had reached their villages.[52]

One episode, more than any other, describes how Cabeza de Vaca consciously manipulates the Native Americans' fear. Wanting to be led to an enemy tribe to which his guides are afraid to go, Cabeza de Vaca and his group go off into the woods to sleep away from the camp. This gesture, along with the "coincidental" sickness and death of several Native Americans that day, suffices to convince the guides to take the Spaniards where they want to go, regardless of the dangers involved in entering enemy territory. After that incident, Cabeza de Vaca writes, "Por toda la tierra donde esto se supo hobieron tanto miedo de nosotros que parescía en vernos que de temor habían de morir" [Through all the land, where this was heard, the Native Americans became so afraid of us that when they saw us, it seemed as if they would die from sheer fright].[53] At this point, Cabeza de Vaca seems to embody the supernatural powers of the shaman over life and death, good and evil, the natural and the supernatural. And although he mostly writes that he heals the sick, that he is kind to the inhabitants, and that he gives as much as he receives (that is, he acts in a Christ-like fashion), here we see him play with the double-edged powers embodied by shamans—particularly with their potential for evil.

The experiences of most Spaniards in the New World were of relatively short duration. Cabeza de Vaca and his group, however, having lived among native tribes for so many years, must have seen the havoc that they wreaked among the inhabitants. Spreading diseases and sowing death wherever they went, the four Spaniards must have been horrified and at a loss. Unaware of the reasons for the many infectious diseases, shamanism provided an explanation for the Native Americans and, through them, the Spaniards as well. When seen in light of the catastrophic effect that the arrival of the Spaniards had in the New World, Cabeza de Vaca's insistence on his "good," Christ-like, healing practices may be understood as a way of minimizing the negative impact that he was actually having on native populations.

Cabeza de Vaca's position within Native American culture is also evident when he writes that no one dares to look at him and that he refrains from talking to anyone in order to maintain his authority. He explains: "Teníamos con ellos mucha autoridad y gravedad y para conservar esto les hablábamos pocas veces. El negro les hablaba siempre, se informaba de los caminos que queríamos ir y los pueblos que había y de las cosas que queríamos saber" [We had much authority and graveness among them and in order to conserve it we spoke to them very little. The black spoke to them always, he informed himself about the route we should follow and the villages that there were on the way and of the things we wanted to know].[54] This tactic coincides with Cabeza de Vaca's arrival among the tribes of northern New Spain. From what we know from Bernal Díaz, the Aztecs never looked at Moctezuma; instead, when in his presence they stared at the ground as a sign of reverence. Cabeza de Vaca seems to have understood this cultural code and manipulated it to his advantage. He also realized that shamans never spoke directly to people; they spoke incoherently or in a language that no one could understand while an interpreter echoed and translated their words. Estebanico seems to have been functioning in that "translating" capacity.[55]

Another clear example of Cabeza de Vaca's conscious mobilization of Native American codes is the episode in which he is given *calabazas* (pumpkins) by a tribe.[56] He realizes the important role that calabazas play as a sign of power and authority among Native Americans. Later in the narrative, when the Native Americans have all fled from the slave raider Diego de Guzmán, Cabeza de Vaca sends a calabaza with the message that they return and re-settle their lands and become Christians. "Y para que fuesen seguros y los otros viniesen les dimos un calabazo de los que nosotros traíamos en las manos (que era nuestra principal insignia y muestra de gran estado) y con éste ellos fueron" [And so that (the messengers) should go safely and so that the others should return, we gave them one of the pumpkins we carried in our hands (which was our main standard/badge and sign of great state) and with this they left].[57] Here we see a remarkable degree of adaptation on the part of the Spaniards, evidenced in their manipulation of the codes of another culture.

The displacement of signs of authority and of wealth (from gold to calabazas) must be situated within the greater context of the ritualistic healings, which entail a handing over of everything that the healed person owns as payment to the shaman. "Después de curado," Cabeza de Vaca writes, "no sólo le dan todo lo que poseen, mas entre sus parientes buscan cosas para darle" [After being cured, not only do they give everything they own to the shaman, but they also search for things from their relatives to give to him].[58] Native Americans therefore fear him not only because of his power over life and death, but also because they know that with his arrival they stand to lose everything. However, Cabeza de Vaca and his group travel so much and heal so many people that they have no use for all the gifts they receive. They therefore redistribute them among those who had guided them from one tribe to another. A custom is quickly established whereby the Native Americans from one tribe give the Spaniards everything they own and then lead them on to the next tribe. There the Spaniards again receive everything, only to redistribute the gifts among their guides, who then go back to their villages, and so on from tribe to tribe. Cabeza de Vaca writes, "y siempre los que quedaban despojados nos seguían" [and always, those who had lost everything followed us].[59] Rolena Adorno argues that the fear of being robbed of everything is at the bottom of Native American fear of the Spaniards. However, I think that Cabeza de Vaca's redistribution of gifts marks a reversal of the relations that until then had characterized the encounter between Spaniards and Native Americans. Now the Spaniards, like the Native Americans, give everything away: "ellos mismos nos ofrescían cuanto tenían y las casas con ello: nosotros les dábamos a los principales para que entre ellos las partiesen" [they gave us everything they had, even their houses, and we redistributed among the leaders (who had guided us) so that they in turn could redistribute the things].[60] Although it was usual for conquistadors to either exchange trinkets of little value for gold or simply to rob the Native Americans outright, here the Spaniards have transculturated an indigenous practice and give away what they receive, taking little or nothing with them.

When they finally encounter other Spaniards in New Spain, Cabeza de Vaca and his men have changed so radically that they are hardly recognized. Cabeza de Vaca writes of their first encounter: "y otro día de mañana alcancé cuatro cristianos de caballo que rescibieron gran alteración de verme tan extrañamente vestido y en compañía de indios" [and on another day I reached four Christians on horseback and the sight of me, dressed so strangely and in the company of Native Americans, caused a great commotion among them].[61] It is striking that he uses the same word, *alteración* (commotion), to describe the Spaniards' reaction to him as well as to describe the Native Americans' reaction upon seeing him, both the first time on the Island of Malhado and later as a white shaman. This foreshadows the gap that opens up between the pronouns "us" and "them" (the other Spaniards). This gap becomes even more apparent when Cabeza de Vaca consistently refers to the other Spaniards as "*los cristianos*," while using an ambivalent "us/*nosotros*" when referring to the Spaniards *and* the Native Americans with whom he was traveling. When describing the first time they see traces of Spaniards, he writes "vimos rastro claro de cristianos" [we saw clear sign of Christians], and later he reports that "Dimos a los cristianos muchas mantas" [We gave the Christians many blankets].[62] In this last example, the "we" is clearly speaking from the American world.

The gap between "nosotros" and "los cristianos" becomes even more significant when Cabeza de Vaca and his group, in true Native American fashion, give everything they have to the Spaniards: "y vinieron seiscientas personas que nos trujeron todo lo más que tenían, mas nosotros no quisimos tomar de todo ello sino la comida, y dimos todo lo otro a los cristianos para que entre sí la repartiesen" [and six hundred people came and gave us everything they had, but we did not want to take anything except the food, and we gave the rest to the Christians so that they could redistribute the things among themselves].[63] Here the chain of redistribution of goods becomes unsettled. It is now no longer from one indigenous group to another via a white shaman, but from Native Americans to Spaniards. Cabeza de Vaca describes the position of his group as indeterminate, belonging with neither the Native Americans nor with the Spaniards, and thereby even further accentuating his intermediate, mediating, shamanic, transcultural position.

The unsteady position of the "us/nosotros" between cultures is also experienced at the level of the body. Having grown used to being clean and naked, Cabeza de Vaca and his companions have difficulty wearing the clothes given to them by the governor of Compostela: "lo cual yo por muchos días no pude traer, ni podíamos dormir sino en el suelo" [for many days I couldn't wear (them), and we couldn't sleep except on the ground].[64] This process has been theorized, in the case of Brazil and the Portuguese experience there, as one instance of the tropicalization of the Europeans. That is, the Spaniards and Portuguese who lived for any length of time in the New World learned to conceive of the body differently than they had before. The New World changed their habits of hygiene: they learned to bathe every day and to wear less clothing. The tropicalization of the body would seem to be applicable in this case, too.[65]

The gap between "nosotros" and "los cristianos" not only results in a split narrative stance, but also in a division between the two groups of Spaniards as to colonial policy in America. Cabeza de Vaca objects to the slave raiders' enslavement and mistreatment of Native Americans. He does not question the superiority of Spanish culture, nor the necessity to Christianize, but, like Father Bartolomé de Las Casas, he advocates a Christianization that *attracts* the native population to a just cause and that does not use force. He therefore uses his authority to bring back many of those who had hidden in the mountains, urging them to resettle their lands and build churches: "los hecimos volver a sus casas y les mandamos que asegurasen y asentasen sus pueblos y sembrasen y labrasen la tierra . . . nos dijeron que harían lo que mandábamos y asentarían sus pueblos si los cristianos los dejaban" [we made them return to their houses and to secure and settle their villages, and to till and sow the land . . . they told us that they would do what we ordered and that they would resettle their lands if the Christians let them do so].[66] In other words, Cabeza de Vaca sees "los cristianos" as the obstacle to Christianization and his own—transcultural—religious practices as the most effective means of evangelization.[67] In this case, however, "evangelization" has become something quite different from what the Catholic church had in mind. It has become a hallucinatory practice of reading the same signs and symbols according to two different cultural codes.

Cabeza de Vaca's idolatrous (from the standpoint of the Inquisition) superimposition of two religions is apparent when he tells Native Americans in New Spain to simply call their god Aguar "Dios" (God). He thus teaches them, in fact, how to disguise their religion within Catholicism: "Nosotros les dijimos que aquél que ellos decían nosotros lo llamábamos Dios, y que ansí lo llamasen ellos y lo sirviesen y adorasen como mandábamos y ellos se hallarían muy bien dello. Respondieron que todo lo tenían muy bien entendido y que así lo harían" [We told them that the god [Aguar] they were telling us about we called God, and that they should call him God too and they should serve and worship him as we ordered and that they would fare well. They answered that they had understood very well and that they would do so].[68]

In other words, what's in a name? Aguar or Dios? Shaman or Christ? The two religions overlap where they coincide, and names begin to hide cultural differences. When Cabeza de Vaca tells Native Americans to merely exchange one name for another, he is only doing what different Andean communities (which I will discuss in the next chapter) would systematically learn to do years later. By hiding indigenous idolatrous practices under Christian rituals, the Native Americans contributed to an uneasy fusion (or confusion) of the two religions. What is noteworthy in this case, however, is that it is a Spaniard, not Native Americans resisting imperialism, who merges the two religions and manipulates the indeterminacy and arbitrariness of signs to his own advantage.

*Naufragios,* then, must be situated as a singular text within that corpus of narratives that constitutes the chronicles. When reading this text with Native American religious practices in mind, it becomes clear that Cabeza de Vaca learned to live between cultures and to understand cultural differences, and that his new understanding of the world situated him both within and outside Spanish culture as well as both within and outside Native American culture. Textually, this meant that the narrative "I" and the experiential "I" do not collapse as readily as they do in most chronicles. In fact, the narrative "I" simply cannot encompass the experiences lived nor the learned biculturalism. This disjunction, felt by critics, perhaps explains the radically dissimilar interpretations of *Naufragios,* which situate the narrative between a medieval hagiographic tradition and the fantastic.

Cabeza de Vaca's apprenticeship in the New World is perhaps best illustrated by a conversation among Native Americans that he overhears and transcribes in the following way:

los indios . . . unos con otros entre sí platicaban diciendo que los cristianos mentían, porque nosotros veníamos de donde salía el sol y ellos donde se pone, y que nosotros sanábamos los enfermos y ellos mataban los que estaban sanos, y que nosotros veníamos desnudos y descalzos y ellos vestidos y en caballos y con lanzas, y que nosotros no teníamos cobdicia de ninguna cosa, antes todo cuanto nos daban tornábamos luego a dar y con nada nos quedábamos, y los otros no tenían otro fin sino robar todo cuanto hallaban y nunca daban nada a nadie; y desta manera relataban todas nuestras cosas y las encarescían; por el contrario de los otros.

[the Indians . . . talked among themselves, saying that the Christians lied, because we came from where the sun rose and they from where it set; and that we healed the sick and they killed the healthy, and that we came naked and barefoot and they dressed and on horseback and with lances, and that we did not covet anything, instead, everything we received we gave away and kept nothing, whereas the others had no other goal than to steal everything they found and they never gave anyone anything. And in this way they described all our habits and doings and praised them, contrasting them to the others' actions, which they criticized.][69]

The gap that had opened up between "us/nosotros" and "them/los cristianos" is clearly apparent in the distinction that the Native Americans make between the two groups. This comparison, perhaps more than any other, shows that the distance Cabeza de Vaca had traveled from Florida to New Spain had created a mental and cultural rift that would henceforth situate him neither here nor there, allowing him to be neither Spaniard nor Native American, neither civilized nor barbaric. As the quincentenary of the "discovery" has come and gone, it is this gap that is increasingly coming to the fore. As more and more critics are pointing out, the colonizer cannot simply impose his culture on a native assumed as a tabula rasa. There are resistances. Furthermore, the experience of discovery and colonization will change not only the colonized, but the colonizer as well.

### NOTES

1. In the sixteenth century, "Florida" comprised a much larger area than it does today. See Robert S. Weddle, *Spanish Sea: The Gulf of Mexico in North American Discovery, 1500–1685.* I thank Michael Greene for mentioning this helpful book and other references used in this study.

2. The account of Álvar Núñez Cabeza de Vaca was probably written by an *escribano*, as were his *Comentarios*. Since conceptions of the text and "the original" were quite different in the fifteenth and sixteenth centuries, the transcribers did not hesitate to interpolate their commentaries or to edit "objectionable" parts, with the predictable result that interpretations of specific texts diverge considerably depending on the sources used.

3. For an excellent analysis of what she has called "el discurso narrativo del fracaso" [the narrative discourse of failure], see Beatriz Pastor, *Discursos narrativos de la conquista: Mitificación y emergencia,* 171–256. For a translation, see Pastor, *The Armature of Conquest: Spanish Accounts of the Discovery of America, 1492–1589.*

4. See Gilberto Triviños Araneda, "Los relatos colombinos," 86; Bernal Díaz del Castillo, *Historia verdadera de la conquista de la Nueva España,* 40; and Leonardo Arroyo, ed., *A Carta de Pero Vaz de Caminha.*

5. "Chronicle" in this case is used as a synonym for "history." It does not designate what Hayden White has called the "naive" chronicle, in which events are simply listed in chronological sequence under the assumption that this temporal ordering "in itself provided a kind of explanation of why [the events] occurred when and where they did." Hayden White, "The Historical Text as Literary Artifact," 93.

6. Walter Mignolo, "Cartas, crónicas y relaciones del descubrimiento y la conquista," 58.

7. Mignolo, "Cartas," 59.

8. Mignolo, "Cartas," 73. Since there was no specified format, many chroniclers chose to write letters, an important discursive genre in the Renaissance. Whether they adhered to the epistolary form or not depended on the level of education they had acquired. Columbus did not follow this format whereas Cortés did, at least initially.

9. Antonio Carreño, "*Naufragios* de Álvar Núñez Cabeza de Vaca: Una retórica de la crónica colonial," 512.

10. Hernán Vidal, *Socio-historia de la literatura colonial hispanoamericana: Tres lecturas orgánicas,* 30.

11. Vidal, *Socio-historia*, 31.

12. For excellent analyses of how this manipulation worked in relation to the writings of Cortés, who was a master at it, see Pastor, *Discursos narrativos,* and Vidal, *Socio-historia.*

13. Mignolo, "Cartas," 71, and Carreño, "*Naufragios,*" 512.

14. Beatriz González S., "Narrativa de la 'estabilización' colonial," 8. González's analysis and critique of colonial literature must be seen in the context of an important new trend in colonial studies that stresses the essential heterogeneity of the literature. Not only are colonial texts read against the grain, but the canon has been expanded to include works that had been excluded from what Ángel Rama has called "la ciudad letrada." See the analyses of Rolena Adorno, Ángel Rama, Hernán Vidal, Beatriz Pastor, and Raquel Chang-Rodríguez.

15. Vidal, *Socio-historia,* 18.

16. Carreño, "*Naufragios,*" 506, 508.

17. For a discussion of Latin American testimonial literature, see Doris Sommer, "Not Just a Personal Story: Women's *Testimonios* and the Plural Self." Sommer argues against the commonly held notion that testimonials are life histories narrated in the first-person that stress development and continuity. She claims that the testimonial narrator speaks from a metonymical connection to a community and thus is very different from the autobiographical first-person.

18. See Irving A. Leonard, *Books of the Brave.*

19. James Clifford, *The Predicament of Culture: Twentieth-Century Ethnography, Literature, and Art,* 14.

20. See Edmundo O'Gorman, *The Invention of America: An Inquiry into the Historical Nature of the New World and the Meaning of Its History.*

21. Renaissance thought, Adorno writes, "resulta inadecuado cuando se mira desde la perspectiva del estudio de fenómenos no europeos" [is inadequate when seen from the perspective of the study of non-European phenomena]. Rolena Adorno, "La *ciudad letrada* y los discursos coloniales," 6.

22. Pastor, *Discursos narrativos,* 212.

23. W. W. Newcomb, Jr., "Karankawa," 359–67.

24. Pastor, *Discursos narrativos,* 224.

25. Álvar Núñez Cabeza de Vaca, *Naufragios,* 59.

26. It is interesting to note that *Naufragios* has been appropriated by the Chicano Movement as the first text to represent the in-between, borderland situation that has come to characterize the position of Chicanos. See Luis Valdez and Stan Steiner, eds., *Aztlán: An Anthology of Mexican American Literature,* and Juan Bruce-Novoa, "Naufragios en los mares de la significación," 12–21.

27. On the radical changes in meaning of the concept of slavery between Native Americans and Europeans, see Michael Taussig, *Shamanism, Colonialism, and the Wild Man: A Study in Terror and Healing.*

28. In fact, with Columbus, the lack of trading ability (together with peacefulness) is interpreted as a lack of civilization and further proof of savagery, since civilized people trade and are aggressive. See Pastor, *Discursos narrativos,* 57.

29. Cabeza de Vaca, *Naufragios,* 76.

30. Cabeza de Vaca, *Naufragios,* 73.

31. Cabeza de Vaca, *Naufragios,* 73.

32. Cabeza de Vaca, *Naufragios,* 74.

33. Cabeza de Vaca, *Naufragios,* 99.

34. Cabeza de Vaca, *Naufragios,* 112.

35. Cabeza de Vaca, *Naufragios,* 122.

36. Enrique Pupo-Walker, "Pesquisas para una nueva lectura de los *Naufragios* de Álvar Núñez Cabeza de Vaca," 524–31.

37. Pastor, *Discursos narrativos,* 238.

38. Pierre Duviols quotes Polo de Ondegardo, who describes, already in the sixteenth century, Peruvian Indian shamans' religious syncretism in a way highly reminiscent of Cabeza de Vaca's practices: "When they find themselves at the bed of a sick person, they give him/her their blessing, make the sign of the Cross and cry: 'Oh, my God, sweet Jesus!' They lay their hands on the patient and, standing or sitting, move their lips, lift their eyes up to the sky and pronounce sacred words. They advise the patient to confess and to follow specific devotions. They cry, say a thousand niceties and make the sign of the Cross, saying all the while that they have received power for that from God himself or from the priests or even from the apostles. But at the same time they make sacrifices secretly and they practice other rites

with guinea pigs, coca, and alcohol. They also rub the stomach of the patient, the legs, or other parts of the body, and they suck out that which hurts. They affirm that they thereby extract blood, worms, and stones which they brandish about saying that the disease has been extracted by the suction." It should be remembered, however, that the Indian shamans practicing these syncretic rites were resisting Christianization, whereas Cabeza de Vaca, a Spaniard and a Christian, was ambivalently merging two religions in order to survive and to gain better efficacy in healing. See Pierre Duviols, *La lutte contre les religions autochtones dans le Pérou colonial: L'extirpation de l'idolatrie entre 1532 et 1660*, 102.

39. Mignolo, "Cartas."

40. Mircea Eliade, *Shamanism: Archaic Techniques of Ecstasy*, 331.

41. Newcomb, Jr., "Karankawa," 366.

42. Eliade, *Shamanism*, 336. Adolph Bandelier's studies of the Aymaras of Lake Titicaca in the early years of this century support Eliade's contention that shamanism must be seen as a universalized phenomenon. Bandelier finds that in Tiahuanaco, "the term *brujo* (sorcerer) appeared to be a household word applied to all Indian medicine-men . . . We were also told of the belief among the Indians that bones of dead 'gentiles' could be introduced into the bodies of persons through evil witchcraft and taken out by some *brujo* through *sucking* . . . Some become 'Yativi' (diviners) because they have been struck by lightning and survived, therefore looked upon as endowed with supernatural gifts; a belief mentioned by older chroniclers and prevailing all over the mountainous districts of Perú." Adolph F. Bandelier, *The Islands of Titicaca and Koati*, 120.

43. Eliade, *Shamanism*, 299. Bandelier's studies again corroborate this assertion. He writes: "the testimony of residents at Copacabana and Puno satisfied us that the influence of the shamans . . . amounts to nearly absolute control of [the Aymara's] actions and thoughts." Bandelier, *Islands*, 122.

44. University of Iowa Museum of Art, *The Art of the Shaman: Northwest Indians*, 14.

45. Eliade, *Shamanism*, 300.

46. Eliade argues that the use of drugs and hallucinogenics is indicative of "the decadence of a technique of ecstasy or of its extension to 'lower' peoples or social groups" and that it is a fairly recent phenomenon. Eliade, *Shamanism*, 477. However, Cabeza de Vaca already mentions drugs when he describes the habits of the Karankawa. He writes: "se emborrachan con un humo y dan cuanto tienen por él" [they get drunk with some kind of smoke and they give everything they have for it]. Cabeza de Vaca, *Naufragios*, 109.

47. Cabeza de Vaca, *Naufragios*, 113.

48. Cabeza de Vaca, *Naufragios*, 112.

49. Cabeza de Vaca, *Naufragios*, 120–1.

50. Willard E. Park, *Shamanism in Western North America: A Study in Cultural Relationships*, 107.

51. Pastor, *Discursos*, 238.

52. As Rolena Adorno has pointed out, this could very easily be explained by the Spaniards' transmission of diseases to the Indians, which ravaged whole populations. However, Adorno and I disagree entirely in our interpretation of Cabeza de Vaca's role among the various Indian tribes. See Rolena Adorno, "The Negotiation of Fear in Cabeza de Vaca's *Naufragios*." See also Cabeza de Vaca, *Naufragios*, 123.

53. Cabeza de Vaca, *Naufragios*, 124.

54. Cabeza de Vaca, *Naufragios*, 130.

55. Eliade, *Shamanism*, 128.

56. "Traían las calabazas horadadas, con piedras dentro, que es la cosa de major fiesta y no las sacan sino a bailar, o para curar, ni las osa nadie tomar sino ellos, y dicen que aquellas calabazas tienen virtud y que vienen del cielo, porque por aquella tierra no las hay" [They brought hollowed-out pumpkins filled with stones, which is a thing held in great esteem and they do not use them except to dance, or to cure, nor does anybody other than them dare hold them, and they say that those pumpkins have virtue and that they come from the sky because in their lands there are none]. Cabeza de Vaca, *Naufragios*, 112.

57. Cabeza de Vaca, *Naufragios*, 144.

58. Cabeza de Vaca, *Naufragios*, 73.

59. Cabeza de Vaca, *Naufragios*, 123.

60. Cabeza de Vaca, *Naufragios*, 123.

61. Cabeza de Vaca, *Naufragios*, 137.

62. Cabeza de Vaca, *Naufragios*, 137, 139.

63. Cabeza de Vaca, *Naufragios*, 139.

64. Cabeza de Vaca, *Naufragios*, 148.

65. See Arroyo, ed., *Carta*.

66. Cabeza de Vaca, *Naufragios*, 140.

67. As Hernán Vidal has pointed out, Cabeza de Vaca here acts in bad faith. The "deal" he strikes with individual Spaniards has no meaning in the context of colonial practices, since it is based on a personal commitment that would not be honored by successive officials: "Cabeza de Vaca diferencia entre individuos mal o bien intencionados éticamente. . . . No tiene conciencia de que el mercantilismo, como sistema total, tiene funciones que están más alla de la voluntad individual" [Cabeza de Vaca draws a distinction between individuals who, ethically, have good or bad intentions. . . . He has no conscious-ness of the fact that mercantilism, as a total system, functions beyond the will of the individual]. In the end, according to Vidal, Cabeza de Vaca uses his authority to subject the native population. See Vidal, *Socio-historia*, 61.

68. Cabeza de Vaca, *Naufragios*, 145.

69. Cabeza de Vaca, *Naufragios*, 140.

## 3 ≈
# DAGON IS THEIR ARK, AND CHRIST THEIR BAAL:
## Christianization, Transculturation as "Contamination," and the Extirpation of Idolatries

*The flag of Castile, in that golden age, always displayed the royal arms on one side . . . and on the other the cross, the image of the Virgin . . . or that of another saint. . . . Spain never advanced forward in her incomparable and overwhelming subjection of peoples without the advancement of the Church.*
— CONSTANTINO BAYLE

*Ye shall utterly destroy all the places wherein the nations which ye shall possess served their gods, upon the high mountains, and upon the hills, and under every green tree. And ye shall overthrow their altars, and break their pillars, and burn their groves with fire; and ye shall hew down the graven images of their gods, and destroy the names of them out of that place.*
— MOSES

*En los refugios distantes, a tiempo fijo, siguen las viejas prácticas y bajo la capa de la liturgia cristiana, debidamente camuflados, están ahí presentes, en el templo o en la procesión los símbolos antiguos.*

*[In distant places the old religious practices continue at fixed times. The ancient symbols are still present in the temple or the procession—properly camouflaged under the veil of Christian liturgy.]*
— PIERRE VERGER

The Conquest and colonization of America can hardly be understood without taking into account the dominant discursive paradigm of conquest as the "conquest of souls." During the colonial period, Christianization played an important role, equal to or greater than military power, in the subjection of native peoples. Indigenous populations were displaced from their lands, reorganized, and relocated in settlements built around Christian churches. The primary function of the *reducciones* (missions) was to control the colonized and force them to adopt Christianity, as well as to extract labor and tribute from them in exchange for evangelization. The upheaval in the Andean world created by these forced displacements was accompanied by the attack on native culture and beliefs. Priests intent on Christianizing very quickly learned that they had to create a religious and cultural vacuum by destroying the idols, worshiping grounds, and religious festivals around which Andean culture was organized in order to then fill it with Christian symbols. Ideally, this meant that Christianization entailed the destruction of Andean culture and beliefs (or des-culturation, in Ortiz's terms), the reeducation of the population, and the adoption of Western practices and beliefs; in short, acculturation. However, in the case of the Peruvian Andean regions of Cuzco (the former Inca capital) and Huarochirí (a region to the east of Lima), the imperial project of Christianization and its actual realization were two different things.

The lack of success in Christianizing different Andean cultures can be attributed to three main reasons. The first lies in the difficulty of erasing telluric religions. As Ruth Gubler Rotsman has pointed out, "la religión de la tierra no muere fácilmente. Una vez consolidada en las estructuras, los milenios pasan sobre ella" [the religion of the earth does not die easily. Once it is consolidated in its structures, thousands of years pass over it].[1] The second reason, related to the first, is that Catholicism was inadequate to take the place of an agricultural religion. The third reason is that a successful Christianization entailed the creation of a cultural and religious vacuum. This proved to be impossible, because it presupposed the complete destruction of indigenous cultures and religions: that is, the extermination of the Andeans.[2] Since this was not achieved (although the population was ravaged by war, brutalization, poverty, and disease), Christianization, in the end, encompassed a series of adaptations, appropriations, and translations of Andean religions on the part of Spanish priests, and a series of resistances to and displacements of Catholic symbols, rites, and rituals on the part of the native population.[3] These accommodations by both sides—which some would call "contaminations" and which I will call "transculturation"—had two different motivations: Christianization and colonization on the side of Spanish priests, and resistance to Christianization on the side of the indigenous Andean population. As Alberto Flores Galindo has shown, "resistance" is an understatement. There have been more than one hundred *violent* Indian uprisings since the Conquest. Critics who insist on the complete and successful subjection of the Andeans adhere to a concept of the "nation" as a homogeneous and exclusive entity. In doing so, they erase a long, turbulent history of indigenous uprisings in the name of a false "unity."[4] Ultimately, these unresolved tensions gave rise to a hallucinatory and refracted form of Catholicism in which religious signs and symbols were destabilized, making meanings oscillate on the borders of the two cultures and religions.[5]

To a great extent, the project of Christianization remained an ideal, not only because cultures cannot be wiped out (unless, as was the case in Cuba and the Antilles, the whole native population is killed or dies), but also because indigenous cultures, however much under attack, never become a tabula rasa upon which another culture can simply and unilaterally inscribe itself. Rather, the Andeans resisted acculturation and evangelization and deployed different tactics in order to maintain and disguise their traditions and beliefs. The Spaniards, for their part, soon realized that knowing was seeing; that is, that they could not even detect, much less destroy, idols unless they learned indigenous languages and studied indigenous culture and beliefs. Michel Foucault's equation of power/knowledge[6] and Todorov's *comprendre/prendre* (understanding/taking)[7] need to be expanded once again to include knowing/seeing, since Andean religious practices—which Father Arriaga ethnocentrically termed "idolatrous"—were invisible to Spanish priests who did not know about them beforehand. Pierre Duviols calls this the "tradition d'incrédulité" [tradition of incredulity] on the part of the conquistadors who, beginning with Columbus, found no evidence of indigenous religions because what they conceived of as religion took an altogether different, and to them invisible, form in the New World.[8]

The "invisibility" of native religions led Spanish priests to become the first ethnographers of the New World. They realized that in order to detect idolatrous practices, they first had to know what to look for. In the process of evangelization, they also realized that they had to approximate and transculturate Catholicism in order to render it accessible to a different culture. They therefore learned an important lesson in cultural relativism and this, to a great degree, allowed them (like Cabeza de Vaca) to question the supremacy of their own culture and religion, if not overtly, at least implicitly in practice. In the process of changing the Other, they inadvertently changed themselves.

One important reason for this change was the fact that in the remote villages of the Andes, priests lived for many years in extreme isolation.

Sooner or later, they began to deviate from Catholic dogma and ritual. Many simply neglected their religious duties, mixed Catholic with "pagan" rites, or ignored the Andeans' tendency to mix the two religions. Many priests, not speaking Quechua correctly, believed they were performing their religious duties when in fact they were deviating from the teachings of the Church. An important text which illuminates these points is Iván Pérez Bocanegra's *Ritual formulario, e institución de curas, para administrar a los naturales de este Reyno*. Written in 1631, this manual was intended to help Spanish priests in the Andean highland city of Cuzco perform Catholic religious rites such as confession, baptism, and confirmation. The Bishop of Cuzco, recommending the book for immediate publication, wrote that it was indispensable not only for the successful Christianization of the native population, but also to help priests "comply with their priestly duties."[9] His recommendation inadvertently acknowledges that priests were unable to perform basic Catholic rites in the New World. Bocanegra's introduction corroborates the bishop's statement and adds that in their efforts to Christianize in the Andes, each priest "quita, y pone, haziendo nuevos Rituales, y viciando las formas de los Sacramentos, sin propiedad. Con solecismos, y barbarismos en el modo delas aplicar a las materias. Y lo mismo en la solene celebración dellos" [takes and adds, creating new rituals and adulterating or contaminating the forms of the Sacraments, with no propriety. With solecisms, and barbarisms in the way of applying them to the rituals. And the same in the solemn celebration of them].[10] Bocanegra's use of the terms *solecismo,* defined as "una composición de oración desbaratada" [the composition of a nonsensical sentence],[11] and *viciar* (to contaminate or adulterate) to describe the disarray and disorder into which Christian dogma had fallen at the hands of priests, is illuminating. When two cultures and two religions meet, order becomes disorder, forms begin to lose their borders and their coherence, and Catholic dogma and ritual begin to deviate from the teachings of the Church. In the language of the evangelizers, ritual and dogma lose their "purity" and become "contaminated" by Andean religious practices. Extrapolating onto a wider context, Spanish culture as a cohesive system or totality is unsettled, forcing reassessments, reevaluations, and readjustments in light of the colonial situation. As we shall see below in the cases of Fathers Arriaga and Ávila, and as Bocanegra's choice of words implies, "contamination" is simply the disorder into which Catholicism falls during, and as a consequence of, the colonial encounter between Christianity and "paganism."[12]

Bocanegra's manual was intended as a corrective guide. Its goal was a return to a form of Catholicism unadulterated not only by Andean beliefs, but also by priests' individual adaptations, their uncontrolled deviations from dogma, and general negligence. Having supervised the evangelization campaigns in Cuzco for more than thirty years and being fluent in Quechua, Bocanegra realized that one of the major obstacles that priests faced was in linguistic competence. He found that many priests did not know what they were saying or doing since they did not speak Quechua properly. To help them, Bocanegra translated Christian prayers, songs, and rituals into Quechua. His translations were accompanied by explanations of the various meanings of words in different cultures and reflections on the difficulty, if not impossibility, of translating not only from one language to another, but also from one cultural context to another. He explains, for example, that the verb "to baptize," generally translated into Quechua by priests as *nocam sutiyaiqui*, actually meant "to name," not to baptize. Since there was no equivalent in Quechua for the Christian concept of baptism, although there was an Andean form of baptism which involved naming, Bocanegra was forced to adopt the term *baptizaiqui*. His neologism in effect combines Spanish and Quechua: to name with holy water. He justifies the necessity for the creation of a new terminology when he writes that "los que en lugar de *Baptizaiqui,* an dicho: *Sutiyaiqui* en ninguna manera an baptizado, sino cometido una grave ignorancia, y sacrilegio: y solo an puesto nombre, aunque ayan tenido intención de baptizar" [those who instead of *baptizaiqui* have said *sutiyaiqui* in no way have baptized; rather, they have committed a grave ignorance and sacrilege. And they have only named, although they intended to baptize].[13]

Understanding the differences between the two religions entailed knowing that the Andeans had a form of baptism that was limited to naming, yet lacked the Christian concepts that were crucial to baptism. Bocanegra therefore created a new word that combined both beliefs and both languages. He realized that Christianization would succeed only if priests learned native languages and translated the Bible and the catechism into those languages. Perhaps most importantly, a "true" Christianization also meant that priests had to understand that words such as "baptize," "god," or "worship" had different—even contradictory—cultural meanings. In effect, Bocanegra's writings reflect a growing awareness of cultural differences. He realized that Spanish language and culture were simply not transparent and universal, as had been assumed by his predecessors. There was no place, then, for literal translations. Rather, translations had to be contextualized culturally.[14] The creation of neologisms such as baptizaiqui shows the degree to which priests attempted to negotiate a tenuous path between the two cultures and beliefs. Bocanegra was not the only one to create neologisms in Quechua and to expand the limits of the language. Father Arriaga, whose work I will analyze below, incorporated more than two hundred Quechua words into Spanish, using them so matter-of-factly that they required no translation or glossary.[15] Both these cases show that "translation" was a practice of transculturation. It actually entailed not only linguistic but also cultural, social, and philosophical negotiations. It included the lexical and conceptual expansion of both languages by the incorporation of foreign words into their vocabularies and by the creation of neologisms.[16]

Aside from important translations of ritual and dogma into Quechua, Bocanegra's *Ritual* contains lengthy lists of questions in Quechua, along with their Spanish translations, which priests were to ask during confession. These questions concerned the Andeans' upholding of the commandments and other sacred Christian rites and rituals. With their minute attention to detail and their knowledge of idolatrous practices, the questions clearly show how aware Bocanegra was of the failure of his evangelization campaigns, although he officially maintained that he had been successful.[17] The questions also reveal the degree to which priests had to be knowledgeable about Andean culture. In order to evangelize in the proper way, they needed to combine Catholic dogma with a knowledge of Quechua that would allow them to say what they meant and mean what they said.

The main idolatrous and sinful practices spanned by Bocanegra's questions include the following:

1. Lying during confession. ("Let the Indians confess all their sins, especially those which they do not want to confess . . . which is easy to see because they swallow saliva often");[18]

2. Confessing to sins not committed, just to please the priest. ("And they confess to things which they never did, nor imagined doing");[19]

3. Confession with *quipus* (counting knots), which in fact reverted back to a form of Andean mass confession. ("Certain quipos or knots and memories which they bring to confession, as a writing");[20]

4. Questions about sexual practices: premarital sex, highly esteemed in Andean culture and a sign of the desirability of a woman, rejected by Catholicism in favor of virginity; homosexual and homoerotic practices; sex with animals;

5. Ritualistic and idolatrous drinking and dancing; not eating salt as a way of asking a favor of the idols; idol worship; worship of ancestors. ("Have you given something to eat to a dead body? . . . Have you worshiped dead bodies?");[21]

6. The interpretation of dreams as omens for the future. ("If you dream of the sun or moon, do you say that a relative is going to die?");[22]

7. Worship of the natural elements. ("Forgetting God, have you worshiped idols, the hills, the springs, the rivers, the sun, the moon, the stars, the morning star, lightning, and all the other things as in times of the Inca?");[23] and

8. General superstitions. ("Have you washed the body of a man or a woman with the grains of maize turned right side up and with white maize?," or, "When you cross a big or small river, do you worship the water and drink of it, so that the river does not carry you away and so that you may cross safely?").[24]

The lists are thorough and lengthy and point to Bocanegra's attempt to classify Andean religious practices into different categories, such as the worship of idols, superstitions, the belief in omens, the interpretation of dreams, sinful sexual practices, and the belief in demons and shamans. Together, these practices form a system of knowledge yet to be analyzed.[25] They show us the extent to which Catholicism was involved in the daily aspects of life, including its attempt to control practices and habits of the most personal and intimate nature. Bocanegra's lists also point to the increasing understanding that Andean religion was inseparable from daily life and that it could not simply be confined to the worship of pagan deities. Therefore, it was not enough simply to destroy all the idols and replace them with the worship of God. Christianization entailed a complete change in the indigenous population's daily actions, beliefs, sexual practices, marriage rites, and death rites.[26] Paradoxically, however, the sense of urgency that pervades Bocanegra's *Ritual* points to the difficulty, if not impossibility, of the Europeans imposing such radical changes on a culture so different from their own. With its emphasis on the faithful adherence of priests to Catholic dogma, it also shows the degree to which priests themselves were contributing towards the transculturation of Catholicism in the New World.

As the *Ritual* shows, the attempt to Christianize inadvertently turned priests into the first ethnographers of Andean cultures. They had to find out what the Andeans believed in order to destroy those beliefs and supplant them with Christian dogma. The first ethnography of the New World, in fact the first book written there, was Father Ramón Pané's *Relación acerca de las antigüedades de los indios,* written as early as 1498—that is, six years after Columbus's arrival in the New World. The *Relación* is an important document because it is the only firsthand study of the original inhabitants of the Antilles that survives. Father Pané was not only the New World's first ethnographer, he also initiated its first literacy campaign. This points to the important role that education and language would play in efforts to Christianize—a role already foretold by Nebrija's dedication of the first Castilian grammar to Queen Isabel.[27]

Other important ethnographies of the Andean region were written as reflections on the process of Christianization in the Andes. These include Father Cristóbal de Albornoz's *Institución para descubrir todas las guacas del Pirú y sus camayos y haziendas* (1570), Cristóbal de Molina's *Fábulas y ritos de los Incas* (1575), Father Bernabé Cobo's *Historia del Nuevo Mundo* (1653), Juan Polo de Ondegardo's *Informaciones acerca de la religión y gobierno de los Incas* (1571), Fray Martín de Murúa's *Historia general del Perú, origen y descendencia de los Incas* (1616), Francisco de Ávila's *Ritos y tradiciones de Huarochirí* (1608), Father José de Arriaga's *La extirpación de la idolatría en el Perú* (1616), and Father Antonio de la Calancha's *Córonica moralizada de la Orden de San Agustín en el Perú* (1639).[28] What all of these texts share is the realization that to know is to see. They are religious texts that yearn for and attempt to recreate a lost Catholic purity, but in the process they have become ethnographic. The mixing of Catholicism and ethnography has, today, transformed these texts into valuable documents about indigenous rituals.[29]

The realization that Andean culture and beliefs had to be well known in order to become visible to Spanish priests is fully articulated by Father Arriaga. His *La extirpación de la idolatría en el Perú* is the account of his experiences traveling from village to village in Huarochirí (which, because of its proximity to Lima, was visited frequently).[30] In these travels, Arriaga followed closely upon the heels of his predecessor, the Jesuit priest Francisco de Ávila. Like Bocanegra's *Ritual*, Father Arriaga's *Extirpación*, written fifteen years before, evidences an early grasp of cultural relativism as well as an attempt to learn Quechua in order to understand Andean culture and beliefs. Unlike Bocanegra, however, whose knowledge derived from thirty years of living and preaching in Cuzco, Arriaga provides us with a rudimentary form of ethnography based on information gleaned from native "informants." As with much ethnography today, the information gained ultimately led to the destruction of Andean culture. In the early days of the Conquest, knowledge of temples and religious shrines allowed them to be plundered by Spaniards searching for gold.[31] The religious sites that were destroyed, however, were the most visible ones and the ones that were thought to contain the most gold. Small shrines and religious sites abounded and were spared. The chronicler Cieza de León, who traveled through Perú a few years after the Conquest, describes the complete destruction of Andean culture: suspen-

sion bridges, temples, and sacred images lay in ruins. However, on his long
travels "Cieza was confronted again and again with the disquieting reality
that God continued to permit the demons to hold dominion over Andean
souls," and that "public idolatry had come to an end with the fall of the Inca
empire, but clandestine idolatry persisted."[32] What happened, in fact, was
that the conquistadors destroyed the official Inca solar cult yet did not realize
until much later that there were innumerable regional and local variants that
were spared.[33] The destruction was also resisted by the indigenous population, who learned to manipulate the cultural codes of Spanish culture
and Catholicism and increasingly dissimulated and disguised their idolatrous
practices. If the Inca solar cult had been massive and public, local Andean
religions had gone underground during the colonial period and were hidden
either in the privacy of the home or in the isolation of distant shrines.

Arriaga's text is crucial within the framework of this analysis of religious
transculturations because it provides us with evidence of colonial attempts
to study and understand Andean culture and religion both systematically and
institutionally. Studies such as his are also useful to the literary critic because
they so clearly demonstrate that to know is to see and that appearances and
reality do not coincide—particularly in bicultural contexts. *Extirpación* is so
important because Arriaga realized that cultural differences and expectations
shrouded Andean religions in invisibility. He argued that Spanish priests
needed to understand Andean culture quite thoroughly in order to actually
see what was going on. He explained that priests had to be well trained in
order to "uncover a deeply rooted, well hidden, and *all-but invisible evil*,"
concluding that "the Indians have been performing their ceremonies and
pagan sacrifices in the sight of all yet they have not been recognized as
such."[34] Arriaga's emphasis on knowing a culture in order to see what is
taking place is an important epistemological step away from cultural comparisons based on assumed similitude and towards an understanding of cultures as different from one another.[35]

Arriaga writes that his book is an attempt to explain why the Andeans,
being Christians "and even the sons and grandsons of Christians," after so
many decades of intense efforts to Christianize them still practiced idolatry.
He wanted to find out why that "evil" had not yet been uprooted and what
means were necessary to do so.[36] In 1616, Father Arriaga realized that "experienced persons . . . believe that [the Andeans] maintain today the same
ceremonies as they did before the coming of the Spaniards, but that they
perform them secretly and that the Devil does not speak to them so fre-

quently nor so publicly as before."[37] Even though Arriaga held that the Devil was less visible in the Andes as a result of intense efforts to Christianize the inhabitants, he nevertheless emphasizes the fact that they had merely learned to disguise and hide their religious practices more successfully from the ever-vigilant priests. Fifty years earlier, the lawyer and Andean historian Polo de Ondegardo had found that the Andeans were shifting their religious practices away from public and visible spaces to the interior of their homes or the seclusion of remote areas. They had also stopped sacrificing llamas, instead sacrificing *cuyes* (guinea pigs) in order to render their practices less visible and to leave no traces of them.[38] More than three hundred years later, Arriaga's suspicions were again proven correct by anthropologists working in the Huarochirí region. María Rostworowski, studying the myths of Huarochirí in the 1960s, discovered that "se comprueba la extraordinaria continuidad, la pervivencia de la tradición" [the extraordinary continuity and the survival and persistence of the tradition is proven].[39] The numerous studies of Huarochirí during the colonial period and in the twentieth century point towards the survival of Andean myths and customs in spite of fierce missionary attempts to Christianize the region (particularly after the two extremely brutal campaigns of extirpation of idolatries in 1545 and 1610), and also as the inadvertent consequence of such attempts. The works of Fathers Ávila and Arriaga, their careful listing and description of idolatrous practices, and their inscription for future reference, actually contributed to the survival of these practices in the modern world, providing contemporary ethnographers with important and valuable data. Studies such as Rostworowski's confirm what Arriaga, Ávila, Bocanegra, Ondegardo, and other priests had already suspected three or more hundred years earlier, and the priests' works enable twentieth-century anthropologists to compare past and present practices.

Bocanegra and Arriaga share the insight that knowing and understanding a different culture not only allow priests to see what is going on, but also allow them to ask the right questions about that culture. Arriaga gives one very clear example of this:

When we ask an Indian whether he has worshiped or adored huacas [idols], this does not mean whether he has seen them or gotten down on his knees before them, because worship does not consist of this, but in coming together for festivals in places chosen for the purpose near the huaca. . . . On such occasions they must wear no Spanish clothing, nor any hat or shoes. Even the caciques [noble leaders], who are generally dressed like Spaniards, wear traditional clothes on these occasions.[40]

Previously, priests had simply asked "do you worship huacas?" and had invariably received a negative response. Father Arriaga, like Bocanegra after him, realized that knowing how to ask the right questions entailed not only a good working knowledge of Quechua, but also an understanding of what different terms meant in the two cultures.

As I have already argued, another obstacle to the successful Christianization of the Andeans lay in the difficulty priests had in identifying idolatrous practices. This was due not only to the general failure of priests to see a different religion at work, as we saw above, but also to the fact that Andean religion did not consist of one set of axioms as did Catholicism, but rather of customs and beliefs that varied regionally. Father Arriaga warns the reader that "Indian superstitions and abuses are as different and diverse as are provinces and towns."[41] He writes that "one should not be astonished that the Indians recognize deity in small things, for it is known that these figures and stones are images representing hills, mountains, and river beds, or even their progenitors and forebears, whom they invoke and worship as their creators."[42] Nature is divine, and even its lowly creatures are worthy of worship. A great part of Arriaga's *Extirpación* is therefore taken up with lists and analyses of all the Andean idols, beliefs, practices, and myths that he discovered, but he warns that the list is inevitably incomplete and should serve only as a guide and not as a definitive study.

Linguistic and cultural obstacles aside, missionaries also faced almost insurmountable physical obstacles. Huarochirí, albeit close to Lima, consisted of many villages, some of which were located in fairly inaccessible areas. Although priests reached Huarochirí more frequently and consistently than they did other regions, particularly during the two great campaigns of extirpation of idolatries, they were still few in number and had difficulty reaching isolated areas. After years of living in remote areas, priests not only tended to deviate from Catholic dogma—as Bocanegra's *Ritual* shows—but also they often simply abandoned the attempt to Christianize the native population. They ignored idolatrous practices and settled for token gestures of acceptance of the new religion, establishing a modus vivendi that allowed them to live peacefully among their parishioners and to profit economically from their services and labor.

At times, local priests actually fostered the Andeans' ignorance of Catholicism, in this way rendering them unequipped to accuse the priests of abuses and deviations from dogma in front of *visitadores* such as Arriaga and Bocanegra.[43] During the early stages of colonization, education played an important role in efforts to evangelize and assimilate the native population to Spanish culture; later, it was knowingly withheld to keep the Andeans ignorant and servile.[44] The visitadores were feared by the Andeans, but priests too did not look forward to these visits, since they were discredited in front of the Church when idolatrous practices were found under their very eyes.

Father Ávila, Arriaga's predecessor, is a good case in point. At the end of the sixteenth century, he was sent to Huarochirí to take charge of the mission in San Damián. Ávila lived peacefully among the Andeans, benefiting economically from their labor and services. When he tried to establish an *obraje* (textile manufacturing plant)[45] in San Damián, he was suddenly accused by "his Indians" of abuses, including sexual and economic exploitation, as well as a poor record of evangelization and adherence to Catholic dogma. Ávila was incarcerated as a result of the accusations against him. This was a rather extreme punitive measure for the colonial administration, which almost invariably sided with the Spaniards against the indigenous population. When he was finally freed and absolved, Ávila returned to San Damián and collected all the information he could about native idolatry. The method he developed, which was later followed by Arriaga and other extirpators of idolatries, was a rudimentary form of ethnography. Ávila coerced and bribed native informants to tell him about Andean myths and beliefs, which he then proceeded to "discover" as he traveled from village to village. As a consequence of his sudden success at uncovering idolatries, destroying idols, and punishing shamans whom he had "befriended" in spectacular *autos-de-fé,* Ávila managed to clear his name and was appointed the first colonial *juez visitador de idolatrías* (judge and visitor of idolatries). In 1610 he orchestrated a campaign of extirpation of idolatries in Huarochirí. Consequently, Ávila became known for his zealousness as an extirpator of idolatries whose cruel methods and punishments shock us today. Just as the Andeans had used their knowledge of Spanish and of the workings of the colonial administration to punish him for his abuses (which they had tolerated until his demands became impossible to meet), Ávila in turn used the information he acquired from bribed or frightened informants to punish them for idolatrous practices that, until his incarceration, he had chosen to overlook.

As a revenge, very lucidly equating power with knowledge, Ávila enlisted the aid of an informant and wrote *Ritos y tradiciones de Huarochirí.* A compilation of Andean myths and cosmogony, this book was intended to help other priests detect native idolatrous practices. It also served to reestablish

Father Ávila's credibility as a successful evangelizer and as a detector and extirpator of idolatries. Today it appears evident that Ávila, until the accusation by the Andean community of San Damián, had actually lived among them quite peacefully. He had preached regularly and had also pursued economic ventures, not only ignoring but actually fostering those idolatrous practices that were financially advantageous to him. For example, Ávila encouraged his parishioners to lay gifts—which he then collected—on the tombs of their ancestors on All Saints Day. This practice was forbidden by the Inquisition because it entailed ancestor worship. The case of the community of San Damián against Ávila seems to have stemmed from his plan to open the textile plant. This project was vehemently opposed by the inhabitants, who were already physically and economically overburdened, because they were to provide free labor.[46]

It seems that the "happy" cohabitation of priests and Andeans, once evidenced in the case of Ávila, was not unusual. Priests often took the place of Indian *caciques* (nobility) within the hierarchies of Andean communities, reaping all the financial benefits to which the latter traditionally had been entitled.[47] As we shall see in the next chapter, Spanish attempts to substitute Andean caciques can also be seen in colonial paintings, where Spanish kings are painted as the successors to the Incas. Similarly, the cross was planted on top of the *apus* (the Andean mountain gods) in order to symbolize the spiritual "conquest" by the Spaniards' God. Ávila, and others like him, simply took the place of the disappeared Inca ruling class and acquired all the benefits that would have accrued to them, disposing of the inhabitants' time and manpower and receiving goods in exchange for their religious services.

Although the people in Ávila's mission had acquired enough knowledge to have him arrested and incarcerated, by the time of Father Arriaga priests were purposefully keeping the indigenous population in ignorance in order to avoid being denounced. Arriaga cites an example of the willful attempt of a priest to actually withhold education from his community. In a large town that he visited, Arriaga found that no one had been taught to read and write or to officiate at mass. He questioned the priest as to this deplorable state of affairs, asking him "why he had not established a school, which would have been easy and profitable to do." The priest answered that "the Indians did not need to read or write, since such knowledge would be of no use to them except to criticize their priests."[48]

Guamán Poma de Ayala corroborates Arriaga's findings. He writes that he had observed that priests: "impiden a que (los indios) no sepan leer ni escribir, ni gusta que ayga maestro de escuela . . . lo hace para que no lo asiente sus bellaquerías y maldades, robos" [prevent the Indians from learning to read and write, nor do they like that there be a school teacher . . . and they do this so as to prevent the Indians from denouncing the priests for their roguery, evilness, and thefts].[49] Like Caliban, who learns to curse his master with the language that the master taught him, the Andeans use their new knowledge to expose the abuses committed by priests, in fact reversing the role knowledge previously had played at the hands of the Spaniards. As Walter Mignolo argues, and as I will show in my analysis of the paintings of the Cuzco School in the next chapter, education not only helps the Andeans accuse the Spaniards of abuses, it also enables them to preserve and stabilize their history.[50] Paradoxically then, "While literacy is conveyed, initially, in order to govern and control the native population, it is prevented, ultimately, in order to have the same results."[51]

As we saw above, the fundamental differences between Andean and Christian religions, which conceived of "worship" and "deity" in very different ways, led to the "invisibility" of idolatrous practices from a Spanish point of view. But there was also the problem of coincidences between the two religions. We have seen in the previous chapter how these apparent similarities were manipulated by Cabeza de Vaca. Christianity and Andean animism coincided in their belief in a creator (God/Inti), both had mediators between this world and the supernatural (the saints, the Virgin Mary, Jesus, priests/the apus or mountain gods, Pachamama or the earth, shamans), both held festivals on special religious occasions (Corpus Christi in honor of the Eucharist/Oncoymita, a celebration of the apparition of the Pleiades in the southern heavens), and both had symbols in the shape of a cross (the cross/the Cross of the South, a heavenly constellation).[52] These coincidences allowed the native population either to assimilate and conflate Christian elements with Andean ones, or to hide their beliefs under the guise of Christianity (seeing, for example, the sun in the golden Eucharist, the Cross of the South in the Christian cross, or the Pachamama in the various advocations of the Virgin Mary).[53]

"It was discovered in Huarochirí," writes Father Arriaga, "that in order to worship an idol in the form of a woman called Chupixamor, and Mamayoc, they celebrated a festival to the image of Our Lady of the Assumption, and to worship a male idol by the name of Huayhuay, they celebrated a festival to a crucifix." He also adds that when the Andeans march in the procession of the Corpus Christi, they not only identify the sun in the Eu-

charist and have hidden their idols under it, but the actual dates of the celebration of the Oncoymita and the Corpus Christi have been made to coincide.[54] Because of this coincidence, Arriaga very slowly and painfully learns
that appearances and reality do not coincide. When the Andeans appear to
be worshiping the cross, for example, they are actually worshiping their idols
buried beneath it. In one such instance, a priest's suspicions were aroused
when the Andeans very willingly, and showing no sign of resistance, worshiped the cross that had been erected on a mountain top. The priest then
dug underneath the cross and found "the *huaca* of the town. It was of liver-
colored stone with a face and eyes and stood upon a stone base with twenty-
five *canopas,* or lesser idols, around it."[55] Hiding Andean idols in or around
Catholic holy sites seems to have been a pervasive practice. Father Arriaga
writes that he found them in and around churches, even in the niches of the
saints.

Four different types of displacements are at work here. The first is a fairly
simple mapping of one cultural symbol onto another. This is the case with
the Eucharist, made of gold and shaped like the sun, which very easily allows
the indigenous population to see in it the god of the sun, Inti. In this case
one symbol lends itself to a bicultural reading. The second is the metonymic
and spatial displacement of a Catholic symbol onto an Andean one, such as
the displacement away from the cross onto the idols buried beneath, or away
from the saints in their shrines onto the idols hidden behind them. The third
consists of temporal displacements in the conflation of religious festivals,
such as when the Andeans make the dates of their religious feasts coincide
with Catholic ones. While they appear to be worshiping the Holy Sacra-
ment in the procession of the Corpus Christi, they are actually celebrating
an Andean religious festival. The fourth displacement consists of a more
complex process whereby several different indigenous cultural symbols are
distilled into the form of a single Spanish symbol. The Andean cult of the
Pachamama and other telluric female and male deities, for example, is subsumed in the cult of the Virgin Mary in all her advocations.[56] Displacements
such as these render the Virgin Mary more complex, since she now represents not only the mother of God, but the apus and the Pachamama as well.
Not only do the Andeans hide their idols in, next to, underneath, or close
to Catholic religious symbols, thereby displacing "worship" from one onto
the other metonymically, but the play of dissimulation and coincidence is
facilitated by the proximity of Andean beliefs with pagan, pre–Christian elements assimilated by Christianity in its formative stages.[57] In the world of

the extirpator of idolatries, not even naming is innocent. This is evident in the use of the name Santiago. As Father Arriaga explains, the Andeans "often give this name to one of their *chuchus* (twins), as a son of lightning, which they call Santiago." And he adds:

I do not think this is because of the name Boanerges, which Christ our Lord gave to the Apostle Saint James and his brother, Saint Thunder, according to the Hebrew phrase. It is probably because the phrase has been brought here or suggested by the young Spaniards who, when it thunders, say that Saint James's horse is running. Or perhaps they have noticed that when Spaniards wage war, they shout before shooting their arquebus, which the Indians call *illapa,* or lightning, "Santiago! Santiago!" However this may be, they have taken over the name Santiago and attach superstition to it.[58]

Teresa Gisbert finds the source for such convergences in biblical apocrypha where pagan attributions of saints and angels remain evident.[59] Arriaga's philological speculations aside, we can say that the Andeans have appropriated a Spanish name and given it an Andean meaning. The signifier "Santiago," therefore, has acquired an additional cultural meaning different from and in contradiction with the Spanish one. Signifier and signified are culturally switched and resonate with the pagan elements assimilated by Catholicism. Aware of the undertones of the Andeans naming their children Santiago, Father Arriaga establishes a prohibition against the use of this name and orders that their sons be called "Diego" instead.[60]

Yet another displacement takes place when the Andeans inadvertently usurp Catholic rites by incorrectly reciting prayers. Father Arriaga once heard them recite the Credo, saying *pucllachacuininta* (the jest or merriment of the saints) instead of *hucllachacuininta* (communion, or gathering of saints).[61] He also found that in church, the Andeans recite "in a parrotlike manner." When asked what they are saying, they reply "in chorus," but if one of them is questioned alone, "not one in twenty knows the Christian doctrine, that is to say the rudiments."[62] This parrotlike going through the motions, without an understanding of their function, empties signifiers of their meanings, leaving only an apparent and hallucinatory Christianization. Yet, as with the above example, meaningless signifiers are sooner or later invested with new meaning (the jest or merriment of the saints) that makes more sense within an Andean context.

An even more prevalent practice, the one that perhaps bothers Father Arriaga the most, is the "contamination" of Catholicism by Andean religions. He describes this process by writing that just as the Andeans "have a tendency to carry water on both shoulders," so too do they "have recourse to both religions at once." We have already examined the case of Cabeza de Vaca, who also had recourse to two religions at once, but here the merging of two different religions is carried out by the indigenous population. "I know of a place," writes Father Arriaga, "where a cloak was made for the image of Our Lady and a skirt for their huaca from *the same cloth.*" As if this were not enough, he also finds that "for the worship of Jesus Christ they generally offer what they offer their huacas."[63] Horrified, Arriaga tries to change this state of affairs, but the Andeans argue back that as "the statues of the saints represent the huacas of the Viracochas (white men) and that as they have theirs, the Indians also have theirs."[64] This naïveté, coming as it does from descendants of the Incas who had conquered and subjected a large number of different cultures, is implausible and must be seen as yet another strategy of resistance.

Afraid of being contaminated by the Other and by the Other's religion, Father Arriaga tries to keep things separate: idols are only idols and God is God, hence his (and the Church administration's) emphasis on confining and isolating witchdoctors and the children of the caciques from their communities. Father Arriaga's almost phobic fear of contamination is shaped by the history of the non-assimilation of the Jews and Moors in Spain, who retained their beliefs and traditions regardless of Spanish efforts to Christianize and acculturate them. Of the Jews, Arriaga writes that anyone could see that they were outsiders in Spain "despite the fact that they came to that country more than 1,500 years ago." His diatribe continues anti-Semitically: "it has scarcely been possible to extirpate so evil a seed in so clean a land, where the Gospel has been so continuously, so carefully, and so thoroughly preached."[65] The Moors, finally expelled from Spain in 1609—not coincidentally one year before the great campaign of extirpation of idolatries—had followed a similar trajectory to that of the Andeans: rather than assimilating Spanish culture and Catholicism, they had persisted in their beliefs clandestinely.[66] Not only that, but Spanish culture had inadvertently assimilated many Moorish elements. Arriaga's horror in seeing the Andeans use the same cloth for both saint and idol and make the same offerings to both Christ and idol is the horror of contamination and, perhaps, the horror of cultural mestizaje. It is based on the imperial dream of a pure, unadulterated culture that represses all the cultural and religious borrowings upon which it is constituted.

Within this context, Father Arriaga's detection of idolatrous practices can be seen as the attempt to eradicate instances of contamination of one religion by another and to keep Spanish culture and Catholicism pure.

*La extirpación de la idolatría en el Perú* is also the record of the failure of that attempt. Arriaga's discourse was itself unable to maintain the purity that it encouraged priests to uphold. His text became a hybrid, oscillating generically between ethnography and religion. Arriaga must be credited, however, for the lucidity with which he perceived what was happening, and for his realization that in the encounter between Christianity and "paganism," appearances and reality did not coincide. For the most part, his conclusion to the 1616 edition of *Extirpación* still holds true today: "Dagon is their Ark, and Christ their Baal."[67]

The attempts to understand and detect idolatrous practices not only offer valuable data to the ethnographer, but also are useful to the literary critic. Inadvertently, these works show how we must proceed if we are to read biculturally and detect traces of Andean culture in apparently hegemonic, non-Andean texts. The tactics used by Arriaga, Ávila, and Bocanegra to detect and extirpate idolatries can be turned around and used productively, not to destroy the Other and not to achieve power through knowledge, but as a point of departure for readings that consider and reveal the intrinsic heterogeneity of Latin American literature. As literary critics, we too must understand that knowing is seeing.

## NOTES

1. Ruth Gubler Rotsman, "La labor misional en Yucatán en el siglo XVI," 33. For an excellent introduction, see also René Jara and Nicholas Spadaccini, "Introduction: Allegorizing the New World," in their *1492–1992: Re/Discovering Colonial Writing,* 17.

2. I have opted for the word "Andean" because, although awkward, it is more indigenous than Amerindian, Native American, Indian, and other available terms.

3. I use the plural "religions." At the official level, the Andeans believed in the sun and in a series of deities that remained constant throughout the Tahuantinsuyo. However, this religion broke down into regional variants at the local level. See Sabine MacCormack, "Demons, Imagination, and Incas," 136.

4. See Alberto Flores Galindo, *Buscando un Inca: Identidad y utopía en los Andes.*

5. See Eric Wolf, *Sons of the Shaking Earth: The People of Mexico and Guatemala—Their Land, History, and Culture,* 170–1. Wolf argues that just as Christianity had assimilated pagan idols and beliefs, it also assimilated Andean ones. In fact, the surprising similarities between Catholicism and Andean beliefs further facilitated this process. However, as I will show, assimilation worked both ways: the Andeans assimilated Catholic beliefs, and the Spaniards Andean beliefs.

6. See Michel Foucault, *Power/Knowledge.*

7. See Tzvetan Todorov, "Comprendre, prendre et détruire," in his *La conquête de l'Amérique: La Question de l'Autre.*

8. Duviols, *Lutte,* 170.

9. Iván Pérez Bocanegra, *Ritual formulario e institución de curas,* "Carta al Ilustrísimo Señor don Lorenzo Pérez de Grado, Obispo de la gran ciudad del Cuzco."

10. Bocanegra, *Ritual,* "Epístola a los curas."

11. Sebastián de Covarrubias, *Tesoro de la lengua Castellana, o Española.*

12. Mary Douglas, comparing "primitive" to Western concepts of pollution, argues that dirt and pollution are culturally relative terms. Dirt is only that which destroys the order of a cultural system; in fact, dirt is simply disorder, disarray, and displacement of things. She writes: "If we can abstract pathogenicity and hygiene from our notion of dirt, we are left with the old definition of dirt as matter out of place." See Mary Douglas, *Purity and Danger: An Analysis of the Concepts of Pollution and Taboo,* 35.

13. Bocanegra, *Ritual,* 46. In his *Nueva corónica y buen gobierno,* the Andean historian Guamán Poma de Ayala points out ironically and critically that priests spoke only those few sentences of Quechua and Aymara that were necessary for their economic and sexual well-being and for their exploitation of the native population. These were: "bring horse," "you shall not eat," "You shall see the priest," "where is the unmarried woman?" (or, a variation of the latter phrase with the same intent, "where are the young women?"), and the final command, "you shall bring them to the mission." See Guamán Poma de Ayala, *Nueva corónica y buen gobierno,* ed. and trans. Franklin Pease, vol. 2. All extracts from *Nueva corónica y buen gobierno* are from this edition.

14. The infamous *requerimiento* was an untranslated document read at full speed to uncomprehending native populations, whereby Spain legally justified its conquest of the New World. See Jara and Spadaccini, eds., *1492–1992.*

15. See L. Clark Keating's preface to his translation of Arriaga's text, *The Extirpation of Idolatry in Peru,* vi.

16. For excellent essays on cultural translation, see Susan Bassnett and André Lefevere, eds, *Translation, History and Culture.*

17. See Duviols, *Lutte,* 173.

18. Bocanegra, *Ritual,* 109.

19. Bocanegra, *Ritual,* 112.

20. Bocanegra, *Ritual,* 111.

21. Bocanegra, *Ritual,* 130.

22. Bocanegra, *Ritual,* 147.

23. Bocanegra, *Ritual,* 130.

24. Bocanegra, *Ritual,* 128, 129.

25. I thank Raúl Bueno for this observation. Bocanegra's classification is an important one and still needs to be studied, because it would provide us with a means of understanding seventeenth-century attempts to classify Andean practices and religious beliefs.

26. Duviols interprets Christianization as a war on Andean culture. See Duviols, *Lutte,* 123.

27. Antonio de Nebrija wrote the first grammar of the Castilian language in 1492, not coincidentally. His dedication to Queen Isabel reads as follows: "Language has always been the companion of empire . . . language and empire began, increased, and flourished together." See González Llubera, ed. *Gramática de la lengua castellana, o española.*

28. For a more complete bibliography and study of the extirpation of idolatries in colonial Perú, see Duviols, *Lutte.*

29. Duviols, *Lutte,* 92.

30. The *visitadores* were highly ranked clergymen who were sent by the Inquisition in Lima to "visit" different provinces in order to evaluate the evangelizing work of priests, to uproot idolatrous practices, and to persecute shamans.

31. As Duviols points out, the historian Cieza de León, traveling around Perú after the Conquest, found most Andean temples plundered and in ruins. Duviols, *Lutte,* 78.

32. See MacCormack, "Demons," 131.

33. The Incas had imposed the sun cult on conquered peoples while allowing the persistence of local cults and even the addition of other deities into the official pantheon. Similarly, Catholicism merely supplanted state sun worship without eradicating local variants. As Franklin Pease writes: "En realidad, antes que la suplantación de los cultos locales por el oficial del Cuzco, lo que se hizo fue sobreponer a las religiones lugareñas la solar cuzqueña pero sin destruir por ello los adoratorios ni prohibir en forma alguna

el culto a los dioses locales. . . . De esta manera se dio inicio a la formación del primer plano . . . el del culto estatal que hallaron los españoles, el mismo que fue reemplazado después de 1533 por el Cristianismo como religión oficial, pero sin destruir la vida religiosa andina en los otros planos, como dan testimonio ininterrumpido los extirpadores de "idolatrías" de los siglos XVI y XVII primero, y los estudios contemporáneos a nosotros, después." [In reality, instead of supplanting local cults with the official one of Cuzco, the Incas superposed the Cuzco solar cult onto that of local religions without destroying local worshiping grounds or prohibiting in any way the adoration of local gods. . . . In this way, the first level was consolidated . . . that of the state cult found by the Spaniards, the same one that was replaced after 1533 by Christianity as the official religion, but without destroying Andean religious life in its other levels. This is witnessed repeatedly first by the extirpators of "idolatries" of the XVI and XVII centuries, and then by studies contemporary to ourselves.] See Franklin Pease, *Los últimos Incas del Cuzco*, 51.

34. Arriaga, *Extirpation*, 103 (emphasis added).

35. See Foucault, *The Order of Things*.

36. Arriaga, *Extirpation*, 6.

37. Arriaga, *Extirpation*, 60.

38. Duviols, *Lutte*, 100. See also Polo de Ondegardo, *Tratado y averiguación*.

39. Maria Rostworowski, "Presentación," 10. Since Huarochirí lay relatively close to Lima, the ecclesiastical center of Perú, it was visited more frequently and consistently than other more remote and isolated regions, which in many cases "suffered" from the benign neglect of the Church. For this reason, Huarochirí has been studied and written about fairly continuously since the seventeenth century. Father Ávila's and Father Arriaga's texts, as well as other studies, provide important ethnographic data about customs, beliefs, and myths in the region, serving as points of departure for anthropological studies in the twentieth century. See Karen Spalding, *Huarochirí: An Andean Society under Inca and Spanish Rule*, and Rostworowski, *Señoríos indígenas de Lima y Canta*.

All these documents have in turn served as a valuable quarry for contemporary novelistic reinterpretations and reelaborations. See José María Arguedas's use of these myths in *El zorro de arriba y el zorro de abajo*, as well as Oscar Colchado Lucio's *Hacia el janaq pacha*.

40. Arriaga, *Extirpation*, 51.

41. Arriaga, *Extirpation*, 52.

42. Arriaga, *Extirpation*, 11. As Sabine MacCormack writes, the Andeans endowed their landscape with life: "The primary Andean process of generation was the transformation of rocks and inanimate matter in general into human beings. This process was held in tension by its opposite, the transformation of humans into rocks. The Andean landscape was thus littered not only with a multitude of places of origin, but also with rocks which had once been human and now acted as guardians of fields and villages . . . places where an Inca had been born or where he had rested or dreamt a dream were thus set aside as holy by periodic sacrifice. Other sacrifices marked sites where battles had been won . . . [thus] With each Inca's reign . . . Cuzco and the surrounding countryside became more richly textured with holy places which projected their sacred power into the present." And she explains the constitution of *guacas*: "Trees, like *illapa*, also attracted cult in their own right, and not only as first ancestor and point of origin of some group of people. In this sense, trees figured among the broad category of worshipful entities which Andeans describe as *guaca*. Stones, springs, caves, indeed any feature of the landscape, could also qualify as *guaca*. So did the three siblings of Manco Capac turned into stone, as well as Manco Capac himself, for his *mallqui* was a stone. As *mallquis* therefore, the Incas shaped on the one hand the historical past, and on the other, they shaped the natural environment, the geographical cosmos." MacCormack, "Children of the Sun and Reason of State: Myths, Ceremonies, and Conflicts in Inca Peru," 8, 15, 22.

43. Duviols writes that a great number of priests "avaient établi avec leurs fidèles un *modus vivendi* où ils trouvaient leur tranquilité et leur profit en acceptant de fermer les yeux" [had established a modus vivendi with their parishioners that allowed them to live peacefully among them and to profit economically by closing their eyes to their practices]. Duviols, *Lutte*, 170.

44. See Mignolo, "Literacy and Colonization: The New World Experience," 72.

45. Eric Wolf, writing about Central American obrajes during the colony, described them as follows: "To obtain the necessary labor force, the *obrajes* frequently made use of forced labor. Workers were prisoners condemned to work off a sentence or a debt, or simply men held against their will . . . The

crown attempted to regulate these prison-like establishments and to improve working conditions, but they continued to flourish in the shadow of the law and of guild regulations . . . Conditions in these prison-like mills did not change until the advent of the first steam-driven machinery in the mid-nineteenth century." Eric Wolf, *Sons of the Shaking Earth,* 185.

46. See Antonio Acosta's recent biography of Ávila, "Francisco de Ávila: Cusco 1573(?)–Lima 1647." Pierre Duviols adheres to the older interpretation of Ávila's actions, whereby the latter is said to have "suddenly" discovered idolatrous practices in Huarochirí. Duviols overlooks his earlier statement regarding the common practice by priests of establishing a comfortable modus vivendi among the Andeans. See Duviols, *Lutte,* 149.

47. Guamán Poma is critical of the practice of Spanish priests taking the place of Andean caciques. See Poma, *Nueva corónica,* vol. 2, 54.

48. Arriaga, *Extirpation,* 66.

49. Poma, *Nueva corónica,* vol. 2, 34.

50. For an analysis of the function of literacy to subvert and criticize the colonial administration, see Adorno, *Guamán Poma,* and Mercedes López-Baralt, *Icono y conquista: Guamán Poma de Ayala.*

With regard to the relation between literacy and Andean constructions of history, Mignolo writes: "As time went on, the European script that the friars were so eager to transmit in order to be more effective in the christianization of the natives was used by the latter to stabilize their past, to adapt themselves to the present and to transmit their own traditions to future generations." Mignolo, *Literacy and Colonization,* 70.

51. Paulo Freire in Mignolo, *Literacy and Colonization,* 72.

52. The cross as symbol seems to have been a known and prevalent form among the Andeans. Duviols cites Miguel de Estete's *El descubrimiento y la conquista del Perú,* in which the chronicler tells of the indigenous practice of displaying cadavers in the shape of the cross ("Estete parle des cadavres qu'on disposait en forme de croix"), Duviols, *Lutte,* 78. The writer Oscar Colchado Lucio, a contemporary neo-indigenista, also plays with this earlier Andean knowledge of the cross when he writes of a shaman killed by the Spaniards during the Inquisition. As the shaman lay dying, he recalled the moment when he had incited his followers to burn a Spanish cross, saying "ella no representaba a la Katachilla, la constelación del sur que en las noches veíamos en el alto cielo del Tahuantinsuyo . . . Que el símbolo de la Katachilla era la cruz cuadrada inscrita en nuestros templos y adoratorios, que no tenía nada que ver con la cruz de los cristianos: dos maderos cruzados soportando a un hombre muerto" [that it did not represent the Katachilla, the constellation of the south, which we saw at night in the high skies of the Tahuantinsuyo . . . That the symbol of the Katachilla was the square cross inscribed in our temples and shrines, that it had nothing in common with the cross of the Spaniards: two crossed pieces of wood holding a dead man]. Lucio, *Hacia,* 16.

53. See Wolf, *Sons of the Shaking Earth,* 171.

54. Arriaga, *Extirpation,* 70. Guamán Poma also corroborates this claim. See Poma, *Nueva corónica,* vol. 2, 44.

55. Arriaga, *Extirpation,* 81–2.

56. See Teresa Gisbert, *Iconografía y mitos indígenas en el arte,* 19–21.

57. Manuel Marzal, in his comparative study of Latin American religions (Mayan, Inca, and Afro-Brazilian), comes up with a similar scheme. See Manuel M. Marzal, *El sincretismo iberoamericano.* He argues that when two religions enter into conflict, there are three possible results: religious synthesis, or the confusing of the two religions into a new one; they overlap, maintaining their own identity and producing a simple juxtaposition; or they integrate into a new one "siendo posible identificar la procedencia de cada elemento de la misma y produciendo así un verdadero *sincretismo*" [it being possible to identify the origin of each element of the new religion and thus produce a true *syncretism*]. Marzal, *Sincretismo,* 175. It is this last option that he finds has taken place in Perú. Syncretism involves four different and simultaneous processes: persistence, loss, synthesis, and reinterpretation. As for the last of these, Marzal argues for three types of reinterpretation. In the first, "Se acepta el rito cristiano y se le da un significado indígena" [The Catholic rite is adopted and given an indigenous signification]. The example he gives is that of the Otomy Indians, who adopt the Christian ritual of "responso" (a prayer said in honor of the dead) in order to liberate them from their sins, but they do it "para librarse de los castigos de los muertos" [to liberate themselves from the punishment of the dead]. In the second, the indigenous ritual is maintained, but it is given a Christian meaning. For example, in Cuzco the "pago a la Pacha-

mama" [paying of Pachamama], which is performed at the beginning of August to thank the goddess for the bounty of the earth and to ensure fertility in the future, is maintained. Now, however, Pachamama has become the Virgin Mary, who tells God: "Yo voy a alimentar a tus hijos" [I am going to feed your children]. In the third type of reinterpretation, the Christian ritual is accepted, but new meanings are added. This is the case when Andeans baptize their newborns so that they become Christians, but also so that Illapa (lightning) does not strike them and so that, in case of premature death, they do not become dwarfs. Marzal, *Sincretismo*, 177, 118.

Marzal also argues that the Andean/Catholic religion that has arisen in the Andes is a new religion, because "están integrados los elementos católicos e indígenas en un todo coherente" [Catholic and Andean elements are integrated into a coherent whole]. Marzal, *Sincretismo*, 192. I disagree with him completely here, since I think one of the first and main tactics of colonial power is the destruction of that "todo coherente" of culture for the colonial subject. That is why transculturation, with its emphasis on the processes of mediation, loss, and reinvention that have arisen since the Conquest, is a far more appropriate concept. To argue for syncretism is, in the end, to argue that the Andean-Catholic religion is a finished product, that it has achieved a state of balance. This is not the case, especially since the Andeans are still very much under attack.

58. Arriaga, *Extirpation*, 54.
59. See Gisbert, *Iconografía*, 86.
60. Arriaga, *Extirpation*, 54.
61. Arriaga, *Extirpation*, 61.
62. Arriaga, *Extirpation*, 60–1.
63. Arriaga, *Extirpation*, 73 (emphasis added).
64. Arriaga, *Extirpation*, 72.
65. Arriaga, *Extirpation*, 9.
66. Duviols, *Lutte*, 177.
67. Arriaga, *Extirpation*, 73.

# 4 ≈
# THE CUZCO SCHOOL OF PAINTING AND ARTISTIC TRANSCULTURATION:
## A Picture Essay

*But culture is always impure, like people. We cannot talk about art by using a static, purely aesthetic conception of it. Impurity is necessary; art feeds on impurities.*

— EDMUNDO DESNOES

The Cuzco School of painting emerged in the eighteenth century as "one of the most extraordinary expressions of art in the Americas."[1] The painting of religious images had been introduced to Perú by the colonial Church at the end of the sixteenth century. As well as decorating churches, these paintings served to help priests in their efforts to evangelize, this time not by coercive means like those employed by the extirpators of idolatries, but rather by letting the persuasion and power of images work on the religious imagination of the native population.[2] As a result, painting flourished in metropolitan centers such as Lima, Quito, and La Paz, but by far the most vital artistic movement arose in the Andean city of Cuzco. Established as a religious center during the early colonial period, Cuzco was a city with a long tradition as center of the Inca world.[3]

The paintings that emerged in and around Cuzco during the colonial period were subservient to the written word in two important ways. Because the values of the Cuzco School were determined by the traditions of European religious art, paintings were to illustrate stories from the Bible and therefore were essentially narrative; furthermore, they were often accompanied by written explanatory or interpellative texts. The paintings, then, were meant to be understood narratively as much as visually. As Rodríguez G. de Ceballos notes:

Más que admirarla [la estampa] se la lee; su mensaje va dirigido al individuo singular, y el hecho culturalmente importante es que el mismo mensaje sea recibido individualmente por cada uno. El grabado tiende, pues, a hacer legibles las obras figurativas. De ahí su aproximación a la obra literaria.

[More than being admired (an engravings is) read; its message is directed to the individual, and the culturally important fact is that the same message be received equally by everyone. The engraving tends, then, to make figurative works readable. Hence its closeness to a literary work.][4]

The Cuzco School's deployment of images-as-narration, following Tridentine policy, allows us to read these paintings as religious allegories. Beyond that, however, they must be situated and understood within the greater narrative of colonial representations of cultural contact and evangelization. We have already seen how the inhabitants of San Damián and Cuzco played with signification by investing symbols with new meanings, thus encompassing two very different and at times incongruent religious systems. In a similar fashion, the Cuzco School painters imitated European forms only to create their own hallucinatory refractions, fusions, and reinterpretations. Their multivalent artistic tradition—a transculturation—is only now beginning to be analyzed.[5]

Four somewhat interrelated events signal the beginnings of what has come to be known as the Cuzco School: the Counter-Reformation, the arrival in Perú of the great Italian Mannerist painter Bernardo Bitti, Cuzco's devastating earthquake of 1650, and, perhaps most importantly, the separation of indigenous artists from the painters' guild.

The Counter-Reformation, which originated with the Council of Trent (1545–63), gave the last stage of Mannerism a new impetus and a different religious theme. With its emphasis on the pedagogical power of images, Tridentine policy attempted to renovate Catholicism and the religious art of the period. One of the decrees of 1563 reads as follows:

Enseñen diligentemente los obispos que por medio de las historias de los misterios de nuestra redención, expresadas en pinturas y en otras imágenes, se instruye y confirma al pueblo en los artículos de la fe, que deben ser recordados y meditados continuamente y que de todas las imágenes sagradas se saca gran fruto, no sólo porque recuerdan a los fieles los beneficios y dones que Jesucristo les ha concedido, sino también porque se ponen a la vista del pueblo los milagros que Dios ha obrado por medio de los santos y los ejemplos saludables de sus vidas, a fin de que den gracias a Dios por ellos, conformen su vida y costumbres a imitación de las de los santos, y se muevan a amar a Dios.

[The bishops shall teach diligently that through the stories of the mysteries of our redemption represented in paintings and other images, the people be taught and confirmed in matters of the faith that shall be remembered and meditated on continually and that from all the sacred images great benefit be drawn, not only because they remind the faithful of the benefits and gifts Jesus Christ has given them, but also because they display for the people the miracles that God has performed through the saints and the healthy examples of their lives, so that they give thanks to God for them, and conform their lives and customs by imitating them and are thereby moved to love God.][6]

Thus, according to the stipulations of the Council of Trent, the representation of scenes from the lives of Christ and the saints serves a double function: as images that illustrate a biblical story and as mnemonic devices to remind the faithful of how they are to live. This was especially important in areas where people were illiterate. Those who could not read biblical texts were taught by the Church to "read" images. However, because the cultural underpinnings that make images definitively readable were missing in and around Cuzco, paintings were often reinterpreted according to an Andean logic and sensibility.[7] When analyzing the paintings of the period, one therefore must keep in mind, as Graham Howes writes, that "when we discuss iconicity in any cultural setting we have to take account of the relation of the sign to the sign-user as well as what is represented by the sign, the referent."[8] This is particularly important when dealing with colonial art, since one sign can have two radically different and even mutually exclusive meanings when interpreted by and situated within two different cultures.

The Italian Jesuit priest Bernardo Bitti arrived in Cuzco in 1583 to paint an altarpiece for the church of his order. Bitti was perhaps the greatest painter working in South America during the sixteenth century. His Mannerist predilection for highly stylized and idealized figures coincided with the pre-Columbian sensibility of native artists whose artistic tradition—embodied in Nazca, Tiahuanaco, and Inca art—also tended towards stylization and a rejection of realism.[9] It was no accident that Bitti became instrumental in the formation of the Cuzco School and that he exerted so much influence among Andean artists. As José de Mesa and Teresa Gisbert point out, Bitti's tendency to the abstract—particularly evident in the geometric designs of his compositions—echoed and revived a submerged pre-Columbian sensibility.[10]

Painted in cold colors and with strong contrasts, Bitti's highly stylized virgins, with their robes falling in exaggerated flairs, were a trademark of his work. Through Bitti, Cuzco artists were introduced to Mannerism, which remained influential in Cuzco well into the mid seventeenth century and left traces in the Baroque of the eighteenth century. But Bitti is also important for having trained the indigenous artists who later formed what we now know as the Cuzco School.[11]

Other important Italian artists who came to Perú were Mateo Pérez de Alessio and Angelino Medoro. The latter worked in Lima around 1600, but his influence was felt throughout the colony. Medoro was crucial in the development of the Andean painter Diego Quispe Tito, who was to become the most famous of the Cuzco School painters. Although initially a Mannerist, Quispe Tito eventually distanced himself from this movement and instead found inspiration in Flemish art, particularly the work of Martin de Vos and Peter Paul Rubens.[12] Another Andean artist, Martín de Loayza, also turned away from Mannerism and found inspiration in medieval Spanish painting. Thus, in the seventeenth century two new tendencies—one Flemish and the other Spanish—arose in Cuzco. But it was the Italians, particularly Bitti, who were crucial to the initial formation and development of the Cuzco School.[13]

The terrible earthquake of 1650, which leveled Cuzco and created the necessity of rebuilding and redecorating the city and its churches, was another important factor in the emergence of the Cuzco School. Because of the earthquake, most of the art produced before 1650 disappeared. There is, therefore, a pre-1650 and a post-1650 artistic period in Cuzco. Much of what we now call the Cuzco School derives from the latter part of the seventeenth century and the reconstruction of Cuzco under the guidance of Bishop Mollinedo. A zealous patron of the arts, Mollinedo arrived in Cuzco in 1673. He remained there for the next thirty years, overseeing the reconstruction and modernization of many of the city's churches and other buildings. Mollinedo attracted artists from all over the colony, creating a renaissance in the arts that was unparalleled in any other Latin American country.[14] He was also instrumental in the introduction of the Baroque to Cuzco.

But perhaps the most important factor in the development of the idiosyncratic and unique style of the Cuzco School occurred in 1688, when Indian and mestizo artist were separated from the artists' guild. At its inception in the sixteenth century, the Cuzco School was a guild of artists and artisans. It was dominated by Italian, Spanish, and creole artists who contracted Indians and mestizos as apprentices; mulattoes and blacks were excluded on racial grounds. The constitution of the guild produced, through the seventeenth century, a curious alliance between Spaniards and Indians. In the eighteenth century, it would eventually become completely monopolized by Indians.[15] Andean artists, having learned the art of painting, were no longer willing to remain subservient to the Spaniards. They separated themselves from the guild and refused to be examined, thus freeing themselves from European artistic and religious standards.[16] De Mesa and Gisbert argue that with the master painter Diego Quispe Tito and his followers, the transition from imitation to freedom of expression took place and a truly American "mestizo" form of painting arose.

Some of the more important transculturations of the Cuzco School came about when indigenous artists began to avoid the strict supervision of European masters in religious matters and to relax in their use of Catholic iconography. However, the Church's attempts to uphold the purity of Catholicism and prevent contamination with Andean elements may explain the relative scarcity of idolatrous paintings. For example, we know through documents that in Cuzco around 1675 there was an image of Jesus as a child, to which native artists had added a *mascaipacha* (symbol of Inca royalty and power) and a sun, which was painted on the child's chest. Bishop Mollinedo ordered these elements removed. Instances such as these would explain, according to Gisbert, "la relativa escacés de motivos autóctonos en el arte virreinal" [the relative scarcity of autochthonous motifs in colonial art].[17] The Church also attempted to use guild examinations to control native artistic production, thus discouraging the production of idolatrous paintings by artists unversed in Catholic dogma. Deviations occurred nonetheless, as in a scene of the Last Supper in which Judas is depicted with a halo, or Quispe Tito's *The Dance of Salomé,* in which the artist suppresses the tragic scene of the decapitation, leaving only Herod and Salomé in what appears to be a courtesan scene.[18]

Regardless of the Church's attempts to constrain the proliferation of religious meanings in the colony, the paintings that have survived Church censorship show how Cuzco artists began to incorporate American elements into their compositions. Native flora and fauna are depicted in these paintings, and elements from Andean cosmology are superimposed upon, juxtaposed with, or disguised within Christian motifs. Artists created completely new versions of Christian iconography, painting archangels with harquebuses and new saints and virgins born on American soil (including Santa Rosa de

Lima[19] and the Virgins of Pomata, Cocharcas, and Copacabana). Sometimes they conflated Andean and Christian elements, depicting mountain-shaped virgins that symbolized the Virgin both as Mother of Jesus and as Pacha-mama (Mother Earth).[20] What we are confronted with, in fact, is a form of artistic transculturation whereby a submerged culture—a culture under siege—appropriates Western forms alien to it in order to express native myths, beliefs, and ideas. In effect, Andean artists created a highly ambivalent iconography in which Andean and Christian beliefs clash or blend to varying degrees, in the end giving rise to new transcultural configurations. As we saw with the inhabitants of Cuzco and San Damián, this merging of religions makes for a proliferation of religious signification that can render an image equally appealing to different systems of belief.

One of the most significant ways in which the Cuzco School artists deviated from Christian religious painting can be seen in their idiosyncratic use of color. Andean artists rarely painted in shades or tones, and the flat colors of their compositions indicate the persistence of Andean artistic traditions, reflecting the use of color in textiles as far back as the Paracas culture.[21] The engravings that inspired so many of the paintings were usually in black and white, and indigenous artists not only enlarged the pictures, but also invented their own—sometimes profane, always divergent—colorings. In Europe, for example, the color blue—symbolic of truth, Heaven, and divine love—was most often used for the Virgin's garments when she was depicted holding Jesus. In many of the paintings of the Cuzco School, however, the Virgin's clothes are white, a color that was conventionally used only in scenes depicting her before the Annunciation and in the Presentation in the Temple. Instead, Cuzco School artists used blue to depict the archangels with their harquebuses. Furthermore, Cuzco School paintings of the Virgin often were brocaded in gold. In Europe yellow was associated with treason, but in Cuzco the use of gold had connotations of Andean divinity and resonated with the indigenous cult of the god Inti/the sun. Red—the color of blood—was the color most often used by Cuzco School painters, especially for the martyrs. This was done in complete disregard of Christian symbolism. Ocher—a symbol of corporeal death—was adopted by the Franciscans and the Capuchins, but was seldom used by indigenous artists except in landscapes, where it represents the color of the Andes.[22] Cuzco School artists also used natural dyes instead of pigments. Because of their brightness, many of these dyes—including cochineal and indigo—later became a highly lucrative export to Europe.

Subverting the intentions of the Church, Andean artists also used oil painting to depict and preserve their own history, as well as to create portraits of the Inca nobility of the day. Thus they continued—in another medium—their tradition of documenting and recalling their history.[23] Not only did Andean artists preserve and glorify their past using painting as a mnemonic device, but they also produced series of paintings—such as those of the procession of the Corpus Christi—that in fact document colonial life in Cuzco and the cultural and racial heterogeneity of the period. Indians and mestizos from the population also commissioned religious works in which they were portrayed as donors at the foot of each painting. In this way, the Andean present and past erupt in paintings that ostensibly reproduce European themes.

In another departure from European tradition, Cuzco School artists emphasized different aspects of certain themes. Few European artists attempted to depict the earthquake that followed the death of Christ, but many of the Cuzco School painters did, living as they did in a zone known for its catastrophic earthquakes. St. Joseph, who is in Europe a mature old man, is handsome and young in Cuzco. In Europe he is very seldom depicted alone with Christ; in Cuzco he is often so. There are also myriad virgins in Cuzco paintings, many more than in Europe. In contrast to Renaissance Europe, they are desacralized, shown in ordinary everyday occupations such as breast-feeding (la Virgen de la Leche) or bathing the child. In other Cuzco paintings the Virgin is depicted as a young Inca princess spinning wool and distinguished by royal Andean garments, or with a lock of hair on her forehead to symbolize fertility (Virgen niña hilando/Virgin of the Distaff). The stress on mundane activities in the religious paintings of the Cuzco School points to the Andean tendency of "dispersing the sacred," an attempt to break the Church's monopoly on all otherworldly matters.[24]

Cuzco School artists also reshuffled Christian hierarchies. They depicted the Apostle Saint James and the archangels with aristocratic elegance while Saint Isidore, whose cult originated in Madrid, became, for all practical purposes, an Andean agricultural saint. In sculptural representations of Isidore, the saint carries a little pouch of coca leaves to combat hunger and fatigue.[25] What we see here is the complete assimilation of a Christian figure into an Andean agrarian cosmogony. We can therefore still refer to "Christianization," but this Christianization was a two-way process: it changed Andean religion by adding more figures to its pantheon (this ideological sleight of hand had already been performed by the Incas, who imposed the cult of the

sun as the official state religion but added the gods of tribes they had conquered to their pantheon and permitted the survival of local religions) and
it also changed Catholicism. The Church added to its pantheon saints born
on American soil, and—as we have already seen with the extirpators of
idolatries—in order to evangelize them, priests ignored or even encouraged
changes in iconography effected by the indigenous peoples. In this way,
Catholicism followed the early Christian tactic of "pouring new wine into
old vessels"; that is, of allowing Christian symbols and beliefs to be articulated within and through pagan semiotics. As Louis Réau writes with regard
to early Christian iconography:

Pour triompher du paganisme fortement enraciné dans le monde antique, l'Eglise
du Christ avait le choix entre deux méthodes: l'abolir ou le remplacer, l'anéantir ou
l'évincer. Avec un sens politique et psychologique très sûr, elle opta pour la seconde.
Il est, en effet, très dangereux et presque toujours inefficace de heurter de front les
croyances anciennes et de les extriper par la violence au lieu qu'il est relativement
facile de leur substituer des croyances et des pratiques nouvelles, pourvu qu'elles
respectent les coutumes ancestrales et les continuent sous un autre nom.

[In order to triumph over a paganism that was deeply entrenched in antiquity, the
Church of Christ had two choices: either to abolish paganism or to replace it; to
destroy it or to oust it. With a sure political and psychological intuition, the Church
opted for the latter tactic. It is, in fact, very dangerous and almost always ineffectual
to attack ancient beliefs frontally and to extirpate paganism violently, whereas it is
relatively easy to substitute ancient beliefs and practices with new ones if these respect ancient customs and preserve them under another name.][26]

This imperial tactic of Early Christianity is reminiscent of Cabeza de
Vaca's strategies. Conquest and colonization can only succeed if the imperialist power is flexible enough to expand its own cultural parameters; consequently, a rigid imperial power is inevitably doomed. In the end, the extirpators of idolatries in Perú, like the fathers of the early Christian church,
learned that their fearful tactics served only to rigidify indigenous populations into positions of resistance, fostering attempts to better disguise native
religious practices. Destruction of the Other's religion was impossible unless
the whole culture and people were eradicated. The only viable form of
Christianization was the one that allowed Catholicism itself to change, assimilating Andean religious symbols while permitting the survival of some
Andean religious practices.

The development of the idiosyncratic style of the Cuzco School is one of
the positive outcomes of the separation of indigenous artists from the guild.
Outside of the context of the guild, however, these artists became eco-

nomically vulnerable, so much so that by the end of the eighteenth century they were forced by economic pressures to mass produce their paintings. The Cuzco School took the concept of the "copy" to an extreme that is very familiar to us today. Although Andean artists did not have at their disposal the means of mechanically producing copies, they nevertheless established studios in which artisans and artists, under the supervision of a master, mass-produced paintings (in the order of 435 paintings in seven months, or more than 2 paintings per day!).[27] Many of these paintings, especially during the late eighteenth and the nineteenth centuries, therefore acquired a hieratic, popular, and artisanal character. They became repetitive and stereotypical.[28] Antonio Casaseca Casaseca's observation that "Es obvio que la Pintura Mestiza es Pintura Cuzqueña pero no toda la Pintura Cuzqueña es Mestiza" [It is obvious that mestizo painting is Cuzco School painting, but not all Cuzco School painting is mestizo] refers to the uneven quality of the Cuzco School paintings at the end of the eighteenth century.[29]

The disregard for individual artistic genius is one of the factors that have contributed to the easy dismissal of the Cuzco School, since the emphasis in mass-produced works was on decoration, not technical innovation. At the same time, this very proliferation saved the Cuzco School from complete oblivion. Because so many paintings were exported around the world, they survived the ravages of time and neglect to which so much Latin American art has been lost. Art historians, who did not distinguish between the different periods of the Cuzco School and who judged the works from a Eurocentric perspective, summarily dismissed the achievements of the movement as archaic, naive, artisanal, and merely decorative.[30] They were unable to account for the cultural ambiguity of Cuzco School painting, with its shifts in signification and its ambivalent iconography. Forgetting that most art in the sixteenth and seventeenth centuries was imitative, art historians and critics dismissed this important artistic movement as merely servile and, at best, a mediocre imitation of European art. Leopoldo Castedo points out that critics who disparage Latin American art do not realize that "in spite of the conquistadors' determined efforts, the New World never became an exact copy of Spain. It was and is an American society."[31] It is only recently, thanks to the important and monumental studies of Teresa Gisbert and José de Mesa, and to the work of other art historians such as Leopoldo Castedo, Pál Kelemen, and Ricardo Mariátegui Oliva, that the achievements of the Cuzco School have begun to be analyzed and its significance appreciated.[32]

Since oil painting did not exist in Latin America before the Conquest,

Indian and mestizo painters had no concept of European artistic *development*. Because they did not follow European developments in technique and artistic sensibility, the artists of the Cuzco School are often criticized for having repeated, well into the eighteenth century, the medieval and Byzantine techniques that they had learned. Critics therefore argue that, in relation to Europe, the Cuzco School is characterized by stylistic anachronisms, particularly in its use of gilt brocade (*brocateado* or *sobredorado*/gold leafing). This technique, which had arrived in Europe from Asia Minor, generally lost favor with the Renaissance. It remained in use in Andalucia, however, and from there it passed to the New World in the sixteenth century.[33] Cuzco School artists' predilection for brocateado can also be attributed to the Andean practice of incorporating tiny gold plaques into cloth woven for the royal Inca family.[34] In Cuzco School painting of the sixteenth and seventeenth centuries, gilt brocade was used to decorate clothes, halos, flowers, and borders. At the end of the eighteenth century, with the mass production of paintings, it tended to pervade the whole composition. The lavish use of gilt made these paintings highly esteemed for their decorative value. As a result, many were sold or stolen from churches and entered private collections.[35]

Appraisals of the achievements of the Cuzco School are plagued by the lack of a specifically Latin American critical apparatus. Western criteria are imposed, with the oftentimes inevitable result that the paintings are found wanting. Cuzco School critics—even those intent on defending the school—oscillate greatly in their evaluations. Even as they try to redeem it, they doom the Cuzco School precisely because of the shortcomings of their critical apparatus. Francisco Stastny is but one such example. He writes: "Cuzco paintings are no half-hearted copies of Renaissance and Baroque models which could be taken for minor European works. In its best moments Cuzco develops a naive style of its own that can achieve extreme refinement."[36] And he continues: "The stylistic difference between the Italian masters and their local pupils is so radical that it is impossible to explain it on the basis of an analysis of individual cases. Only a broader explanation which takes into account the differences in mentality and of *Weltanschauung* between the New Colonial World and Europe will make it understandable."[37] Thus, even though Stastny argues for an independent spirit of creation operating in the Cuzco School, he undermines his own argument by characterizing the school as naive, thereby implicitly comparing it to Europe's assumed artistic sophistication. Stastny not only stresses the school's refined naïveté, he also points to its presumed archaic nature: "We have the impression that history is going backwards as time goes on and as the painters of the Cuzco School manage to bring out the hidden seeds of the fourteenth-century prototypes that were stored away in the sixteenth-century models. Only then do they stop in their quest. They have arrived at a pre-Renaissance stage that corresponds to their own mentality."[38] Statements such as these betray the Eurocentric bias of many critics: the Cuzco School is evaluated in the light of European art history and not according to its own Weltanschauung, as Stastny had advocated. Furthermore, criticism of the Cuzco School as "archaic" also overlooks the fact that Spain itself remained a medieval nation for much longer than the rest of Europe, entering the Renaissance gradually and incompletely.

Even as insightful a critic as the architect Emilio Harth-Terré hints at the Cuzco School's supposed archaism. Writing on architecture in the New World, Harth-Terré calls for the application of Latin American standards to Latin American art:

el arte tenía que sufrir la torsión por los factores telúricos y demográficos. Torsión que no desfigura sino que al contrario, configura una nueva forma en la que aparecen los rasgos típicos y estéticos que caracterizan la arquitectura hispanoamericana. El tiempo y el espacio son otros sin contemporaneidad ni paralelismo metropolitano. Si es un nuevo espacio el de América, también es un nuevo tiempo en el fluir de los estilos que rompe el orden cronológico con *arcaismos* y florecimientos regionales. No hay por consiguiente una sucesión histórica al modo clásico occidental.

[art had to be shaped by telluric and demographic factors. It is a torsion that does not disfigure but that, on the contrary, constitutes a new form in which the typical features and aesthetic sensibility that characterize Latin American architecture appear. Time and space are other without contemporaneity nor parallelism to the metropolis. If America is a new space, it is also a new time in the progression of styles. With its *archaisms* and regional flowerings, Latin American art breaks with chronological order. There is therefore no historical succession according to the classical western model.] (Emphasis added.)[39]

While arguing for the creation of a new, specifically Latin American artistic language and periodicity, Harth-Terré—like Stastny—characterizes Latin American art as archaic. Statements that call for consistency in and with a unique Latin American context are invariably inconsistent with the critical parameters they attempt to establish. This can be readily explained by our neocolonial situation and status, as well as by the fact that the call for a new critical apparatus has to be framed within—and concomitantly is subsumed by—the terms of the old apparatus that is being criticized.

Another form of criticism, which sees artistic transculturation as miscegenation, falls prey to the racist theories that underlie much of the writing on race relations in Latin America. These theories see miscegenation as degeneration. As Graziano Gasparini writes:

por su misma condición de "coloniales," regidas por un sistema de inevitable dependencia, [las ciudades americanas] no tuvieron la posibilidad de producir expresiones artísticas autónomas y autóctonas. Hasta en las ciudades coloniales de cierta jerarquía, como México y Lima, las actividades artísticas derivan siempre de los modelos europeos. Por eso, lo que irradia de ellas tiene un nivel artístico provincial que sufrirá ulteriores deformaciones toda vez que se propaga hacia los lugares periféricos.

[because of their "colonial" status, and ruled by an inevitable system of dependency, (Latin American cities) did not have the opportunity of producing autonomous and autochthonous artistic expressions. Even in colonial cities of certain hierarchy, such as Mexico and Lima, all artistic manifestations always are derived from European models. That is why they irradiate an artistic level that is provincial and that will only be deformed further upon reaching peripheral areas.] [40]

This critique of the school's "provinciality" is echoed by Antonio Bonet Correa: "su primitivismo hace pensar en una escuela arcaizante y provincial en la que se degradan tipos hispánicos y europeos" [its primitivism makes one think of an archaic and provincial school in which Hispanic and European forms are degraded]. [41] Inevitably, "imitation" is equated with "deformation" and "degradation." What Ángel Rama considers the normal flow of influences from the cities, which tend to acculturate more, to the provinces, where transculturation is more common, is discussed by most of these critics—informed as they are by racist theories of miscegenation—as deformation. They place little emphasis on the ability of the native imagination to modify foreign or inherited forms.

The deviations, the "bad" or "deficient" or "degraded" copies, can in fact be attributed to native liberties taken in the reproduction of European models. As Teresa Gisbert points out, the paintings of the Cuzco School are examples of an American art that has managed to be creative "pese a haber sido realizado en condiciones de dependencia" [in spite of the fact that it has been produced under conditions of dependency]. [42] Furthermore, the creation of a mestizo art form to express a typically American sensibility—so often attributed to technical limitations or lack of information—must, in fact, be situated within the context of a concrete political "voluntad de rechazo" [deliberate rejection]. [43] That is, Cuzco School artists were selective in what they chose to appropriate and what they chose to discard. In this way, a new and typically American art form arose. As we shall see in the next chapter, a similar process occurred with regard to the novel. A Western genre with a long tradition unknown in the New World, the novel was appropriated by American writers only to be adapted to indigenous oral, lyrical, and theatrical traditions. When seen within a Latin American context, these new media—oil painting and the novel—become part of long-standing native traditions. When viewed through Eurocentric eyes, however, they appear anachronistic because they do not follow the development of those media in the West.

The Cuzco School is easily dismissed by art historians largely because most of its paintings were copies of Spanish, Italian, and Flemish engravings that were sent to the New World. Since they were imitations, their divergences from the originals were—and still are—easily overlooked. Furthermore, as we saw with regard to the extirpators of idolatries, knowing is seeing. Until recently, most art historians knew little about pre-Columbian Andean religious beliefs, culture, flora, and fauna, and thus were unable to detect native transculturations of European symbols. They did not see how Cuzco School artists created a space for themselves, their world, and their cosmology while apparently imitating European religious engravings. Because of this, art historians continue to make uninformed yet apodictic statements such as those reached by the XXXVI International Congress of Americanists, which one critic summarized as follows: "la conclusión a la que se llegó . . . es que en pocas líneas puede resumirse el balance de las obras del Arte Hispanoamericano en las que encontramos aportaciones verdaderamente indígenas" [the conclusion that was reached . . . was that the balance of works of Latin American art in which there were real indigenous contributions could be summarized in a few lines].[44]

However, given that during the sixteenth, seventeenth, and eighteenth centuries all art was to a greater or lesser degree imitative, it is surprising that so much of the Cuzco School was dismissed as mere imitation. Artists simply followed and elaborated upon an established religious iconography, with little leeway or emphasis upon individual creativity. Cesare Ripa's *Iconologia*, reedited seven times between 1593 and 1630, set down the rules for the new science of iconography.[45] Although Cuzco School artists followed Ripa's iconography, they deviated from the dictate that perspective is there to tell a story, which Ripa included in his introduction to *Iconologia*.[46] Diego Quispe Tito, for example, emphasizes American nature rather than the narrative by systematically painting his subjects smaller than their surroundings and by including tropical birds in his compositions. Another work that served as inspiration to many artists was Father Nadal's *Evangelicae Historiae*

*Imagines,* published in Antwerp in 1593. Nadal combined engravings of religious scenes with a written text, explaining his sources and giving reasons for the iconography chosen.

The art of the engraving differed from other religious art in that engravings could be reproduced mechanically. They could thus be made available more readily to the population at large. The invention of engraving permitted the Counter-Reformation Church to use the new technique "a efectos de una propaganda visual a escala prácticamente universal" [to the effects of a visual propaganda at a practically universal scale].[47] Engravings were sent from Antwerp to the Spanish colonies in the New World. Because visual images were less alien than writing and therefore much more accessible to the Andeans, they allowed the colonial administration to evangelize more effectively.[48] Given the Baroque *horror vacui,* religious images literally swamped the New World, either as paintings filling the walls of churches or as engravings in the hands of individuals.[49] Bitti and other European artists were sent to Latin America by the Church in order to decorate churches and religious buildings. They arrived with "portfolios full of engravings," most of which were supplied by the famous printer Christophe Platin of Antwerp.[50] In Cuzco, therefore, many paintings were copies of imported works of art.[51] At times they were removed three or four times from the original, having been copied from small religious stamps, which in turn were copied from black-and-white engravings, which themselves were inspired by compositions like those in Ripa's *Iconologia.* Cuzco School artists therefore not only enlarged the stamps—sometimes more than a hundred times their original size—but also invented color schemes for the compositions, using color symbolism either inconsistently or idiosyncratically. As de Mesa and Gisbert point out, to talk of these paintings as mere copies is to stretch the point, since they are indigenous interpretations that followed only the formal arrangement of figures in the engravings. Once this arrangement was copied, the painters of the Cuzco School enjoyed great freedom of expression in all other aspects of their compositions.[52] Furthermore, works of art were never considered finished products as they are today. For all practical purposes, they were perpetually works-in-progress. Often they were repainted, with figures added or obliterated by other artists. Sometimes a whole painting was painted over and used as an empty canvas. These practices—like the sale or theft of paintings from churches—further complicate the evaluation of art during the colonial period.

Misconceptions about the Cuzco School are further exacerbated by the rapid destruction and disappearance of Inca and pre-Inca art after the Conquest. Many art historians simply concluded that the indigenous culture had not possessed an artistic tradition prior to the arrival of the Spaniards. To put it rather crudely, art was thought to belong exclusively to what was considered the civilized world. Although oil painting, in the narrow Western sense, was not known to them, the Incas and pre-Inca tribes had a long tradition of painting. They created murals, painted on *keros* (wooden ceremonial vases) and on ceramics, and designed intricate patterns with textiles. According to Inca Garcilaso, Inca Viracocha once had a painting made on one of the hills overlooking the city of Cuzco. This was to celebrate his victory over the *chancas,* the tribe that had vanquished his father. The painting depicted two fierce birds of prey (the *cuntur*), one with its back to the city and its head bent in submission, representing Viracocha's father, and the other with spread wings ready to attack and defend the city and the whole Inca empire. Garcilaso reports that he saw the painting in 1580 before he left Perú and that it was in good condition. By 1595 it had disappeared.[53]

Testimonies such as Garcilaso's, along with modern archaeological discoveries, indicate that the Incas and pre-Incas had a rich artistic tradition. Oil painting, even though a new medium, was a continuation of that tradition.[54] Art historian Leopoldo Castedo writes that oil painting, particularly as evidenced in the Andean use of natural dyes, must be seen as the "persistence (rather than the survival) of the indigenous in art."[55] The continued failure of critics to recognize and appreciate the rich pre-Columbian artistic tradition has led to unidimensional art histories that overlook the important interactions and intersections between pre-Columbian and European artistic traditions. It was this cross-fertilization that gave rise to the Cuzco School.

## PICTURE ESSAY

### 1. Guamán Poma de Ayala

Felipe Guamán Poma de Ayala's *Nueva corónica y buen gobierno* (1585–1615), with its juxtaposition of narrated text and visual representation, is a very early and clear example of Andean transculturation. As his adoption of a hybrid name—Quechua puma/Poma and Spanish Ayala— suggests, Guamán Poma thought of himself as an Andean mediating between two worlds. In his account addressed to King Philip III, he argues for the restitution of indigenous lands and for self-determination. In Andean fashion he conceives of the colony as an upside-down world (*pachacuti*)[56] that must be reversed. To assist in this reversal, he will contribute suggestions for good government. Guamán Poma writes a history of his people in order to counter the colonial perception that they were without history, without religion, and without culture, an argument that was used by the Spaniards to ideologically justify the Conquest as a "just war" waged against the natives of the New World. He also added a lengthy critique of political and religious abuses on the part of the Spanish colonizers.

Guamán Poma's manuscript combines text written in Spanish, Quechua, and Aymara with drawings that illustrate specific scenes and that are themselves accompanied by written captions. Examining the relationship between the written text and the illustrations, Rolena Adorno argues that Guamán Poma considers visual images a means of communication more powerful than written language.[57] The drawings in *Nueva corónica* were inspired by European engravings sent to the New World. In turn, they served as models and inspiration for later mestizo artists of the Cuzco School.[58] In these images Guamán Poma followed the Counter-Reformation's understanding of art as an effective means of moving the beholder, in this case an implied Spanish reader. But the semiotic disposition of the drawings brings a non-Western culture into play. In true transculturating fashion, Guamán Poma appropriates writing, historiography, and the literature of religious devotion[59] in order to reach a Western reader, yet the necessity of presenting his own—Andean—vindications within the framework of Western media leads him to subvert these from within. Guamán Poma not only appropriates foreign forms, he also continues the Andean tradition of oral and painted historiography (*qelqas*), in which paintings function as narration.[60] His transcultural text is part New World chronicle, part history, part ethnography, part Spanish, part Quechua, part Aymara, part autobiography, part testimony, and part written and part pictorial treatise.

The most striking yet least visible characteristic of Guamán Poma's manuscript is that the disposition of many of the drawings actually reproduces the spatial and cosmological organization of the Inca empire, thus undermining their explicit "message." In the Andean conception of space, Cuzco lay at the center of the world. It was shaped like a puma and surrounded by four provinces, which were divided into upper and lower in relation to the center. The position to the left of the center axis is *hunan;* to the right of the center is *hanan.* Hunan is associated with the left, the lower, the female, and with complementarity or subordination; hanan is associated with the upper, the right, the male, and with superiority.

In many cases this Andean semiotic disposition emerges as subversive subtext. In figure 1, *Pontifical mundo,* for example, Guamán Poma depicts the Andean world under colonization and situates Spain on the lower and therefore left, inferior, and subordinate position, with Cuzco on the upper and therefore right and superior position. As if to make his "hidden" meaning even more clear, the sun shines only on Cuzco and not on Castile.[61] In figure 2, *Indios/dormilón, perezoso,* he criticizes the sloth that colonialism gives rise to and puts the sun in the space left of center, suggesting that the colony is a "world upside down."

In figure 3, *Crió Dios al Mundo Entregó a Adán y Eva,*[62] God (Father and Creator) is situated at the center. Masculine elements are located to his right with the sun on top and Adam underneath; feminine elements such as the moon (on top) and Eve (underneath) are to his left. Implicit in this scheme is the notion that humanity will arise out of the conjunction of the sexes. Mercedes López-Baralt, analyzing the disposition of the figures, finds that there are binary categories at work (Adam and Eve/the two sexes), but because they are mediated by God they form a typical Christian trilogy. Seen as a whole, however, the drawing actually proves to be organized according to the typical Andean semiotic disposition of space. That is, a fivefold division: sun, moon, Adam, Eve, God. Therefore, as López-Baralt concludes: "se trata . . . de una trasposición evidente del esquema cosmológico andino a términos cristianos" [it is an example . . . of an evident transposition of the Andean cosmological scheme into Christian terms].[63]

As is evident in Guamán Poma's strategy, and as we will see repeatedly in the Cuzco School, God is either covertly or overtly identified with the sun. In this case, God is situated underneath the sun and is therefore regarded by the author as implicitly subservient to the Andean sun god. In other cases, God is substituted by or conflated with the sun. The persistence of this identification throughout the seventeenth and eighteenth centuries (and even today, as evidenced by the coincidence of Inti Raymi and Corpus Christi) indicates that even though the official Inca cult of the sun was destroyed in its most visible manifestations (including temples and idols), it was never completely eradicated.

The continuation of Andean animism under the cloak of Christianity coincides with the fact that, even today, Western Christianity still contains ancient pagan elements. These are manifest in the coincidence between Christmas and the cult of the Persian god Mithra; in the use of the nimbus,

FIGURE 1. Pontifical mundo / Las Indias del Perú en lo alto de España / Castilla en lo abajo de las Indias /Castilla [Pontifical World / The Indies of Perú on top of Spain]. Guamán Poma. *Nueva corónica y buen gobierno,* ed. Franklin Pease. Courtesy Biblioteca Ayacucho.

FIGURE 2. Indios / dormilíon, perezoso, punuyeamayoc quilla caicuypacnacama punucunqui quillaspa quitaconayquipac mana chacrayquita ilamecasqunche ilamayquita riconquicho ualota apanquicho llamtata ychuta auanquicho mana puchacánqui auanquicho causanayque pac quilla [dormilón, flojo (holgazán, ocioso), duermes hasta el momento de comer, no has llevado guano, ni leña, ni paja, ni has tejido para vivir. Flojo] / pereza [Indians / sleeping, lazy . . . you sleep until you want to eat, you have not taken guano, nor wood, nor straw, nor have you woven to live. Lazy]. Guamán Poma. *Nueva corónica y buen gobierno,* ed. Franklin Pease. Courtesy Biblioteca Ayacucho.

FIGURE 3.    Crió Dios al Mundo / Entregó a Adán y Eva / Adán, Eva / mundo /
papa [God created the world / Gave to Adam and to Eve / Adam, Eve / world /
potato]. Guamán Poma. *Nueva corónica y buen gobierno,* ed. Franklin Pease.
Courtesy Biblioteca Ayacucho.

which had previously served to crown Greek and Roman kings, to signify divinity;[64] in the belief in and representation of the Trinity; in the eastern orientation of churches; and in many other ways as well.[65] The pagan under-pinnings of Christianity are perhaps best exemplified in the Sistine Chapel frescoes, where Michelangelo depicts God throwing thunder and the damned crossing the River Styx in Charon's boat.[66] In the Andes, indigenous reli-gious beliefs and the submerged paganism within Christianity come into conjunction. In effect, two different pagan belief systems from two different historical times and circumstances reverberate with one another in this new period of Christianization.

The simultaneous coincidence of religious symbols from different cultures creates a great ambiguity in signification, for the same symbol can mean very different things in different cultures. For example, the triangle that promi-nently marks God's head in figure 3, *Crió Dios al Mundo,* can be interpreted in terms both Christian (as the Trinity) and astrological (as the symbol of fire),[67] and also as a remnant of the Greco-Roman world's way of represent-ing their rulers. Furthermore, throughout Asia the triangle or the number three has mystic significance "symbolic of the supreme Being."[68]

Figure 4, *La octava Coya, Mama Yunto Cayan/reinó Lima, Jauja, Chinchay-cocha,* is one of Guamán Poma's many depictions of Inca rulers.[69] This paint-ing, like many portraits of Inca princesses, provides a clear precedent to the triangular or mountain-shaped virgins that would become a favorite theme of the Cuzco School. It was an Andean custom for women rulers to be shaded by a parasol held by a dwarf.[70] In the procession of the Corpus Christi, this same custom has been transferred to Christian virgins and saints, who are now shaded by a parasol instead of the traditional Christian pano-ply. Today, however, an angel rather than a dwarf holds the parasol.

Another clear precedent to the Cuzco School can be seen in the self-portraits that Guamán Poma incorporated into his *Nueva corónica* (figure 5). This is but an early example of the Andean appropriation of painting not for religious ends, but to continue the tradition of recollecting and recording Inca history. The painting of self-portraits also allowed artists to document the times in which they lived. Thus, the Andeans themselves need to be seen as the first indigenistas, as practitioners of an "interior" indigenismo that created representations of the Andean world by and for an Andean com-munity. This interior indigenismo needs to be juxtaposed with the more commonly known exterior exoticising indigenismo practiced by writers and ethnographers who were exterior to the world about which they wrote.

In Guamán Poma's work, the deployment of two culturally specific

FIGURE 4. La octava Coya, Mama Yunto Cayan / reinó Lima, Jauja, Chinchaycocha [The eighth Coya, Mother Yunto Cayan / ruled Lima, Jauja, Chinchaycocha]. Guamán Poma. *Nueva corónica y buen gobierno,* ed. Franklin Pease. Courtesy Biblioteca Ayacucho.

# CAMINA EL AUTOR

con su hijo don fran.co de ayala sale de
sp. rovincia a la ciudad delos Reys de
Lima a dar quenta asumag.d ysale pobre desnudo y camina en vierno

amigo · autor · dō juan de ayala · Iautaro

a cabo

FIGURE 5.  Camina al autor con su hifo don Francisco de Ayala, sale de
la provincia a la ciudad de Los Reyes de Lima, a dar cuenta a Su Majestad, y
sale pobre, desnudo, y camina en invierno / guiado [?] /autor / don Francisco
de Ayala / amigo / Iautaro [The author walks with his son don Francisco de
Ayala . . .]. Guamán Poma. *Nueva corónica, y buen gobierno,* ed. Franklin Pease.
Courtesy Biblioteca Ayacucho.

semiotic codes in one drawing gives rise to two possible and divergent readings. One way of reading the drawings is to pay attention to the literal message or the events depicted. Another is to notice the symbolic message underlying each composition. This second reading takes into account Andean ideology and allows the reader to see how the literal message is subverted by the underlying structure.[71]

This double reading of Guamán Poma's text can only take place if the reader knows both cultural codes very well. Otherwise, only a literal, monocultural reading is possible. In a sense then, Guamán Poma's text lay in waiting for more than three hundred years before it found its readers.

## 2. Fray Martín de Murúa's *Historia general del Perú, origen y descendencia de los Incas*

A strange parallel to Guamán Poma's manipulation of two cultural codes—this time effected by a Spaniard—is Fray Martín de Murúa's seventeenth-century *Historia general del Perú*.[72] A Spanish priest (Mercedarian) and Guamán Poma's contemporary, Murúa wrote *Historia* to document various aspects of Inca culture, including customs, royal genealogy, and religion, as can be seen in figure 6. There is a great similarity between both artists' depictions of the Inca princess and their use of the parasol, although Murúa's drawing departs from convention in that the parasol is not held by a dwarf.[73] Like Guamán Poma, Murúa used Western means (drawing and writing) to depict a world alien to those forms. A comparison between the Andean and the Spaniard shows that whereas Guamán Poma translated his cultural experience into European forms, Murúa does the reverse, using early-sixteenth-century Spanish and Flemish iconographic conventions with which he is familiar to describe an alien world. As de Mesa and Gisbert point out, "se ve con claridad un curioso mestizaje cultural en ambos" [a curious cultural miscegenation is seen very clearly in both].[74]

## 3. Inca Portraits

The Cuzco School created traditions that are among the most important indigenous deviations from European religious painting. Artists of the school painted genealogies of the Incas, portrayed contemporary male and female Inca nobles, included portraits of Andean donors within religious paintings, and incorporated self-portraits into their works. In fact,

FIGURE 6.    Modo da caminat las coyas y keynas, mujeres de los Incas
Chuquillante, mujer de Huasear Inca [Way of walking of the coyas and queens,
wives of the Incas / Chuquillante, wife of Huascar Inca]. Fray Martin de Murúa,
*Historia general del Perú, origen y descendencia de los Incas,* ed. Manuel Ballesteros
Gaibrois (Madrid: Romero Delecea, 1962). Courtesy Manuel Ballesteros Gaibrois
and Romero de Lecéa.

the overwhelming majority of Cuzco School portraits are of descendants of the Incas and not of Spaniards or creoles, as one would expect given colonial hierarchies. Like the drawings of Guamán Poma, they are an important example of how the Cuzco School managed to subvert the exclusively religious understanding of art that the Church tried to impose in the New World. The Cuzco School artists shifted the emphasis from moving the souls of the onlookers to commemorating past and present glories.[75] As these paintings make clear, the first indigenistas were the Andeans themselves, insisting as they did on portraying a glorious past.[76]

The practice of painting Inca genealogies and portraits must be situated within a tradition of Andean millenarian thinking. This belief, which led to hundreds of rebellions during and following the colonial period, was essentially driven by the dream of reversing the miserable conditions of the colony and reinstating Inca rule. The myth of Inkarrí (Inca plus rey, or Spanish king), who died by decapitation (which conflates the death of Atahualpa with the uprising of Túpac Amon), tells of the slow reconstitution of Inkarrí's body from the head down, promising that when he has become whole again the Inca world will be restituted. The eerie symmetry by which the past is understood as a paradise to be regained by reversing the conditions of the present (pachacuti) forms the subtext of all these portrayals and genealogies.[77] As already seen in the work of Guamán Poma, this is a typically Andean reversal. It has little in common with the Christian promise of a heaven or hell where the believer will be rewarded or punished for his or her sins. Here, the conditions of the present (poor, exploited Andean peasants and rich, sadistic Spaniards) will be simply and clearly reversed: the poor will become rich, the exploited will become exploiters (see chapter 5). For the Andean masses, portraits of the Inca elite sustained the possibility of a restitution of Inca rule. Paintings of the Incas and their descendants became extremely popular in the eighteenth century. It was not until after the 1781 uprising, when leaders had themselves portrayed bearing Inca arms and shields, that the colonial administration understood how subversive these portraits were. They were legally banned according to the decree of 1782.[78]

There was another way in which Cuzco School artists incorporated themselves and their world into an alien medium. Being a good Catholic entailed the commissioning of religious works of art, and it was common practice in Renaissance Europe to portray donors at the foot of a painting.[79] The sheer preponderance of such paintings in Cuzco makes it possible to suspect that the religious subject was only an excuse for the inclusion of portraits. The wonderful portrait of Mateo Pumacahua (figure 7), an erudite

FIGURE 7.    Artist unknown. *Portrait of Brigadier Mateo Pumacahua and His Family.*
Cuzco School. 18th century. Courtesy Instituto de Investigacion y Conservacion
del Patrimonio Cultural "Diego Quispe Tito" and the Museo Histórico
Regional del Cuzco.

FIGURE 8.    Antonio de Herrera y Tordesillas. *Historia General de los Hechos de los Castellanos. en las Islas y Tierra Firme del Mar Oceano.* Courtesy Baker Library, Dartmouth College.

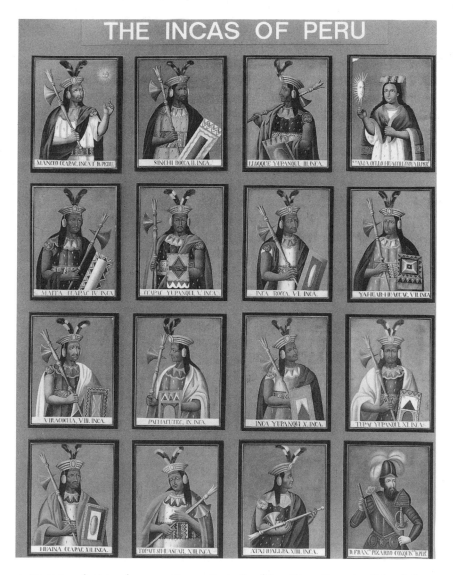

FIGURE 9. Artist unknown. *Sixteen Portraits of Inca Kings*. Peruvian School. Late 19th century. Courtesy Denver Art Museum.

Andean, is but one such example. Situated in the lower right-hand side of the painting, Pumacahua is shown in more detail than the ostensible subject of the painting. In effect, he dominates the composition.

Following the historical and ethnographic tradition evident in the work of Murúa, many Inca genealogies were painted by Spanish and creole historians. In Antonio Herrera's *Historia General de los Hechos de los Castellanos,* also known as the *Décadas,* the Spanish historian reproduces engravings of the Inca genealogy. He begins with Manco Cápac, founder of the empire, and ends with Huáscar, who, along with his brother Atahualpa, was fighting for the empire at the time of Pizarro's arrival (figure 8).

Some Inca genealogies also served the imperial aim of legitimating Spanish rule. In these works, Spanish and creole painters followed the tradition of painting Inca genealogies, but ended their genealogies with a Spanish leader as heir to the Inca world. In *The Incas of Perú* (figure 9), the genealogy starts with the first Inca and ends with Pizarro. Such works are a clear example of how the colonial administration attempted to naturalize and justify colonization by using the traditions of the colonized. During the period of Independence, the creole heroes Simón Bolívar and San Martín employed the same tactic to justify and strengthen their position.

Regardless of Spanish attempts to subvert Andean traditions, the huge number of Inca portraits is a testament to the will to resistance. Through these paintings, a subjected people proudly affirm their heritage and project their continuity into the future.

## 4. The Corpus Christi Procession Series

The fifteen paintings of the Corpus Christi procession, long considered anonymous, are now attributed to Diego Quispe Tito, the most famous of the Cuzco School painters. The series, which falls within the tradition of portraying the Incas and their descendants, constitutes a veritable sociological and historical document of the times. The portrait genre is taken to its full implications, becoming the "portrait of a period."[80] The images that constitute the series represent the participants and the public with extraordinary detail, making it possible to distinguish people by class and race. These paintings (see figures 10, 11, and 12) are important not only as artistic masterpieces, but also as documents of the times.

The Corpus Christi procession in honor of the Holy Eucharist was offi-

FIGURE 10.   Diego Quispe Tito. *Corpus Christi Procession, Procession Leaves the Cathedral.* Courtesy Arzobispado del Cusco.

cially instituted in Cuzco by Virrey Francisco de Toledo in 1573.[81] It began in the main square of Cuzco when the Eucharist was taken out of the Cathedral, stopped before all major religious buildings in the city, and ended with the return of the Eucharist to the Cathedral.[82] The entire population of Cuzco and surrounding areas took part in the celebration. Descendants of the Incas were chosen as standard bearers and led the procession. It was they, apparently, who commissioned the series of paintings.[83]

FIGURE II.  Diego Quispe Tito. *Corpus Christi Procession, Carriage of Saint Sebastian*. Courtesy Arzobispado del Cusco.

Because most of Cuzco's Catholic religious buildings were built upon former Inca temples, the procession actually consisted of a geographical palimpsest. Christian markers also indicated Inca religious sites, making possible their commemoration. The Cathedral, for example, had formerly been the palace of Inca Huiracocha, known as Corincancha or "enclosure of gold," which represented the sun.[84] The church of the Jesuit order, Iglesia de la Compañía, had been the palace of Inca Huayna Cápac, known as Amarucancha.

The procession also created a religious palimpsest. The dates of the Corpus Christi coincided with those of the Inca Inti Raymi, readily allowing an

FIGURE 12.    Diego Quispe Tito. *Corpus Christi Procession, the Jesuit Fathers Leave Their Church*. Courtesy Arzobispado del Cusco.

identification of the cult of the sun with that of the Eucharist shaped as the sun. From an Andean perspective, however, the Inti Raymi is only the central event in the series of celebrations beginning in April and May with the maize harvest and ending in August with ploughing.[85] The conflation Corpus Christi/Inti Raymi allowed the resemanticization of the Catholic festival, incorporating it into that Andean "interconnected fabric of sacred time."[86]

The Catholic practice of carrying religious figures in processions allowed for further coincidences, since it probably coincided with the Inca cult of the dead. During the Inca festivals, which were witnessed and described by the chroniclers, the mummies of former Incas were paraded around the center of Cuzco. Echoing the Inca tradition, Catholic Virgins were—and still are—carried on litters and sheltered by parasols, as was the case for Inca *coyas.* The cult of the Virgin is thus associated with the Andean cult of Inca princesses, except that whereas the parasol was once held by a dwarf, now it is held by an angel. This practice also deviates from the common use of a dais or canopy to shelter the saints, martyrs, and other important religious figures.[87] After 1702, Indian dancers wearing masks and dressed as Spaniards accompanied the Corpus Christi procession.[88] These dancers recall the *sijllas* (traditional Andean dances) in which Spanish colonial rule is mocked and spurned.[89]

All of these elements point to an Andean reinscription of the festival of the Eucharist—one of the most important Catholic rituals—within an Andean context. As William Rowe writes, the procession is an example of how the Christian festival of Corpus Christi is "surrounded by native ritual and reinterpreted by it." Just as Christianity had appropriated and reinterpreted pagan elements, so too in the procession of the Corpus Christi "a whole Andean cosmology is shown to be mobilized in order to control Christian meanings."[90] This particular ritual readily lends itself to the process of transculturation, given the coincidences of the date on which the two festivals are celebrated and the symbolic representation of the Eucharist made of gold and in the shape of the sun. These coincidences were already noted by Arriaga and are discussed in chapter 3.

Teresa Gisbert found yet another unequivocal example of the pervasive way in which the Andeans identified God with the sun. The Church of Andahuailillas was decorated in 1628 by Luis de Riaño, a disciple of the Italian painter Angelino Medoro. De Riaño followed the design of Iván Pérez de Bocanegra, who, as we saw in chapter 3, wrote a Catholic religious manual in Quechua and Spanish. The artist placed a hole in the wall behind the choir so that the sun would shine through at dawn. The wall was painted with a scene from the Annunciation, with the sun's rays assuming the place of the Holy Trinity. The following words were inscribed around the aperture: *Adonai, Radix, Clavis, Rex Oriens* (Lord, Root, Key of Everything, King of the Orient). This text is given in Latin, Spanish, Quechua, Aymara, and Puquina, showing that the priests were aware of the need to translate Christian concepts into the various languages of the highlands. In this important and unique example of religious and artistic transculturation, God, described as King of the Orient, becomes God the Sun. Facing East as it does, the church at Andahuailillas also reminds us that Christian churches of the fourteenth century were built to face the rising sun. This practice, Louis Réau argues, is evidently a "souvenir des *cultes solaires,* de l'antique adoration du soleil levant: en Egypte et en Grèce, les fidèles se tournaient vers l'Orient pour adorer le dieu du Soleil, et, morts, ils se faisaient inhumer face à l'astre divinisé. Dans le Christianisme, le Soleil n'est plus adoré comme un dieu, mais il reste le symbole de la divinité du Sauveur" [a remnant of *solar cults,* of the adoration of the rising sun in antiquity: in Egypt and in Greece, the faithful turned towards the Orient to adore the Sun God, and, when they died, they were buried facing the divine heavenly body. In Christianity, the sun is no longer worshiped as a god, but it remains the symbol of the divinity of the Saviour].[91]

The series of paintings of the Corpus Christi procession is noteworthy not only as an important historical document, but also for its artistic singularity. The inclusion of tropical birds in these paintings has become a signature of the Cuzco School. Towards 1660, paintings were invaded by tropical birds in bright colors, including the Huáscar Kente (*Patagonia gigans*), the Tunki (*Rupicola peruviana*), the Pusti (*Psarocolius decumanus*), the Guacamayo (*Ara chloroptera*), and the Macaw.[92] The birds are usually bigger and much brighter than other objects in the paintings. In Christian religious iconography, birds symbolize either the spirit of the painter or the spirits of all Christians. However, the pervasiveness of birds in Cuzco School paintings seems to indicate an Andean symbolism that has not yet been explained. Their use has baffled art historians because tropical birds do not form part of the fauna of the Andean highlands. They are therefore apparently quite "other" to the experience of the painters. Furthermore, the condor—ever present in the Andes—is all but absent. Gisbert argues that the only artistic antecedent to the painting of tropical birds is to be found in the keros, where "the Inca conquest by Túpac Yupanqui may be seen, and this is why the jungle is depicted schematically with many birds and some trees. The landscape backdrop and the placing of figures in a single plane, so typical of the keros, is transferred by the Indian artists to their paintings."[93] If this is the case, then Andean painters were simply continuing an Andean tradition, replacing the ceremonial vases with canvas. Other critics have attributed the proliferation of these birds to an Andean "nostalgia for the tropics," an explanation that seems implausible. Still others argue that they are not as foreign or exotic as is commonly held, since it is well known that the Incas used different "ecological floors" in agriculture and were therefore familiar with the flora and fauna of the jungles as well as the highlands. For whatever reasons, tropical birds seem to have been held in high esteem and were even collected: archaeologists found a house in Cuzco that contained more than one hundred thousand specimens. In artistic terms, the addition of tropical birds to Cuzco School paintings, as well as the pervasive use of brocateado, falls within the tendency of indigenous artists to enrich European compositions and to stress the decorative aspect of art.

A parallel to this invasion of the tropics in painting can be found in colonial architecture, where monkeys and diverse kinds of parrots were sculpted into churches, convents, and monasteries. This form of American architecture has come to be known as the "barroco mestizo." One of the many "hidden" forms of idolatry that surprised Arriaga concerned the monkeys that were sculpted at the bases of churches in the region of Huarochirí. Arriaga discovered that these were not Christian symbols of sinners or images of the Devil, as monkeys traditionally signified in Christian iconography, but instead depicted Andean gods who held up those structures.

### 5. The Virgin Mary/Pachamama

Paintings of virgins in their various advocations were a favorite theme of the Cuzco School and were a pervasive cult in the colonies. A great number of Cuzco School paintings depict the Virgin Mary in the shape of a mountain. A clear precedent to this type of iconography can be found in Guamán Poma's depictions of Inca coyas, the triangular shapes of which later became so characteristic of the Cuzco School (see figure 4).[94] A literal example of the Andean conflation of the Virgin and Pachamama is the anonymous painting of the Virgin in Potosí, in which the mountain forms her dress (figure 13). In this painting, the mountain of Potosí is given the face of the Virgin Mary, with the Virgin's hands, palms up, at her sides. The mountain-virgin is crowned by the Trinity. At her feet are King Charles V, a cardinal, a bishop, and another figure—generally believed to be Inca Mayta Cápac—with the Cross of Alcantara on his cape.

The mountain shape of so many Cuzco School virgins conflates the Catholic cult of the Virgin Mary and the Andean cult of Pachamama. A telluric divinity common to all peoples of the Andes, Pachamama originally represented only the flat earth. In identifying her with the Virgin Mary, the Andeans merged the cult of Pachamama with that of the *apus* (Andean mountain gods), male regional divinities thought to have been living gods in antiquity. In the creation of this new image, different processes of transculturation are at work. With the conflation of Mary and Pachamama—

FIGURE 13. Artist unknown. *The Mountain Virgin.* 18th century. Courtesy Museo de la Casa Nacional de Moneda, Potosí, Bolivia.

both female deities—and then the extension of the meaning of Mary/ Pachamama to encompass the apus, there is a collapse or condensation of many different religious symbols into one—apparently Christian—symbol. At the same time, however, this single religious symbol—the Virgin Mary— has acquired several new meanings and iconographies in her Andean- Christian resemanticization. Mary is now no longer solely the mother of Jesus; she is also a telluric divinity and a mountain goddess. That is, she is no longer solely a Christian religious symbol.

Interestingly enough, it was not only the indigenous population who contributed to the transculturation of the Virgin Mary. Priests themselves assisted the process by drawing parallels between idolatry and Christianity in order to facilitate the process of evangelization. The Christian identifi- cation of Mary with a mountain is already present in the writings of biblical exegetes such as St. Augustine, who equates her with a mountain of jewels.[95] In the New World, Alonso Ramos Gavilán, Augustinian chronicler of Copacabana, preached that "as the Sun deposits its rays on Earth making her a mother, for the benefit of man; so God deposits his rays in Mary, making her also a mother, to benefit man." Here we see, as Gisbert argues, the "origin of the identification Earth-Virgin-Mary, both as mother of men."[96] As we saw with Arriaga, this kind of intercultural logic—"as the Mamapacha . . . so too the Virgin Mary"—is established by priests in order to make Ca- tholicism accessible and comprehensible to non-Christians. However, the causal and temporal genesis of these parallels is difficult to pinpoint. Gisbert's assertion may need to be corrected, since it would seem likely that evangel- izers such as Ramos Gavilán are not the creators of the conflation Virgin Mary/Pachamama, but are instead appropriating and attempting to neutral- ize an idolatrous Andean conflation. In the same way, St. Augustine may only have been appropriating pagan symbols into his Christian discourse.

There are many other examples of Andean transculturations of Christian virgins. The Virgin of Cocharcas (figure 14) derives from the Virgin of the Candlestick, who through regional miracles became an American virgin in her own right. She acquired her own iconography, which has spread and become popularized through native engravings and religious stamps.[97] Like- wise, the Virgin of Pomata, protector of natives and slaves, holds an S and a nail (esclavo/slave) in many paintings.[98] Her assimilation into the Andean world is seen in the feather headdress she wears (figure 15).

Even when European and Andean virgins seem greatly similar, Cuzco School paintings often show slight adaptations that reveal the virgins' as- similation into an Andean context. In many cases, for example, the vases

FIGURE 14.    Artist unknown. *Our Lady of Cocharcas Under a Baldachin.*
18th century. Courtesy New Orleans Museum of Art.

FIGURE 15.    Artist unknown. *Our Lady of Pomata*. Peruvian School (Colonial).
1675. Courtesy Brooklyn Museum.

FIGURE 16. Artist unknown. *Virgin of the Distaff*. Courtesy Denver Art Museum.

FIGURE 17.    Artist unknown. *Madonna de la Leche*. Peruvian School. 1750.
Courtesy Brooklyn Museum.

below the virgins contain the *nukchu* (lily of love), a sacred flower associated with the "chosen women" who live to render service to the Inca. As Carol Damian points out, "to this day [the nukchu] are strewn before the Virgin's litter on processional days, as they have been strewn before the litter of the Inca's mummy on Inca festival days honoring the 'Cult of the Panaca.'"[99]

In other paintings of the seventeenth and eighteenth centuries, depictions of the Virgin clearly deviate from Christian dogma. Unlike their European contemporaries, Cuzco School artists often show the Virgin breast-feeding Jesus, or engaged in mundane occupations such as spinning wool. These depictions refer back to European medieval and pre-medieval iconographies, which were later forbidden because they underline submerged pre-Christian and pagan meanings. Images of the Virgin breast-feeding have a clear precedent in ancient scenes of the goddess Isis breast-feeding Horus.[100] In paintings of the Virgin of the Distaff (figure 16), Cuzco School painters depict her as a young Inca princess. She has a curl on her forehead, an Inca symbol of fertility, and she wears the royal *llauto* (a band around the forehead) as a sign of Inca nobility.[101] The Virgin wears an Indian shawl held by a *tupo* pin and European-style lace sleeves. That she is engaged in spinning can be related to one of the Inca legends of origins, according to which Mama Occllo, the wife of Manco Cápac, taught women how to spin and weave. These skills became a special service to the Inca and one of the main occupations of the "chosen women." The Christian Virgin has in this case been very clearly resemanticized by the Inca symbols with which she is painted. The Virgen de la Leche is yet another example (figure 17). Depictions of the Virgin engaged in everyday occupations defy the Church's attempt to distance the human from the divine. Instead, they must be understood within the Andean tendency of humanizing the divine, which followed the Inca custom of turning the Inca into a God when living, and into a living being when dead.[102]

## 6. Archangels with Harquebuses

One of the differences between European and American art lies in the prevalence of different themes. Archangels and virgins were a favorite theme of the Cuzco School, but not of Spanish artists. The Cuzco School archangels are usually armed with harquebuses and dressed in seventeenth- and eighteenth-century brocade-and-lace costumes (figures 18 and 19). Because of the extreme elegance with which they are depicted, they are like

FIGURE 18. Artist unknown. *Angel with Harquebus*. Cuzco School. Courtesy Museo de Salamanca, Spain, with assistance from José Colmeiro and Patricia Greene.

FIGURE 19.   Artist unknown. *Angel with Harquebus*. Cuzco School. Courtesy
Museo de Salamanca, Spain, with assistance from José Colmeiro and Patricia
Greene.

"the lords of the heavens."[103] These archangels derive from the series of engravings representing the *Seven Archangels of Palermo,* which were produced in Antwerp by Hieronymus Wieriex.[104] However, by arming the archangels, the Cuzco School artists make them a truly American creation. Given the Marian emblems included in many of these paintings and the archangels' warrior-like stance, they represent the defense of the Virgin of the Immaculate Conception in Christian iconography.[105]

Archangels are also associated with natural phenomena such as hail, rain, and the stars. As such, they assume the place of the ancient celestial gods.[106] As Gisbert argues, in cabalistic knowledge the archangel Michael is connected to the sun, Gabriel to the moon, the angel Zamae to Mars, Zachariel or Zadquiel to Jupiter, and Cassiel to Saturn.[107] The association of archangels with the stars apparently also derives from the apocryphal *Book of Henoc.*[108] In the case of Michael, for example, Louis Réau has found that, almost without exception, the temples named for him were formerly temples to the pagan god Mercury.[109] Because of these associations with natural phenomena, Gisbert concludes that we find ourselves confronted with a very ancient way of viewing celestial phenomena.[110] The American archangels are derived not from the mainstream of Christianity, but from its margins—in this case the apocrypha—as were so many other borrowings from Europe in Latin America. Priests in the Andes apparently knew this and, playing with the coincidences between both, allowed it in the attempt to substitute the pagan cult of the stars with the Christian cult of the angels.[111]

In figure 20, the Archangel Raphael is holding a fish, an allusion to his rescue of Tobias as narrated in the apocrypha.[112] According to the *Book of Tobit,* Tobias set out on a journey in search of his blind and dying father. He was accompanied and protected by the archangel Raphael, who rescued him from being devoured by a great fish. With the gall of the fish and the help of the invisible Raphael, Tobias cured his father of blindness and thus Raphael became patron of doctors, healers, and medicine men. His ready adoption into Andean iconography can be explained by the fact that Andean medicine men also healed by extracting organs from animals and rubbing them on the affected parts of their patients (see chapter 2). This transculturation of Raphael was perhaps also made possible by the fact that Raphael's Hebrew name means "medicine of God" or "God has healed." In the coloring of his wings we see Cuzco School deviations from Christian color

FIGURE 20.    Artist unknown. *The Archangel Raphael*. Peruvian School. Late
17th century. Courtesy Brooklyn Museum.

symbolism. In Europe, the wings of archangels were usually painted in solid color with discrete gradations of tones at the tips, but in Cuzco they were painted with borders in red or ocher.

## 7. Santiago Mataindios/St. James Killer of Indians

St. James the warrior is an Iberian figure in European hagiography. After returning to Judea from the Iberian peninsula in A.D. 44, he became the first of the apostles to be martyred. His remains were transported back to Santiago de Compostela and in the eleventh century his myth was reincarnated in El Cid. The Milky Way was then named El Camino de Santiago de Compostela [The Road to Santiago de Compostela]. With the Reformation, the chivalric fame of St. James was eclipsed, leaving only a nostalgic remembrance of him as captain of the Christian militia fighting against the Moors in A.D. 700. St. James Slayer of Moors (Santiago Matamoros) was taken by the Spaniards to America, where he became a different symbol for two cultures. For the Spaniards he was transformed into St. James the slayer of "bad"—that is, rebellious—Indians (Santiago Mataindios), and for the Andeans he came to symbolize *Illapa,* the god of thunder and lightning.[113] That is, he was transferred from the Spain of the reconquest to the New World and a different context and conquest. In the process of being moved from one world to another, St. James is transculturated and acquires an Andean subtext as god of thunder.

By associating him with thunder, the Andeans were equating St. James with the roar of the Spaniards' harquebuses, thus creating an Andean correspondence between both. But this association also referred back to the submerged pagan meaning of St. James as Son of Thunder.[114] The curiously circular movement that is operating here shows the extent to which Christianity incorporated other religions and was itself the result of transculturations. In its constitution as a coherent religious ideology, Christianity appropriated pagan elements and infused them with new meanings. During the colonial period, the Andeans in turn reappropriated what had become a Christian symbol and resemanticized it back to its pagan origins. To argue, then, for the upholding of purity in religion and against its contamination—as the extirpators of idolatries did—is to overlook important historical transculturations in the constitution of Christianity.

The tradition of depicting St. James trampling an Indian underfoot arose during the earliest days of the colony. The motif returned in one of the first

Cuzco School paintings, a mural by Juan Iñigo de Loyola, which was dated 1545 and destroyed soon after.[115] Another early depiction is Guamán Poma's *Conquista/milagro del Santo Santiago Mayor* (figure 21). Yet another St. James Mataindios, painted in 1650 by an anonymous artist of the Cuzco School, is in the Museo Histórico Regional del Cuzco (figure 22). Gisbert finds that the ancient pre-Inca motif of depicting lightning as a serpent and the Inca tradition of depicting it as a warrior who broke a large pitcher of rainwater with his sling disappears to be substituted by the Apostle James on a white horse.[116]

Irene Silverblatt, in her study of Andean transformations of Santiago, points out that even though Santiago was considered helper of the Spaniards, he was nevertheless appropriated by the Andeans in order to help them: "Thus Santiago, the warrior-saint who was to redeem the New World for the Spanish, could do battle for those whom he was commissioned to vanquish." In this uncanny and twisted logic possible only under colonialism, Santiago Mataindios becomes a native deity urging the Andeans to resist Spanish rule.[117] However, internal contradictions persist in the composition of the new deity. As Silverblatt continues: "Seventeenth-century Christianized mountain gods (Santiago as god of thunder also rules over mountains) challenged colonialism's moral ascendancy and cultural dominance; and they decried any characterization of Indian peasants as passive victims of European rule. Andeanized Santiagos encouraged resistance, but it was a resistance contained within the boundaries of colonial power relations."[118]

It is only within this complicated scenario of power and powerlessness that religious transculturation can be understood. As Silverblatt argues, "divine Spanish and native images of power sputteringly fused as colonized Quechua created a new Andean religion inseparable from the political realities in which it was spawned. The new religion carried colonization's complexities, incongruities, and conflicts at its core, and it brooked difficult burdens."[119] Her proviso is well taken and her point is all too often overlooked by critics writing about syncretism and hybridism. However, it should also be remembered that the Andes were geographically isolated and a long distance from Lima, the seat of colonial and post-colonial power. As a result, Andean communities had to a great degree fallen by the wayside of colonial rule. Silverblatt's point, then, needs to be applied in such a manner that degrees of subjection to power are kept in mind. Anthropologists have repeatedly shown that, even as late as the early part of this century, Andean communities have been able to maintain their traditions because of their extreme isolation and thus evasion of colonial control.[120]

FIGURE 21.    Conquista / milagro del Santo Santiago Mayor, apóstol de Jesucristo / en el Cuzco [Conquest/miracle of Saint James]. Guamán Poma. *Nueva corónica y buen gobierno*, ed. Franklin Pease. Courtesy Biblioteca Ayacucho.

FIGURE 22.    Artist unknown. *Saint James Slayer of Indians*. Courtesy Instituto de
Investigacion y Conservación del Patrimonio Cultural "Diego Quispe Tito"
and the Museo Histórico Regional del Cuzco.

As was also true in the case of the Virgin of Guadalupe in Mexico,
"miracles" serve to naturalize and render acceptable the very violent acts of
aggression committed against the religions of indigenous people. Since evangelization partly entailed Christianity's appropriation and resemanticization
of Andean religious symbols, the transposition can be effected and justified

by means of the miracle. In the case of Mexico, the Virgin of Guadalupe is said to have appeared to an Indian on the very site on which the temple of the goddess Tonantzin had stood. The miracle in this case justifies the suppression of the native religion. Miracles show that one set of gods is more powerful than another, and they are therefore crucial in the rhetoric of evangelization. However, miracles do not seem to occur randomly and indiscriminately; they seem to take place at the ideologically and emotionally loaded intersections of the two religions.

The equation of St. James with thunder survives to this day, becoming part of what the Church denigrates as popular superstition. It can be seen in the Andes, where the countryside is dotted with shrines erected to St. James on sites where lightning was seen to have hit.[121] Anthropologists have also been informed that "when lightning strikes a house, it is abandoned for the day and night following, for [the Indians] believe that 'Santiago' [Saint James] has stumbled and made a mistake."[122] Michael Taussig has argued that one of the ways in which indigenous religions survive in spite of colonization is by going underground into what the West dismisses as superstition.[123] This submersion of native religions into superstition would account for the survival, in the case of St. James, of the saint's identification with thunder and lightning. This association could easily be dismissed by priests as mere superstition, and thus appeared to pose no threat to the Church.

## 8. St. Isidore the Laborer

Tradition has it that Isidore, a poor laborer who served a rich landowner, was lost in prayer and unable to finish his work when an angel appeared and plowed the land for him. When Isidore took up his pick and started to work again, a spring burst forth and irrigated the land.

Figure 23 shows St. Isidore as an Andean farmer, thus combining the saint's story with the agricultural miracles ascribed to Mama Occllo in pre-Columbian religious thought.[124] In this painting of the Cuzco School, European and Andean traditions are combined. There are indigenous flowers and crops, yokes of oxen pulling plows, and the humble man kneeling and praying. The humble man in the foreground wears the creole—that is, the Europeanized—fashion of the early nineteenth century. A number of indigenous birds appear, from a variety of families.[125]

Pierre Verger has photographed the modern-day ceremony performed on

FIGURE 23.　Artist unknown. *The Legend of San Ysidro*. Peruvian School. 1750.
Courtesy Brooklyn Museum.

FIGURE 24.    Artist unknown. *Trinity as three identical figures.* Courtesy Museo de
Arte, Lima. Photo credit: María Teresa Bustamante.

the day of St. Isidore, the farmer. He described it as "a typical Indian-
Catholic ceremony" in which "the priest blesses the yokes of oxen and these
symbolically plough in the square."[126] In this ceremony, the priest has very
definitely taken over an Andean idolatrous practice, showing the negotiations that Catholicism had to make in order to fulfill some kind of meaning-
ful role in a predominantly agricultural community.

## 9. The Holy Trinity as Three Identical Persons

Until the fifteenth century, the Trinity had been represented as
three identical figures, an iconography that referred back to the ancient
practice of representing the synchronic rule of two or three rulers.[127] However, because this practice deteriorated into the grotesque and the monstrous (God painted with four eyes, three mouths, and three noses), it was
forbidden by the Church.[128] Since the Renaissance, the Church had insisted
that the Trinity be represented by God the Father as an old man, the Son/

FIGURE 25. Artist unknown. *Trinity as three-fold face*. Courtesy Museo de Arte, Lima. Photo credit: María Teresa Bustamante.

Jesus as a young man, and the Holy Spirit as a dove. Given the Andeans' history of idolatrous animal worship and animal sacrifices, the practice of representing the Trinity as three identical figures or faces—banned in Europe—was reinstituted in the New World (figures 24 and 25). However, in the Andes it recalls the pre-Columbian cult of a three-headed idol.[129] This deviation is a clear example of some of the compromises that the colonial church engaged in so as to circumvent native idolatrous practices, and of the impossibility of controlling different culturally coded meanings.

## NOTES

1. Leopoldo Castedo, *The Cuzco Circle,* 41. See also Mary Grizzard, "Four Eighteenth-Century *Mestizo* Paintings from Cuzco," 3.

2. In part, this effort stemmed from the stipulations of the Council of Trent and the Counter-Reformation and therefore belonged to a larger European politico-religious scheme. For a contemporary religious treatise and a history on the power of images to move the spirit, or "eyesight as insight," see Margaret R. Miles, *Image as Insight: Visual Understanding in Western Christianity and Secular Culture.*

3. Felipe Cossio del Pomar argues that the confrontation between the long and rich Andean tradition and Hispanic culture was the factor that led to the development of such a vital artistic movement. See Felipe Cossio del Pomar, *Peruvian Colonial Art: The Cuzco School of Painting,* 30.

4. Rodríguez G. de Ceballos, "Las *Imágenes de la historia evangélica* del P. Jerónimo Nadal en el marco del jesuitismo y la Contrarreforma," 13.

5. As Mario Barata, in his short survey of Latin American artistic periods and styles, writes: "Durante cinco siglos la asimilación de las contribuciones externas resulta—en el campo de los impulsos artísticos—una constante. En cambio, las formas de adaptación y rechazo eventuales son aún poco conocidas" [During five centuries there was a constant assimilation of external artistic impulses. However, the modification and rejection of these has hardly been studied]. Mario Barata, "Epocas y estilos," 128.

6. Quoted in de Ceballos, "Las *Imágenes,*" 8.

7. Graham Howes argues that this situation has been reversed in the twentieth century: we have become literate textually but can no longer read paintings or stained-glass windows. See Howes, "Religious Art and Religious Belief," 335. Howes also studies cases of "escalation," in which religious images lose their power of reference and are worshiped for themselves. Thus, Greek islanders who were studied by anthropologists "certainly speak of and act towards the icon as if it *were* powerful in itself. The tissues and pieces of cotton wool with which church icons are dusted are kept for amulets and for use in the household cult of icons" (333). Escalation often occurs in the Andes, as well. During an earthquake, for example, the statue of the Señor de los Temblores is taken out so that he can perform a miracle and stop the disaster. The statue is venerated and imbued with magical qualities, ignoring the Church's dictate that icons be worshiped not for themselves, but for what they represent.

8. Howes, "Religious Art," 331.

9. See José de Mesa and Teresa Gisbert, *Historia de la pintura cuzqueña,* 86.

10. De Mesa and Gisbert, *Historia,* 270.

11. De Mesa and Gisbert, *Historia,* 62. De Mesa and Gisbert also trace the artistic development of Bitti in America. They find that over time he lost his ties with Italy and was influenced by the American continent—although it remained absent figuratively, it became latent in his paintings. He eventually painted more personal, less Mannerist, and more "American" works. De Mesa and Gisbert, *Historia,* 58.

Cossio del Pomar also argues that Spanish artists were changed by America and ended up painting very American works. For him, it is irrelevant whether a painting was executed by a Spaniard, a creole, or a mestizo, because the Spaniard could paint a true "American" painting and a mestizo or Indian painter was perfectly capable of painting a "European" painting. I think that that is true in exceptional cases. Generally, however, an American mestizo art tended to be created by mestizo and Indian artists and not by European ones, even though a certain "loosening" of form and content is apparent in the works of European artists.

12. Diego Quispe Tito actually went through three artistic phases: first as a Mannerist, then as a truly exceptional American artist, and finally, towards the end of his life, as a servile imitator. See De Mesa and Gisbert, *Historia,* 142.

13. De Mesa and Gisbert, *Historia,* 82–3.

14. De Mesa and Gisbert, *Historia,* 84.

15. De Mesa and Gisbert, *Historia,* 125. Breaking down the figures of the composition of the guild, Leopoldo Castedo finds thirty-five Indians, seven creoles and mestizos, four Spaniards, and one Italian, as well as countless anonymous Indian artists and artisans. Castedo, *Cuzco Circle,* 34.

16. The Church had decreed that no artist would be allowed to paint religious images without having first been examined. The exam followed a long apprenticeship of between one and five years and the candidate had to be well versed in Western artistic principles such as figure drawing and classical perspective. De Mesa and Gisbert, *Historia,* 227, 271.

17. Gisbert, *Iconografía,* 84.

18. De Mesa and Gisbert, *Historia,* 146.

19. Isabel Flores de Oliva was sanctified by Pope Clement X in 1671 as Santa Rosa de Lima. She was the first saint born on American soil. Ricardo Mariátegui Oliva, *Pintura cuzqueña del siglo XVII: Los maravillosos lienzos del Corpus existentes en la Iglesia de Santa Ana del Cuzco,* 26.

20. Furthermore, the newly Christianized did not uphold the Catholic differentiation between icons and what they represent. In many cases, icons of new saints and virgins acquired miraculous value in a way that would seem idolatrous, since in all religious art there is the problem of distinguishing between the "physical representation of the sacred as an art product and as a cult object." See Howes, "Religious Art," 332.

21. Castedo, *Cuzco Circle,* 42.

22. Castedo, *Cuzco Circle,* 51. On the evolution of the treatment of landscape by artists of the Cuzco School, Castedo writes: "From the mannerist period on, urban and wooded landscapes had been Flemish, but with *mestizaje* in painting, the local environment begins to exert its influence, albeit very timidly. Salamanca [a priest who covered every square inch of the walls and ceiling of his cell with murals] painted 'his own' snow-capped mountains, and many narrative paintings show the ocher barrenness of the landscape in the high Sierra and the Altiplano." Castedo, *Cuzco Circle,* 52.

23. The chronicler Sarmiento de Gamboa mentions that "la historia incaica fue pintada por lo menos a partir del reinado de Pachacutec" [Inca history was painted at least as far back as the rule of Pachacutec]. De Mesa and Gisbert, *Historia,* 45. As Mercedes López-Baralt writes, Sarmiento interviewed thirty-two descendants of the Incas and asked them how they preserved their tradition. "Los entrevistados contestaron que la tradición se transmitía a través de narraciones y cantos memorizados por especialistas o *amautas,* con la ayuda de quipus e imágenes pintadas en tablas" [Those who were interviewed answered that tradition was transmitted by means of narratives and songs memorized by specialists or *amautas,* with the help of *quipus* or knots and images painted on boards]. Important is the fact that with colonialism, the emphasis in the Andean world shifted away from paintings and songs as mnemonic devices to the appropriation of writing as a way of maintaining tradition and history. López-Baralt writes: "Pese a la intención manifiesta de servir a la evangelización y a la extirpación de la idolatría, el manuscrito se convirtió en el medio idóneo para que el indio aculturado pudiera preservar su pasado" [Despite the fact that the overt intention was that of evangelization and the extirpation of idolatries, the manuscripts became the ideal means through which acculturated Indians could preserve their past]. López-Baralt, *Icono y conquista,* 100.

24. Rowe and Schelling, *Memory and Modernity,* 29.

25. Castedo, *Cuzco Circle,* 51.

26. Louis Réau, *Iconographie de l'Art Chrétien,* 50.

27. Castedo, *Cuzco Circle,* 50.

28. De Mesa and Gisbert, *Historia,* 271.

29. Antonio Casaseca Casaseca, *Pintura cuzqueña en el Museo de Salamanca,* 14.

30. Another useful way of thinking about this is to consider that the Latin American literary [read artistic] tradition needs to be subjected to what Antonio Benítez Rojo calls a "second reading." Whereas

a first reading only allows the reader to recognize his or her self in a text, a second reading allows more of the text's structure and meaning to be rendered visible. This Barthesian notion is very nicely applied by Benítez Rojo to the necessity of having always to reread Latin American literature in order to understand its cultural subtext and ambivalence. See Benítez Rojo, *Isla que se repite,* xxvii.

Leopoldo Castedo writes that errors and false aesthetic judgments have been made by art historians "who have inflexibly applied the standards of 'Western culture.'" However, falling into the trap of defining art in terms of high versus popular art, he argues that critics cannot account for the Cuzco School because it is "a subject that cannot be considered strictly as a work of art within the stereotypes of 'European' culture, for the simple reason that the fundamental motivations of the two cultures vary widely in many respects." See Castedo, *Cuzco Circle,* 19. Castedo also quotes Erwin Palm, who writes: "As far as the colonial 'schools' of painting are concerned [of course this includes the Cuzco School] . . . their decorative grace and naïveté . . . are very far from being creative qualities—and one doubts that even the naïveté was intentional. The eagerness to reproduce forms and themes, the incapacity to contribute in terms of reality, the lack of creative freedom, all serve to keep this painting obviously at the level of mere craftsmanship." Castedo, *Cuzco Circle,* 141, n. 54. Another critic writes: "The baroque quality of colonial painting in the seventeenth and eighteenth centuries, as well as its basis in engravings, resulted in a cultivated manifestation of an insipid art without much substance. . . . Its primitivism makes one think of an archaizing, provincial school in which the Hispanic and European types were degraded." Antonio Bonet Correa, "Integración de la cultura indígena en el arte hispanoamericano," 15.

For Louis Réau, the difference between medieval and Renaissance art lay in the fact that in the Middle Ages, art was subjected to religious concerns. During the Renaissance, however, aesthetic considerations were more important. This would mean that Cuzco School paintings, when they are dismissed for being "merely decorative," are being judged according to a criterion that was not even upheld in Europe. Réau, *Iconographie,* 442.

31. Castedo, *Cuzco Circle,* 33. As Mary Grizzard writes, "it was not more degenerate for Cuzqueñan artists to have adapted forms from European artistic prototypes than it was for so many European artists to have done so throughout the history of art." Grizzard, "*Mestizo* Paintings," 7.

32. See de Mesa and Gisbert, *Historia;* Teresa Gisbert, *Iconografía;* Cossio del Pomar, *Peruvian Colonial Art;* Pál Kelemen, *Art of the Americas, Ancient and Hispanic;* José Antonio de Lavalle and Werner Lang, eds., *Pintura Virreynal;* Mariátegui Oliva, *Pintura cuzqueña . . . Cuzco* and *Pintura cuzqueña del siglo XVII en Chile.* For important studies on the mestizo in architecture, see the numerous works of Emilio Harth-Terré, particularly his *Las figuras parlantes en la arquitectura mestiza de arequipa* and *Por una arquitectura contemporánea que sea nuestra.* I thank Raúl Bueno for bringing the excellent studies of Harth-Terré to my attention.

33. Castedo, *Cuzco Circle,* 47. See also de Mesa and Gisbert, *Historia,* 271.

34. See figure 9 in MacCormack, "Children of the Sun," 31.

35. A work such as de Mesa and Gisbert's deals only with those paintings that are still hanging in their original sites. This makes for two very different types of scholarship on the Cuzco School: theirs and that of art historians who deal with exported works the world over.

36. Francisco Stastny, "The Cuzco School of Painting: A Gothic Revival," 20.

37. Stastny, "Cuzco School," 22.

38. Stastny, "Cuzco School," 27.

39. Harth-Terré, "Resumen histórico de la arquitectura peruana," 51.

40. Graziano Gasparini, "La ciudad colonial como centro de irradiación de las escuelas arquitectónicas y pictóricas," 10.

41. Bonet Correa, "Integración," 15.

42. Gisbert, *Iconografía,* 11.

43. De Mesa and Gisbert, *Historia,* 271.

44. Bonet Correa, "Integración," 12.

45. See López-Baralt, *Icono y conquista,* 128. She also writes "estamos ante todo un sistema visual aceptado colectivamente por la Europa culta" [we have before us a total visual system collectively assumed by Europe's elite] (129). As Edward A. Maser points out in the introduction to his new edition of Ripa's *Iconologia,* it was itself a very eclectic work: "a blend of antique mythology, Egyptian pictorial writing arbitrarily interpreted, biblical motives, and medieval Christian allegory, with all sorts of recon-

dite meanings being assigned to human expressions and actions, to the animals, plants, prescribed colors, and all objects natural and artificial which were their symbolic attributes." See Cesare Ripa, *Baroque and Rococo Pictorial Imagery: The 1758–60 Hertel Edition of Ripa's "Iconologia" with 200 Engraved Illustrations,* x.

46. As Ripa explained: "The esteemed reader is herewith advised, with all respect, that on each page of this work, the primary or main figure appearing in the so-called foreground always indicates the general title of the subject at hand, whereas the somewhat more distant representations indicate the associated histories and allegories." See Ripa, *Baroque and Rococo,* figure 2, "The Messenger."

47. De Ceballos, "Las *Imágenes,*" 13.

48. As session XXV stipulates, Catholicism would be renovated and given new impetus by emphasizing the production and proliferation of religious images, which were to serve as "salutory examples . . . set before the eyes of the faithful, so that they may give God thanks for those things, [and] may fashion their own life and conduct in imitation of the saints and be moved to adore and love God and cultivate piety." As Mercedes López-Baralt concludes, "[l]a Contrarreforma entendió que la revitalización de la sensibilidad católica sólo sería posible mediante el bombardeo simultáneo de los sentidos del cristiano con un mismo lenguaje redundante" [the Counter-Reformation understood that the revitalization of a Catholic sensibility could only be achieved by means of the simultaneous bombardment of the senses of the Christian with the same redundant language]. López-Baralt, *Icono y conquista,* 124.

49. This continued well into the nineteenth century. A painting commissioned for a church in the Andes reads "para el adorno de esta Yglesia, que totalmente estaba desnuda e indecente—año de 1803" [for the adornment of this church, which was completely naked and indecent—year of 1803] . De Mesa and Gisbert, *Historia,* 220.

50. Stastny, "Cuzco School," 23.

51. In an extreme case of the denial of indigenous transculturation, Bonet Correa writes that "Los frailes que le proporcionaron los modelos no hicieron más que utilizar la habilidad mecánica del artista para reproducir los grabados europeos" [Priests who provided the models did nothing more than to use the mechanical ability of the artist in order to reproduce European engravings]. In Bonet Correa's racist interpretation, priests as Spaniards possess the brains and the creativity, whereas Indians provide only the work. See Bonet Correa, "Integración," 13.

52. De Mesa and Gisbert, *Historia,* 146–7.

53. Inca Garcilaso de la Vega, *Comentarios reales,* 261. See also Luis Enrique Tord, "La pintura virreinal en el Cusco," 167, and Duccio Bonavia, *Ricchata Quellcani: Pinturas murales prehispánicas.*

54. Artistic transculturation has already been much studied with regard to colonial architecture. Teresa Gisbert in her *Iconografía* often alludes to it and draws comparisons between colonial painting and architecture. However, the most thorough investigation has been done in numerous works by Emilio Harth-Terré.

55. Castedo, *Cuzco Circle,* 36.

56. The reversal of a world that is upside down is best exemplified by the Inkarrí myth recounted by Rowe and Schelling: "History is referred to in the Inkarrí cycle through the idea of a temporal series of three ages: of God the Father, of the Son and of the Holy Spirit. The idea derives from the millenarian teaching of Joaquin de Fiori (1142–1202), whose belief system was the most powerful in European history until the rise of Marxism, and was brought to the Andes by Franciscan missionaries. He was condemned as a heretic for preaching that the future age of the Holy Spirit would bring salvation on the earth, and at a particular time. The Joaquinite third age becomes in the Andes a utopian future, in which existing power structures established by Spanish colonialism will be reversed. Here the Andean concept of *pacha kuti,* the turning upside down and inside out of time and space. In all of these versions, Inkarrí's dismembered body (whose severed head has been taken, variously, to Cuzco, Lima or Spain) is coming together with the idea that the lower or inside world (*manqhapacha* in Aymara, *ukhupacha* in Quechua) will exchange places with our present world." Rowe and Schelling, *Memory and Modernity,* 55.

57. Adorno, *Guamán Poma,* 81.

58. As de Mesa and Gisbert argue, it appears that Guamán Poma was an apprentice of the early Cuzco School. His drawings "son de lo mejor que ha producido el arte indígena en el Perú. En su esquematización y abstraccionismo provienen directamente de la herencia precolombina, en tanto que su iconografía y composición deben mucho a lo europeo. Formado en la escuela cuzqueña, su arte es el primer testimonio de la mezcla indoeuropea que iba a eclosionar un siglo después en la llamada escuela mestiza. El aprendizaje del dibujo lo debió realizar Guamán en algún taller del Cuzco hacia 1560" [are the best

that has been produced by indigenous art in Perú. In their schematic and abstract nature they are direct heir to a pre-Western tradition, whereas their iconography and composition owe much to Europe. Formed in the Cuzco School, his art is the first testimony we have of the Indian-European mixing that was to develop, one century later, into the so-called Mestizo School. Guamán must have learned to draw in some Cuzco workshop towards 1560]. De Mesa and Gisbert, *Historia*, 87.

59. Adorno, *Guamán Poma*, 14.

60. López-Baralt, *Icono y conquista*, 101.

61. The complete written text in the drawings reads as follows: "Pontifical mundo/Las Indias del Perú en lo alto de España/Castilla en lo abajo de las Indias/Castilla" [Pontifical world/The Indies of Perú on top of Spain/Castile in the lower part of the Indies/Castile]. Notice again the fivefold division of both sections and the Andean sun god shining down on the world. Cuzco is again in the center of the Inca world, whereas Castile is put in Andean fashion at the center of its world and surrounded by four provinces.

62. The full written text reads as follows: "Crió Dios al Mvndo/Entregó a Adán y Eva/Adán, Eva/mvndo/papa."

63. López-Baralt, *Icono y conquista*, 203–4.

64. As Adolphe Napoleon Didron points out, given its pagan use to crown rulers, the nimbus was absent from Christian iconography until the fifth and sixth centuries. Its use was revived because enough time had elapsed to erase memory of such idolatrous practices. See Adolphe Napoleon Didron, *Christian Iconography: The History of Christian Art in the Middle Ages*, 97–8.

65. Réau, *Iconographie*, 48, 54, 69.

66. Réau, *Iconographie*, 438. As Réau writes: "l'art païen, imprudemment ressuscité par les humanistes de la Renaissance, contamine l'art chrétien à un moment où il se trouve en état de moindre résistance et ne peut échapper à la contagion" [pagan art, imprudently resuscitated by the humanists of the Renaissance, contaminates Christian art at a moment when it finds itself able to offer least resistance and hence cannot escape the contagion] (439).

67. Carl G. Liungman, *Dictionary of Symbols*.

68. Didron, *Christian Iconography*, 61.

69. Notice the regularity of the symbols of the *coya*'s skirt and scarf: *, o, 2 or z, 4, and a square with a point in the middle. The significance of Guamán Poma's use of these symbols has not yet been studied, but they all point to pagan meanings. The *, for example, is the sign of Venus as well as of women's fertility; o symbolizes eternity; 2 represents dualism and the moon; and 4 is symbolic of the earth and also is associated with the square and with the cross that points to the four cardinal directions. See Liungman, *Dictionary of Symbols*.

70. Art historians write that the person holding the parasol is a dwarf and not a shift in perspective to denote a less important character.

71. López-Baralt, *Icono y conquista*, 195.

72. Fray Martín de Murúa wrote his *Historia general del Perú, origen y descendencia de los Incas* . . . between 1600 and 1611, according to Ballesteros Gaibrois.

73. It is difficult to tell whether Murúa's deviation from convention is attributable to him having witnessed an exception in which the parasol was not held by a dwarf, or whether the dwarf in traditional portrayals of Inca royal women invoked European traditions and the use of perspective, with size being an indication of power and importance.

74. De Mesa and Gisbert, *Historia*, 88.

75. Gisbert, *Iconografía*, 13.

76. This commemoration of the Inca past can also be seen in the numerous theatrical and popular representations of events such as the death of Atahualpa, the founding of the Inca empire, and the glories of Inca Huayna Cápac, which are represented in the Andes to this day.

77. For an outstanding study of Andean messianism, see Flores Galindo, *Buscando un Inca*. I thank Juan Epple for having referred me to this invaluable book. See also Juan M. Ossio, ed., *Ideología mesiánica del mundo andino*.

78. Gisbert, *Iconografía*, 13.

79. Réau, *Iconographie*, 441.

80. De Mesa and Gisbert, *Historia*, 278.

81. Mariátegui Oliva, *Pintura cuzqueña* . . . *Cuzco*, 12. In medieval Spain, the Corpus procession was

closely related to the *autos sacramentales*. These were dramatic pieces in one act "que tiene[n] por tema el misterio de la Eucaristía y que se representaba[n] en la antigua España el Día del Corpus" [Their theme was the mystery of the Eucharist. They were represented in former times in Spain on the Day of the Corpus]. Initially, the Corpus procession served as a pretext for the representation of the auto sacramental, and only later did the Eucharist become its theme. See Alfonso Reyes, "Los autos sacramentales en España y América," 117, 119.

82. For a description of the Corpus Christi celebration in México/Tlaxcala in the year 1538, see Fray Toribio de Benavente Motolinía, *Historia de los indios de la Nueva España*, 122–5. Notice especially Motolinía's description of the Tlaxcalans' construction of four artificial hills along the route of the procession, which certainly had pagan roots (123–4).

83. De Mesa and Gisbert, *Historia*, 177.

84. MacCormack, "Demons," 140.

85. MacCormack, "Children of the Sun," 23.

86. MacCormack, "Children of the Sun," 24.

87. Gisbert, *Iconografía*, 83–4.

88. Mariátegui Oliva, *Pintura cuzqueña*, 14.

89. See chapter 5 for José María Arguedas's study of these dances.

90. Rowe and Schelling, *Memory and Modernity*, 53–4. Rowe bases his argument on anthropologist Tristan Platt's "The Andean Soldiers of Christ: Confraternity Organisation, the Mass of the Sun, and Regenerative Warfare in Rural Potosí (18th–20th Centuries)," 139–46. The extirpator of idolatries Pedro de Villagómez was well aware of the Andean religious subtext of the Corpus Christi when he wrote in his *Exortación contra la idolatría del Perú* (Lima, 1649): "Si en las fiestas del Corpus Christi, ó en las otras fiestas de la Iglesia fingiendo los Indios que hace fiestas de los Cristianos, an adorado, ó adoran ocultamente, á sus idolos, ó an hecho ó hacen otros ritos" [If in the festivities of the Corpus Christi or in other Church celebrations, the Indians have pretended to celebrate with the Christians but have adored their idols, or have performed other rites instead]. Quoted in Bandelier, *Islands*, 160.

91. Réau, *Iconographie*, 69.

92. De Mesa and Gisbert, *Historia*, 272.

93. Gisbert, "The Andean Gods throughout Christianity," 86–7.

94. For a discussion of this precedent, see Barbara Duncan, "Statue Paintings of the Virgin," 15.

95. As Gisbert points out, St. Augustin in his *City of God* "plantea la dualidad entre el mundo cristiano y el pagano ante el cual [demuestra] la primacía del cristianismo afirmando que las verdades cristianas se hallan latentes, tanto en la naturaleza circundante como en la cultura pagana de griegos y romanos" [postulates the dualism between the Christian and the pagan worlds. Before the latter he argues for the primacy of Christianity, affirming that Christian truths are found latently in nature as well as in the pagan cultures of Greeks and Romans]. Gisbert, *Iconografía*, 12. This same form of argumentation-as-appropriation was to be copied by evangelizing priests and the extirpators of idolatries and repeated tirelessly.

96. Gisbert, "Andean Gods," 89.

97. De Mesa and Gisbert, *Historia*, 263. Gisbert's *Iconografía* is an excellent analysis of the development of the Virgin of Copacabana into an American religious symbol. See also Carol Damian, "The Survival of Inca Symbolism in Representations of the Virgin in Colonial Perú," 21–31.

98. Gisbert, *Iconografía*, 83.

99. Damian, "Survival," 22.

100. "Ce type de Virge nourrice est le plus ancien de tous. On le trouve dès le IIe siècle dans l'art del Catacombes (Fresque de la catacombe de Priscille) et ses origines iconographiques remontent au groupe égyptien d'Isis allaitant Harpocrate, christianisé par l'art copte (Fresque de Baouit)" [This type of nourishing virgin is the most ancient of all. It is found after the second century in the art of the Catacombs (Fresco of the Catacomb of Priscilla) and its iconographic origins go back to an Egyptian tomb where Isis is represented breast-feeding Harpocrates, which is Christianized in Coptic art (Fresco of Baouit)]. Réau, *Iconographie*, 44.

101. Damian, "Survival," 22.

102. In fact, as Sabine MacCormack writes, "an Inca's career was shaped by a twofold set of forces. While alive, he was set apart from humankind by an elaborate courtly ritual. When by contrast an Inca became a *mallqui* (the deceased Inca's embalmed body), courtly ceremonial endeavoured to emphasize

his human characteristics. . . . In short, the living Inca's human life was extended into divine life, while the deceased Inca's divine life was extended into human life." MacCormack, "Children of the Sun," 20.

103. Gisbert, "Andean Gods," 92. For a general discussion of the archangels, see Guy Brett, "Being Drawn to an Image."

104. Castedo, *Cuzco Circle,* 56.

105. Gisbert, *Gloria in Excelsis: The Virgin and the Ángels in Viceregal Painting of Peru and Bolivia,* 61.

106. Gisbert, *Iconografía,* 92.

107. Gisbert, *Gloria in Excelsis,* 63.

108. Gisbert, *Iconografía,* 86.

109. Réau, *Iconographie,* 50–1.

110. Gisbert, *Iconografía,* 87.

111. Gisbert, *Iconografía,* 87. See also Casaseca Casaseca, *Pintura cuzqueña,* 20. There is another series of paintings by Diego Quispe Tito, "Serie del Zodiaco," which was commissioned by the Church in order to assimilate and neutralize the Andean cult of the stars. In this series, each astrological sign and therefore each month is related to Christ's parables. The Latin heading to the series affirms that the paintings were expressly made to banish the adoration of heavenly bodies. Gisbert, *Gloria in Excelsis,* 63.

112. As Castedo points out, Raphael is the protector of the young, of travelers, and of pilgrims, which is why he always carries a walking stick. Castedo, *Cuzco Circle,* figure XXIII. My discussion of the Archangel Raphael is also indebted to the Brooklyn Museum description of the painting reproduced here as figure 20.

113. Castedo, *Cuzco Circle,* 57.

114. Gisbert, *Iconografía,* 197.

115. López-Baralt, *Icono y conquista,* 283.

116. Gisbert, "Andean Gods," 86–7.

117. Irene Silverblatt, "Political Memories and Colonizing Symbols: Santiago and the Mountain Gods of Colonial Perú," 187.

118. Silverblatt, "Political Memories," 191. As we will see in chapter 6, my feminist critique of transculturation, women's modes of resistance to and rearticulation of male discourse take place within the parameters established by a male tradition.

119. Silverblatt, "Political Memories," 183.

120. As Pierre Verger observed: "En los refugios distantes, a tiempo fijo, siguen las viejas prácticas y bajo la capa de la liturgia cristiana, debidamente camuflados, están ahí presentes, en el templo o en la procesión los símbolos antiguos. Este proceso de indianización de lo europeo se produjo desde el día siguiente a la conquista española" [In distant areas, at specific times—appropriately camouflaged—the old practices, former symbols, remain present in the temple or the procession and continue under the guise of Christian liturgy. This process of Indianization of the European took place right after the Spanish conquest]. Pierre Verger, *Fiestas y danzas en el Cuzco y en los Andes,* 14.

121. De Mesa and Gisbert, *Historia,* 307.

122. Bandelier, *Islands,* 100, 122.

123. Taussig, *Shamanism.*

124. Castedo, *Cuzco Circle,* figure XXVI.

125. Castedo, *Cuzco Circle,* figure XXVI.

126. Verger, *Fiestas y danzas,* figure 96.

127. Réau, *Iconographie,* 54–5. See also Didron, *Christian Iconography,* 219.

128. Didron, *Christian Iconography,* 58. Adolphe Napoleon Didron also writes: "It was a heresy to make the Trinity incarnate; it was audacious to depict the three hypostases fused and commingled in so monstrous a manner. Pope Urban VIII, on the 11th of August, 1628, prohibited representations of the Trinity under the figure of a man with three mouths, three noses, and four eyes; he proscribed also some other similar images. Disobedience to this command was threatened with the pope's anathema, and it was commanded that all Trinities of that description should be burned" (61).

129. De Mesa and Gisbert, *Historia,* 305. See figures 24 and 25.

# 5 ≈
# JOSÉ MARÍA ARGUEDAS: Entre Dos Aguas

*We must respect the one God at the heart of the sky which is the Sun.*
— RIGOBERTA MENCHÚ

*Y el Río Sagrado, el Vilcanota, expandiendo su garganta, grita con la fuerza entera de sus aguas para adorar al Creador.*

*[And the Sacred River, the Vilcanota, expanding its throat, screams with the whole strength of its waters to worship the Creator.]*
— JOSÉ MARÍA ARGUEDAS

To read Arguedas's work from the early *Agua* stories (1935) to his last, unfinished novel *El zorro de arriba y el zorro de abajo* (1971), is to follow an ever-expanding conception of Peruvian reality in which the initially Manichean universe of *Agua* gives way to increasingly comprehensive and complex views of Perú.[1] To read Arguedas's critics is to follow yet another trajectory, from an emphasis on the indigenista aspect of his work to an appreciation of his creativity and inventiveness. This shift in the appraisal of Arguedas's work can be clearly seen in two divergent views given by Mario Vargas Llosa. In 1969, Vargas Llosa made a now well-known distinction between the *novela primitiva* and the *novela de creación*. The so-called primitive novel was flawed, because it confused art and folk art, literature and folklore, information and creation;[2] it was a novel that was informed by foreign models and that rendered the local exotic. The novel of creation, on the other hand, was cosmopolitan and technically innovative. Because it transcended the realm of the rural and the regional, which had been the focus of the primitive novel, Vargas Llosa argued, the novel of creation went beyond the boundaries of America. It was universal, not regional.[3]

Needless to say, Vargas Llosa was thus positioning himself on the side of the novel of creation, with José María Arguedas on that of the primitive novel (although he absolved Arguedas of some of its worst shortcomings). His move, of course, should be understood as an ideological sleight of hand whereby writers of the "boom" attempted to emphasize their Adamic originality at the expense of the previous generations of writers.[4] Almost ten years later, however, in his acceptance speech upon admission to the Academia Peruana de la Lengua in 1977, Vargas Llosa upheld the radical originality and inventiveness of Arguedas's work and situated him on the side of the novel of creation.[5]

What had happened in those years? It seems that Arguedas had managed to create—and thus to find—his readers. In fact, Vargas Llosa's radical change follows in the wake of two seminal studies written by prominent Latin American critics: Antonio Cornejo Polar's *Los universos narrativos de José María Arguedas* (1973) and Ángel Rama's first essay on transculturation, which appeared as the preface to his compilation of Arguedas's ethnographic essays, *Señores e indios: Acerca de la cultura quechua*.

These works, among others,[6] rescued Arguedas from earlier, simplistic versions of indigenismo in which writers had positioned themselves as both exterior and superior to the culture they were writing about. In contrast, Cornejo Polar and Rama both argue that Arguedas, as a bilingual and bicultural writer, allowed Andean oral culture to inform and shape his writings. Thus, Arguedas opted to write in Spanish and chose the nineteenth-century realist, bourgeois novel to explore a world foreign to that genre. In the process of adopting the novel to write about Andean culture, he transculturated it. Arguedas not only made of language yet another fiction by forcing Spanish to conform to Quechua syntax and rhythms of speech, but also organized his novels according to the structure of Andean music rather than Western logic. This is where Arguedas, these critics argue, made his greatest contribution to the creation of an American—specifically Peruvian—literature.

Although critics have contributed to the recovery of Arguedas's works from a much-maligned indigenismo, they continue to overemphasize his political and artistic compromise with the Indians. In doing so, they disregard his conceptualization of Perú as a mestizo nation. Critics therefore con-

tinue to categorize Arguedian characters as either Indians or whites (*mistis*).[7]
Thus, while saving Arguedas from a flawed indigenismo, they unwittingly
recontextualize him within a "good" indigenismo. In fact, in Arguedian
narratives there are no "pure" Indians and no "pure" mistis. Everyone, to a
greater or lesser degree, is situated along a continuum of mestizaje. Part of
the reason why critics have not realized this, and still write about Arguedian
characters as "Indians," lies in that the key to Arguedas's idiosyncratic cod-
ing of characters is to be found in his ethnographic studies. To fully understand his work, Arguedas's novels and his ethnographic works must be read
in conjunction with one another.

Arguedas's career spans almost four decades, from the 1930s until the late
1960s. This was a period of vertiginous change throughout Latin America,
and particularly in the Andean nations. Arguedas constantly transformed his
conception of Perú, adapting his ethnographic and novelistic writings to the
changes that were taking place around him. As such, his work can be considered a faithful—although personal—seismographic record of the times.
This chapter will focus on the links between Arguedas's novels and the ethnographic theories that they so carefully register. It will also examine how
Arguedas's ethnographic theories of transculturation, or cultural mestizaje
(he used both terms interchangeably), informed his novelistic endeavour and
a conception of the subject—and hence novelistic characters—as split between two worlds.

## The Ethnographer of a World in Transition

If the whole of Arguedas's life and work could be reduced to
answering one question, it would be that of explaining how Andean culture
has managed to survive—and even to thrive—despite the devastation in-
flicted upon the Peruvian Andes by the Conquest. Although 70 percent of
the native population had been wiped out in the first eighty years of colonization, by the twentieth century most of the population of Perú could,
once again, be called "Indian." Not only had the Andeans survived, but
they had managed to maintain a vigorous culture despite all odds. In Arguedas's time—particularly between the two world wars—industrialization and
modernization led to mass migrations from the Andes to the coastal cities.
Arguedas lived to see what he called the "second great catastrophe" befall
Perú. Like the Conquest, modernization was bringing about the rapid dis-

integration of traditional rural Andean societies. Arguedas's question there-fore had two components: How had the Andeans managed to survive his-torically, and how were they negotiating their relation to modernity?

If one term could be used to answer Arguedas's question, it would be transculturation. By transculturation, Arguedas understood both loss and gain: the terrible and painful loss of native cultures, languages, and bodies; and the appropriation and adaptation by those very same cultures, languages, and bodies of what colonialism and neocolonialism had imposed on them. Arguedas's ethnographic studies show that Andean cultures had been con-tinually adapting and transforming themselves since the Conquest: what was perceived as Indian was actually a highly transculturated form of Andean culture. Within this context, the denomination "Indian" only served as a marker of greater identifiable closeness to that original Quechua culture, while "mestizo" signaled distance away from that culture.

That assimilation can spell gain is easily overlooked by the critic situated in the late twentieth century and writing in the United States, where as-similation, from a "minority" position, has invariably come to mean loss. In Arguedas's work we see a different conception at work. Assimilation is situated within the greater context of transculturation, where nothing is adopted passively and everything is changed and adapted—recontextualized and resemanticized—to fit a native mold. Over time, the incorporation of new and altered elements gradually changes the whole matrix of what once was the pure indigenous culture. That is, with each new addition the whole is changed, if only slightly, and with every slight change, Andean culture becomes more transculturated. Furthermore, it should be remembered that, as Ángel Rama has pointed out, not everything is adopted indiscriminately by the colonized.

In order to demonstrate how indigenous elements were preserved in new mestizo configurations, Arguedas used as examples of transculturation the Andean bullfight and Andean architecture. In the Andean bullfight, a con-dor is tied to the back of a bull, replacing the picadors of the traditional Spanish bullfight. Analogous to the relation between superior and inferior or hanan and hunan in Guamán Poma's work, the condor promises the tri-umph of the Andean world over the Spanish, since the bull invariably dies and the condor—symbol of Quechua culture—is adorned with bright rib-bons and let loose to fly freely into the mountains. In this way, the Spanish spectacle of the bullfight is transplanted to Peruvian soil, where it is trans-formed and resemanticized.

Colonial architecture provided Arguedas with another example of trans-culturation. In the Andes, Spanish colonial buildings rise on Inca founda-tions. Colonial architecture, with its Inca base and Spanish superstructure, has therefore unwittingly become "un símbolo y una imagen del futuro mundo peruano" [a symbol and an image of the future Peruvian world].[8] In this case, unlike with the bullfight, the superior position of Spanish co-lonial architecture symbolizes the triumph of the culture of the colonizers. Whether superior or inferior, triumphant or subjected, for Arguedas these two examples each illustrate the processes of transculturation. In the bull-fight, substituting a condor for the picador changed the whole significance of the spectacle. Similarly, Inca foundations determined the siting and shape of Spanish colonial buildings. Both these examples also served as symbols of the intercultural negotiations that were shaping modern Perú.

Other examples that clearly show the processes of transculturation in Perú include the *charango,* now considered a "typical" Andean musical instrument but actually derived from the Spanish *bandore* and re-created with autoch-thonous materials; the *sijllas,* carnivalesque Andean dances in which the dancers criticize the imposed Spanish legal system and reverse colonial hi-erarchies;[9] and Andean myths, which Arguedas collected from the oral tra-dition and then transcribed. Myths such as those of Inkarrí and Adaneva betray their double origins even in the constitution of their names (Inka/rey/king, Adam/Eve). For Arguedas, the most striking aspect of this trans-culturation is that these myths both arise from and promise an end to colo-nial social hierarchies.[10]

In the process of transformation and adaptation, native cultures suffered losses but they also made gains. The charango, for example, provided the Andeans with a new musical instrument that enriched the configuration of indigenous music.[11] Likewise, the sijllas and the myths of Inkarrí and Ada-neva proved to Arguedas that Indian culture was a configuration of diverse elements and that it was well on its way to becoming a mestizo culture:

El folklore peruano es . . . muestra elocuente de la vitalidad de la cultura india que no se ha anquilosado ni detenido, como se supone, sino que, asimilando constan-temente cuanto le ha sido necesario de la cultura occidental, se transforma y alienta paralelamente a la misma, creando con ella, como zona de confluencia, al mestizo inestable y dinámico.

[Peruvian folklore is . . . an eloquent proof of the vitality of Indian culture, which has not become rigid nor stopped in its tracks, as is assumed. Rather, it has continu-ally assimilated Western elements that it found useful. It has transformed itself and fosters, parallel to and creating with it, as a zone of confluence, the unstable and dynamic mestizo.][12]

Within Arguedas's scheme, Indian culture ceased to exist with the Conquest. All things labeled "Indian" were actually only markers for the different stages of transition away from that original culture and towards a mestizo one. Since the Conquest, it had become impossible to determine what was truly indigenous and what was Spanish, even in the most isolated regions. Thus, Arguedas argued that Peruvian folkloric manifestations "constituyen formas complejas de lo mestizo indoespañol. No existe casi ninguna expresión folklórica que pueda ser considerada como rezago puro de la cultura pre-hispánica-peruana" [constitute a complex form of the mestizo Indo-Spanish. There is hardly any folkloric expression that can be considered a pure remainder of pre-Columbian culture].[13]

Arguedas derived immense relief and hope from finding that the processes of transculturation had been at work since the Conquest and that Indian culture would be "saved," in one way or another, in cultural mestizaje. But he also realized, to his dismay, that transculturation did not take place uniformly throughout the Andes. In fact, the degree to which individual Andean communities had changed was proportional to their relative isolation from urban centers, particularly Lima.[14] In isolated communities, including the one in which Arguedas had grown up, the colonial feudal organization created a stark confrontation between powerful misti landowners and Indian serfs. With the Andes acting as an impassable barrier, these communities maintained a way of life that changed little from the days of the Conquest until well into this century. However, this isolation now worked against them.[15] As Arguedas put it, they were unable to resist the assault of Western, bourgeois capitalism from Lima. Modernization, in fact, condemned isolated bastions of Andean culture "a la desintegración social y espiritual" [to social and spiritual disintegration].[16]

Borrowing a metaphor from biology, Arguedas writes that these areas had not developed the "antibodies" needed to resist Western culture. In Arguedas's scheme, therefore, the more geographically isolated a community and the more oppressed it had been, the less able it was to register productively the impact of the West. However, even those regions that had little contact with the West and that seemed most purely Andean had been transformed to some degree. In those areas, there had been a micro transculturation taking place between Indians and Spaniards. For just as the *gamonal* (feudal landowner of Spanish descent) had shaped the Indian community under his control, so too had that community "Indianized" him.

In the 1930s, the period of the "second great catastrophe," Arguedas saw the world of his childhood, the world of the isolated Indian community that had sheltered him, suddenly disappear.[17] One of his aims, both as an ethnographer and as a novelist, became the preservation of that world through writing. With a great sense of ethnographic urgency he collected myths, legends, and stories of the region, believing that they were "en peligro de muerte, de extinción absoluta, de esas extinciones que no dejan huellas" [in danger of death, of absolute extinction, of those kinds of extinction that leave no traces].[18]

Arguedas's attempt to save and preserve an oral culture that was rapidly being lost made him engage in what James Clifford has criticized as "salvage" ethnography. The rhetoric of salvage, Clifford argues, legitimates the practice of ethnography: "The other is lost, in disintegrating time and space, but saved in the text." This kind of ethnographic stance is driven by the underlying assumption that "the other society is weak and 'needs' to be represented by an outsider (and that what matters in its life is its past, not present or future)."[19] Like Western ethnographers, Arguedas urgently attempted to save a world from disappearance. Unlike them, however, he was much too interested in the dynamics of the present to compose what Clifford calls "requiems" in the name of science.[20] Furthermore, Arguedas never quite fit the role of the ethnographer-as-outsider. Instead, he enjoyed a privileged position as insider both to the culture that served as his field of inquiry and to the culture from which he obtained the ethnographic impulse. Although he shared with Western ethnographers a sense of urgency, his position was further complicated by the fact that it was both more personal and more ambiguous.

In fact, Arguedas's ethnographic stance was paradoxical and at times even contradictory. On the one hand, he wanted to preserve a world from disappearance, as is evident in posthumous publications such as *Indios, mestizos y señores, Señores e indios: Acerca de la cultura quechua,* and *Formación de una cultura nacional indoamericana.* However, he realized that the Andean world imagined in all its pathos by the indigenistas of his time was but a mirage, a folkloric romanticization based on a static understanding of cultures, the inability to grasp the moment, and the desire to glorify a once-great past at the expense of the present. The impulse to preserve and "museumize" was therefore tempered by his conception of culture as a vital process that was constantly changing and adapting to foreign impulses. Arguedas's increasing interest in the mestizos and the new cultural configurations that were arising in his time constitute the other side of his ethnographic focus.

One series of studies in particular helped shape Arguedas's conception of transculturation and demonstrated the vitality of the transformations that were affecting Perú. His studies of the Mantaro river valley were undertaken in the 1950s and published as *Formación de una cultura nacional indoamericana,* edited by Ángel Rama.[21] They became the basis for his theory of the adaptability of the mestizo and the survival of vital forms of Andean culture in new mestizo cultural configurations. Arguedas found that the communities of the Mantaro, unlike those of isolated regions, had not been subjected to colonial institutions of serfdom[22] because the Spaniards had needed the Indians' assistance in combatting an invading tribe from the North. Spaniards and Indians had therefore become allies and had worked closely together and intermarried. Because the area was poor in natural resources, the Spaniards eventually moved away. They left behind communities that were included in the colonial organization, but lacked the rigid feudal conditions of serfdom that were imposed elsewhere.[23]

Given their economic insignificance to the Spaniards, the mestizo communities of the Mantaro had been allowed to evolve peacefully. Cities such as Huancayo, strategically located at the crossroads between north and south, had prospered, becoming centers of diffusion for mestizo culture.[24] Unlike isolated areas, these communities actually benefited from the building of the Central Railway at the turn of the century and of the Central Highway in the 1930s. Improved communications between the Andes and the coast allowed them to flourish by raising the prices of their products and opening new markets. The communities of the Mantaro, with their ongoing and easy adaptability, proved that cultural survival would be possible through transculturation, even if indigenous cultures were greatly changed and transformed in the process. Mestizo communities were more readily able to implement new technologies and standards than were those communities in which the rigid, feudal relations of power instituted during the colony had survived into the present.[25] However, despite the differing abilities of communities to adapt, the studies of the Mantaro had proven that transculturation was possible. Those communities that were most fragile in terms of their ability to resist Westernization were destined to suffer the greatest losses, but they would not be irremediably lost, as had been generally held and sometimes feared—even by Arguedas himself.[26]

Arguedas's studies of the transculturation of the Mantaro, as well as his own refusal to cling to the past and to museumize, inevitably led him to explore the new culture being formed by the mestizos. His early studies of the mestizos centered on those living in larger Andean towns, where they formed a group that belonged neither to the dominant class nor to that of the Indians. Often, a mestizo in this situation would leave the Andes for the cities rather than remain and become foreman for a landowner. As such, a mestizo was a *cuña* (wedge) between both groups and would, as Arguedas writes, "bajo el silencio de los cielos altísimos sufrir el odio extenso de los indios y el desprecio igualmente mancillante del dueño" [under the silence of the very high skies, suffer the immense hatred of the Indians and the equally tarnishing contempt of the owner].[27]

As a result of the mass migrations to the coastal cities and the new cultural configurations that were arising, Arguedas's interests began to shift. Towards the end of his life, his ethnographic studies turned increasingly away from the Andes. Instead, he began to examine the mestizos in Lima and other large urban centers along the coast. Being neither white nor Indian, neither here nor there, mestizos were universally held in contempt. Arguedas realized that they did not merit this treatment, and that they in fact represented a truly Peruvian "third path," since they embodied both the salvageable aspects of Andean culture and the useful aspects of Western culture. However, although Arguedas made categorical statements concerning the survival of vital and viable aspects of Andean culture in the newly emerging mestizo culture of his day, his position was not devoid of a great ambivalence.[28] At times he positioned himself on the outside, as the ethnographer saddened by the turn of affairs, but more generally he included himself in the category "mestizo" and wrote about the anguish of being in process between two different cultures and languages.[29]

Arguedas studied members of another group in the *barriadas* (shanty-towns) around Lima. These were the Indians who had been forced to migrate to the urban coastal centers when they lost their lands and could no longer make a living in the Andes. Their transculturation, once they settled in coastal cities, began to take place at a vertiginous rate and involved both positive and negative aspects. Arguedas found that they tended to regroup in the barriadas according to origin. In this way, what to the uninitiated eye appeared as total demographic chaos, actually proved to be a duplication of Andean space and ethnos. Furthermore, lacking basic infrastructure such as running water and electricity, newly arrived Andeans banded together and continued to work according to traditional communitarian forms they had practiced in their villages. Describing the continuation of Andean forms of social organization and work in positive terms, Arguedas writes:

Cuando se habla de "integración" en el Perú se piensa invariablemente en una especie de *aculturación* del indio tradicional a la cultura occidental; del mismo modo que cuando se habla de alfabetización no se piensa en otra cosa que en castellanización. Algunos antropólogos . . . concebimos la integración en otros términos o dirección. La consideramos no como una ineludible y hasta inevitable y necesaria *aculturación,* sino como un proceso en el cual ha de ser posible la conservación o intervención triunfante de algunos de los rasgos característicos no ya de la tradición incaica, muy lejana, sino de la viviente hispano-quechua que conservó muchos rasgos de la incaica. Así creemos en la pervivencia de las formas comunitarias de trabajo y vinculación social que se han puesto en práctica, en buena parte por la gestión del propio gobierno actual, entre las grandes masas no sólo de origen andino sino muy heterogéneas de las "barriadas," que han participado y participan con entusiasmo en prácticas comunitarias que constituían formas exclusivas de la comunidad indígena andina.

[When people speak of "integration" in Perú, they invariably think in terms of a type of *acculturation* of the traditional Indian to Western culture. Likewise, when people speak of literacy, they only think of learning Spanish. Some anthropologists . . . like myself, understand integration in other terms and as taking another direction. We understand integration not in terms of an inevitable and necessary *acculturation,* but as the process whereby some of the characteristic features of Hispano-Quechua culture—the originary Inca being so distant—are conserved and intervene triumphantly. Thus, we believe in the persistence of communitarian forms of work and social interaction which have been put into practice, to a great extent by the government today, among the great masses, not only those of Andean origin, but also those very heterogenous groups living in the poverty belt who have participated and continue to participate with enthusiasm in communitarian forms of work that formerly pertained exclusively to the Andean world.][30]

In the barriadas, therefore, Arguedas finds the conflation of two phenomena with very different origins: early Andean "communism" and Latin American Marxism as it was developed in its transculturated form.[31] Whereas communitarian forms of work formerly had been practiced exclusively by the Andeans, in the poverty belt around Lima many of the poor have banded together to provide for basic necessities. A formerly Andean conception of work now predominates in some of them. However, these new forms of Andean "grass roots" organization function in some barriadas and not in others. Where they do not persist, the atomization under capitalism in its worst form comes into play.

The communal organization of work is seen as a positive impact that the

Andeans have had on the city, but the city has had a negative effect on them. The newly arrived peasants are despised for being Indian. Since they inhabit an in-between and ambivalent cultural space, they rapidly interiorize negative judgments and try to erase all trace of their origins. In their desire to fit in, they mimic everything Western and act in grotesque ways, which further fuels the contempt in which they are held. In popular fiestas organized by their local organizations, for example, they try to dance fashionable Western dances, only to look comical and out of place. When a little drunk, they give up all pretense and go back to dancing traditional Andean dances. On the basis of observations like these, Arguedas concludes that Indians who migrate from the Andes to coastal urban centers are in a state of confusion. On the way to becoming cultural mestizos, they find themselves at the intersection of two cultures.[32]

The confusion between languages and cultures creates situations of tension and social chaos, especially in the context of extreme poverty and marginalization. When there is no common set of values against which a person's life and work can be measured, there is a concomitant loss of morals or scruples that effectively tears at the social fabric. The axiom "every man for himself and God against all" becomes the order of the day. On the other hand, when people are freed from narrow local social constraints, they begin to rethink social priorities. Everything is reshuffled and re-created anew. In Lima today both options coexist: on the one hand, social chaos and the brutal Sendero Luminoso war; on the other, heroic examples of communitarian social organization such as those of the shantytown Villa El Salvador.[33]

In the end, however, the confusion between cultures and languages revolves around conceptions of subjectivity and the subject, which are also in transition. Whereas previously culture and cultivation of the land or the close connection between ethics and ethnos went hand-in-hand,[34] in cases of mass migration a disjunction between place and identity takes place. In the trajectory of the *huayno* (song) as it is transplanted from the Andes to Lima, Arguedas finds evidence of the process of preservation and loss that accompanies any transculturation and new cultural formation. Arguedas's observations also shed light on the redefinition of the huayno, which was taking place during his time. As Arguedas writes: "El wayno es como la huella clara y minuciosa que el pueblo mestizo ha ido dejando en el camino de salvación y de creación que ha seguido" [The huayno is like the clear and precise mark that mestizo culture has been leaving on its way to salvation and creation].[35]

When transplanted from the Andes to the coastal urban centers, one of the first things that happens to the huayno is a loss of anonymity. The attribution of authorship to the songs parallels the mestizo's painful efforts at self-definition and individuation. In this Arguedas finds traces of the development of "un pueblo diferenciado y nuevo" [a new and differentiated culture].[36] Moved from rural villages to the coliseums, huaynos begin to be heard via records and radio stations. The displacement from the rural—Walter Benjamin would say "auratic"—sphere to an attribution of authorship, the concomitant creation of a star system, and the adoption of mass-production and distribution methods once again bring about a resemanticization of what once was a solely Andean art form.

The distance between urban mestizo and Quechua songs also can be seen at the level of content. In Indian huaynos,

los seres amados se simbolizan en una nube, en un árbol, en una piedra . . . de tal manera, con tanto olvido de diferenciar, con tanto afán de hacer saber que igual se puede amar a los pájaros y a la tierra, como a la mujer y a los padres, que no se sabe para quién es el canto.

[loved ones are symbolized by a cloud, a tree, a rock . . . in such a way, with such a desire to forget differences, with such eagerness to make others know that one can love birds and the earth as much as a woman and one's parents. This is so much the case that the listener, in the end, no longer knows to whom or to what the song is addressed.][37]

In other words, in Andean cosmogony "la naturaleza envuelve aún, como un manto vivo al hombre" [nature still envelops people, like a live cloak].[38] Thus, in a Quechua song, nature is a subject like any other. In contrast, the mestizo love song is unambiguously addressed to a woman: the world has lost its immanence; the love for a woman and the love for a bird, a flower, or nature are no longer interchangeable. Arguedas sees this dichotomy (Spanish and Quechua lyrics mixed with a mestizo content) embodied in the mestizo singer Gabriel Aragón. When he needs to express the life of the villages in its entirety, Aragón chooses Quechua and drama or comedy.[39] He is unable to express all of this in Spanish. But when it is "un solo sentimiento el que necesita expresar, entonces prefiere el canto, y para eso el español le es mejor" [a single feeling that he needs to express, he prefers to sing, and then Spanish serves him better].[40] In Arguedas's scheme, Quechua serves to give voice to a whole world and to a world that is whole. Spanish expresses only fragments of that world and only isolated feelings. Thus, Andeans who migrate to the coast not only begin to oscillate between two different languages and conceptions of the world, but also between two different understandings of subjectivity.

Arguedas also finds that a trademark of the mestizos who sing huaynos in Lima is that they know the melody but in many cases have forgotten the lyrics, which they then must invent. As a result, the melody remains age-old and traditionally Andean, but the content and language are different. One song contains the line "con qué ternuras tapu kuni-kayakuskay . . . ," which begins in Spanish but adds the very intimate and familiar Quechua *s* to the Spanish *ternura,* and from then on continues in Quechua.[41] For Arguedas, this mixing of languages as well as of cultural codes and cosmogonies is the exclusive form of expression of the Peruvian who is culturally mestizo. This observation is fundamental to an understanding of how Arguedas conceived of mestizo subjectivity, which, as I will show in the next section, in turn affected the way in which he coded his characters.

Arguedas learned from the transculturations that he studied and he attempted to reproduce them at a narrative level. However, the degree to which he translated ethnography into fiction varied. In some cases Arguedas directly transposed one onto the other; in others, he used his findings— particularly about the transitional character of indo-mestizo culture—as a means of characterizing the "new" Peruvian. A clear example of direct transposition appears in *Todas las sangres.* In this novel, Arguedas's ethnographic observations regarding the bicultural development of the charango are transposed into a poetic query. When a woman is serenaded by a charango player in the middle of the night, the narrator asks: "¿Désde qué honduras de la tierra y del hombre andino y europeo confundidos llegaban esas notas en que el universo nocturno se recreaba llorando?" [From what depths of the earth and the confusion between Andean and European man did these musical notes, in which the night universe re-created itself crying, arise?].[42]

In the story "El sueño del pongo," Arguedas uses the Andean messianic dream voiced by the myth of Adaneva, which he had collected and transcribed in its different versions, as a structuring device. The myth tells of how the god Adaneva slept with the Virgin of Las Mercedes and left her when she became pregnant. She gave birth to Téete Mañuco, who destroyed ancient humanity (pre-Inca civilizations) and created the modern world. Today's humanity is divided into Indians and mistis. Each year, Téete Mañuco dies on a Friday and is resurrected on a Saturday. He is therefore immortal. Téete Mañuco created Heaven as an exact replica of the world, but with one difference: "allí los indios se convierten en mistis y hacen trabajar por la fuerza y hasta azotándolos, a quienes en este mundo fueron mistis" [there the Indians become mistis and force to work—even by whipping—those who were mistis in this world].[43] In this myth, the rigid and unchangeable opposition between masters and slaves replaces the Christian ideal of justice and peace for all. The myth also shows the extent to which elements from Spanish and Quechua cultures are entangled, giving rise to new post-Hispanic cosmogonies that usurp the Christian elements from which they derive. The dream of the liberation of the Andean world is framed in terms of the absolute reversal of the conditions of the colony: oppressor will become oppressed, and vice versa.[44] In "El sueño del pongo," Arguedas merely fictionalized the Andean belief in the colony as a world upside down, with heaven as the place where wrongs will be righted. In that story, el pongo, a young Indian serf, dies and meets his master in heaven. God covers the pongo with shit and the master with honey and orders them to lick each other off.

Spanish and Quechua, and the different conceptions of the world that they each express, act as poles of tension between which the narrators in Arguedas's novels move. Spanish, adulthood, ethnography, and a rational and sociological understanding of the world coincide at one level. Quechua, childhood, the autobiographical, and an animistic, musical, and magical conception of the world coincide at another. In fact, many of Arguedas's protagonists are children. This is the case in *Agua, Amor mundo,* and *Los ríos profundos.* When Arguedas opts for the child protagonist (and the adult narrator who reminisces), as in *Los ríos profundos,* metonymic associations of Quechua words and a non-Western conception of the world—which is itself equated with childhood—predominate. As Cornejo Polar and Rama have shown, the structure of these novels is musical rather than rational. Plots advance by means of word association rather than by logical continuity. When, as in *Todas las sangres,* Spanish and a rational conception of the world predominate, myths and magical events from the Andean world irrupt in the text and disrupt the flow of the Western rational structure.

The dichotomy between Quechua and Spanish, between Andean animism and a "rational" Western interpretation of the world, is translated in Arguedas's narratives into a constant struggle with language and a determined effort to have his narrators embody and represent both worlds. The merging of two worlds and two languages can be seen clearly in *Todas las sangres,* in which all the different facets of Peruvian reality are incorporated into a moment of crisis.[45] The novel takes place during the years in which

Andean isolation begins to break down. It is the time when North American imperialism is increasingly felt, even in the remotest areas. *Todas las sangres* shows the rapid pace of disintegration experienced by villages and towns. It also shows the conditions that force the migration of Andeans to the coastal cities in search of work, a subject that became the focus of Arguedas's last novel, *El zorro de arriba y el zorro de abajo*. Because of these dynamics, Arguedas's characters and narrators are torn between a traditional, rural way of life and the modern, urban world of the coast; between Spanish and Quechua; and between the Andes and the metropolitan centers. Situated along what I call a "continuum of mestizaje," they are linguistically and culturally unstable. In order to be understood in all their intercultural complexity, they demand a new interpretive mode.

## Todas las sangres / All the Worlds

Somos miles de millares, aquí, ahora. Estamos juntos; nos hemos congregado pueblo por pueblo, nombre por nombre, y estamos apretando a esta inmensa ciudad que nos odiaba, que nos despreciaba como a excremento de caballos. Hemos de convertirla en pueblo de hombres que entonen los himnos de las cuatro regiones de nuestro mundo, en ciudad feliz, donde cada hombre trabaje, en inmenso pueblo *que no odie.*

[We are hundreds of thousands, here, now. We are together, we have congregated people by people, name by name, and we are squeezing that immense city that hated us, that despised us as horse dung. We shall turn this city into a city of people who sing hymns to the four regions of our world, into a happy city, where everyone will have work; we shall become an immense people *that does not hate.*] (Emphasis added.)

— JOSÉ MARÍA ARGUEDAS

Arguedas's ethnographic works and his novelistic writings parallel and inform each other. At the same time, like finely tuned instruments, they both respond sensitively to the changes taking place in Perú. Arguedas never confined himself to one position; his work constantly expands both in scope and in depth. Ethnographically, he moved from an exclusive focus on the Indians to encompass the mestizos and life in the big cities. Novelistically, he attempted to merge the Western and the Andean worlds—to effect, at a narrative level, the transculturations he saw taking place in Perú.[46] Arguedas appropriated the nineteenth-century European novel and displaced it to write about a world where the novel had no place; he assumed Andean cosmogony as an interpretive scheme; he interpellated a rich Andean tradition of oral history, storytelling, and drama; he played with both the Western understanding of the individual and the Andean understanding of subjectivity; he introduced huaynos and Quechua words and syntax into his narratives; he created characters who are in transition, like the mestizos he studied in Lima; and he assumed a narrative voice that is itself unstable and in process, split between two worlds and moving back and forth between them.[47]

Because they lack familiarity with Arguedas's ethnographic works, many critics have failed to see the different ways in which he culturally coded the narrators and characters in his novels and stories. Indians, Spaniards, and mestizos in various stages of transculturation inhabit his narratives. Arguedas's characters and narrators are all in one way or another engaged in radical change in a radically changing world. In his ethnographic writings, Arguedas claims that no one can avoid transculturation, not even the white hegemonic class that claims direct descent from Spain. "Los españoles y sus descendientes, rodeados por la masa indígena que a todo lo largo del país habla una sola lengua y aislados por gigantes montañas . . . se indigenizan mucho más de lo que hasta ahora se ha descubierto" [The Spaniards and their descendants, isolated by gigantic mountains and surrounded by the mass of Indians who speak one language throughout the country . . . are Indianized to a much greater extent than has been found until now].[48]

This point is made clearly in *Todas las sangres,* in which Arguedas insists on showing how white landowners have become Andeanized, despite their efforts and assertions to the contrary.[49] Aragón de Peralta, the patriarch with whose suicide the novel begins, is a case in point. His name clearly positions him as a white landowner, a misti of noble Spanish lineage, but his discourse undermines any pretensions to purity of race, language, or culture. Aragón de Peralta insults the village priest as a useless "traga hostias" [swallower of church bread], thus appealing to a Quechua traditional competition in which two men insult each other publicly in order to amuse the onlookers, the funniest one winning.[50] Although white, by calling the priest a host-swallower the old man is operating within this Andean tradition and speaking from within the Andean world.[51] Arguedas reinforces this characterization when he has Aragón de Peralta slip from Spanish into Quechua without even being aware of it: "Y ya no volvió a hablar en castellano" [And he did not speak Spanish again].[52] The text, however, continues in a Spanish translation, showing that Quechua has become, unconsciously, the language through which even the white, Spanish, landowning elite can best express themselves. With the slow corrosive action of the centuries, Quechua has colonized them, despite their efforts to position themselves as exterior to and unaffected by the Andean world. In this manner Arguedas debunks the notion of racial and cultural purity both for the Indians and for the Spaniards.

Not only does Arguedas show the inevitable pervasiveness of Quechua, he also extends his argument to the religious and cultural realms. The old man's religion is presented as a transculturated form of Catholic-Andean animism. Aragón de Peralta admonishes the priest for his inability to still the crying of a child, a sound said to be heard in the stone walls of the parochial house on a particular night of the year. He suggests that the priest listen to the advice of the *layk'as* (Andean witchdoctors), who recommend that he bathe the stones of the wall "con el zumo rojo del k'antu" [with the red juice of the *k'antu* flowers]. The child would feel the warmth of the slopes of the mountain where the k'antu flowers grow and would go to sleep.[53] In other words, if Catholicism (praying to God) does not work, then the power of the mountains (*Apukintu*) should be invoked. The old man's suggestion is reminiscent of Cabeza de Vaca's tactic: to heal using the chants and herbs the indigenous healers had taught him, and to say an Our Father, just in case.

The old man's speech, shouted down from the church steeple, is his public last will. He again makes use of the two cultural systems to validate his words, telling the crowd: "Pongo de testigos al pueblo y a su cura; al 'Apu-kintu' padre" [I make the people, the priest, and father 'Apukintu' my witnesses].[54] He calls on two different worlds—the priest and the Apukintu—to serve as guarantors to his last wishes. His demise signals the end of a (feudal) way of life, since an appeal to the Indians in such a matter (one's death and testimony as a misti) would have been unthinkable even ten years before.

The cultural split and paternalistic authoritarianism towards the Indians that characterize the old man are echoed in different degrees and with different variations in his two sons, Fermín and Bruno. The brothers, along with three other figures—Cabrejos, Cisneros, and Rendón—represent the different paths that Arguedas envisioned Perú could take in the 1960s. Although they inhabit different cultural spaces and are shown at different stages of negotiation between the rural Andes and the metropolitan centers of Perú, the United States, and Europe, these five figures are allegorical and characterized schematically. This is principally due to the fact that *Todas las sangres* is, more than anything else, a thesis novel, a sociological attempt to work out and understand the different ideological positions of the time. These shortcomings make of *Todas las sangres* a novel that has been bypassed by critics and readers alike. Lacking the musical structure of *Los ríos profundos* and the chaotic configuration of people and cultures of *El zorro de arriba y el zorro de abajo,* it is, nevertheless, an interesting novel, because the Andean world either subverts or affirms the novel's sociological explanatory system.

Aragón de Peralta's sons stand for a Spanish descendant ruling class that has been acculturated to the Andean world to varying degrees. Bruno, the youngest, is the one most influenced by Andean culture. He fights to maintain a feudal way of life in which money and a market economy are absent, calling the Indian serfs who work for him "his" Indians and positioning himself as their alternately benign and punishing father. Bruno fears the West with its market economy and the different shape it gives to work and to interpersonal relations.[55] His brother Fermín, on the other hand, despises Andean culture for its backwardness and for what he calls its "witchcraft." He wants to modernize the economy, bring new machines and technologies to their isolated region, and transform everything into a *dínamo,* an anthill of industrial work under his control.[56] In keeping with Fermín's Western orientation, English words appear in the novel: "caterpilares," "yanqui," "yanquilandia." However, even Fermín, with all his Westernizing ideas, is shown as having been influenced by his milieu to a greater extent than he acknowledges or realizes. His lawyer in Lima gives voice to the almost comic intercultural space that Fermín inhabits when he tells him: "Tiene usted un aire de aristócrata con tintes de yanquilandia y andilandia" [You have the manner of an aristocrat with shades of yanquiland and Andeland].[57] In other words, his body too has been "written" by the Andes, even though he is white and appears Western to himself and to the people in his town.[58] Fermín's ambiguous position with regard to the Andes translates, at times, into seeing the world he inhabits with the eyes of a tourist. He uses words such as "magic" and "witchcraft" to describe a way of life that seems exotic.

Both Fermín and Bruno, regardless of their orientation, act out of the conviction that what they are doing is best for them and for the country: what is good for General Motors is good for the United States. They are different in that Bruno is intent on preserving intact a feudal system inherited from the colonial period. Fermín, on the other hand, wants to destroy the way of life that Bruno clings to in order to institute a capitalist system that he, naively, thinks he can control. The brothers are similar in that neither has sold out to foreign interests. But as the novel shows, by the late 1960s even the most remote Andean regions are under the control of Western multinational corporations. These are likened by Arguedas to a giant octopus sucking the lifeblood of the country. Thus, the position of the white Andean ruling class, embodied by the two brothers, is naive and is not viable. Bruno and Fermín's situation is contrasted to that of Cabrejos, a mestizo engineer from Lima; Cisneros, the prototype of the mestizo as wedge between landowners and peasants; and Rendón Willka, Bruno's foreman and Arguedas's voice in the narrative.

Cabrejos, who has been hired by Fermín to work in the mines, represents the type of mestizo who has no allegiances. He is solely interested in furthering his own position and his own interests, regardless of the negative impact that his actions might have on others. As one who has sold his soul to the multinationals, and who actually works for a foreign company that wants to sabotage the project in order to bankrupt Fermín, Cabrejos is consistently characterized by the others as someone who has no soul (nor does he have a country). He advocates the institution of "individualism" as an ideology in order to turn everyone against everyone, and so undo Andean communitarian forms of work and subjectivity.[59] For Cabrejos, the aim of those like himself should be to destroy Indian communities, that "nación metida dentro de otra" [nation within another nation], and to teach them "el veneno de la ambición personal . . . y luego el del predominio del individuo" [the poison of personal ambition . . . and then that of individualism].[60] Arguedas here has merely transposed into Cabrejos's words an observation that he made in an ethnographic context: namely, that Peruvians with Westernizing tendencies "intentan convertir a estos 'comunistas' (por sus métodos comunitarios de trabajo) en *individualistas*" [try to convert these "communists" (because of their communitarian forms of work) into *individualists*].[61] In other words, capitalism can only take hold in societies in which personal ambition, competitiveness, and greed have become positive and generalized characteristics.

Cisneros is the flip side of Cabrejos. He too is a mestizo who embodies Arguedas's worst fears. As a wealthy and greedy Andean landowner, he can best be understood by Arguedas's theorization of the mestizo as a wedge between mistis and Indians. Cisneros stands alone against everyone and is universally despised. He has no allies and no friends, describing himself as "de nuevo cuño" [a new kind of man].[62] Like his father before him, he profits from the regional infighting between landowners and Indians. Since he has no allegiances and no friends, Cisneros plays one group off against the other to his advantage. His position is best described by another character. "Cisneros no es cristiano mestizo, ni cristiano indio, ni misti blanco. Nu'hay regla para él. A todos odia, a todos quiere desollar. Siquiera, pues, su padre le habría dado instrucción. Le dejó sólo su pistola, azote y rabia" [Cisneros is not a Christian mestizo, nor a Christian Indian, nor a white misti. There are no rules for him. He hates everyone, he wants to fleece everyone. Had his father at least educated him. He only left him his gun, his whip, and anger].[63]

Cisneros embodies the anger, resentment, and violence to which colonialism inevitably gives rise. Recalling the epigraph at the beginning of this section, which voices Arguedas's hope for a new people with no hate, he is the man who hates everyone. Described in terms of sheer negativity (his semen is "pus"), Cisneros does not belong anywhere and therefore does not adhere to any social code. He inhabits a new topology alien both to the dominant classes and to the Indians.[64]

These four characters—Bruno, Fermín, Cabrejos, and Cisneros—are in turn contrasted to Rendón Willka, whose affiliation with the Indian world is strong. A fellow worker describes him as incorruptible: "nadies lo agarra. Él va como libre. Cholo bueno; sólo que parece que tiene algo de brujo" [nobody will get him. He goes as if free. Good *cholo;* only he seems to have something of the sorcerer about him].[65] Rendón comes from a community of Indians who have managed to hold on to their land and who continue to work cooperatively as they have for generations. His father had enrolled him in the town's school so that he would learn to read and write, but Rendón was harassed so much by the landowners and their children that he went to Lima and Huancayo instead. In Lima he made his apprenticeship in the slums and garbage dumps, learning his lessons in racism and marginalization, "comiendo basura con perros y criaturas" [eating garbage with dogs and children].[66] There he also learned to demystify Andean superstitions. Like many of the *serranos* (inhabitants of the sierra) in Arguedas's novels, he returns trying to convince his community that "el cerro es sordo . . . la nieve es agua . . . el cóndor wamani [a representative of the mountain god] muere de un tiro" [the hill is deaf . . . snow is water . . . the condor god dies when shot].[67]

Rendón attempts to disenchant and deconstruct Andean beliefs in order to free his community from fear.[68] In Lima he had learned that the Indians' fearfulness was used by the mistis to enslave them. When Cabrejos tries to frighten the workers by paying a miner to imitate the Amaru, a mythical bull-monster thought to live in the bowels of the earth, Rendón goes into the mine and unmasks the culprit. His knowledge, acquired in Lima, allows him to function within two cultural codes and to understand how the dominant culture has manipulated the fears and superstitions of the Andeans. This knowledge permits him, like Arguedas, both to operate in a new world and to preserve valuable elements from his own culture. Rendón is therefore characterized as a mestizo-in-process.[69] He sometimes wears Western clothes, he understands two belief systems, and he knows two worlds. Like the mestizos Arguedas studied in Lima, Rendón has forgotten the words to Quechua huaynos. When he sings, he does so "improvisando la letra" [improvising the lyrics].[70] A reader not familiar with Arguedas's ethnographic works would overlook this important detail and read Rendón as an idealized Indian. He is, in fact, an idealized mestizo who embodies the best of two worlds and whose vision of the future corresponds very closely to that of the author.

Because Rendón has lived in Lima and experienced the atomization of society under capitalism, he defends Andean beliefs concerning communal labor and the subjection of the individual to the community. In doing so, he is literally the type of Peruvian that Arguedas had studied in the barriadas, only he has been transported from Lima to the Andes and from an ethnographic context to a fictional realm. As Rendón tells Bruno, the point is to realize that "la alegría viene de ver en cada comunero a un hermano que tiene derecho igual a cantar, a bailar, a comer, a trabajar" [happiness comes from seeing each communal worker as a brother who has an equal right to sing, dance, eat, and work].[71] Rendón is thus associated with what has been called the early agrarian "communism" of the Andes.[72]

It is very clear with which mestizo Arguedas's sympathies lie. Cabrejos, Cisneros, and Rendón are all mestizos-in-process and on trial, but Rendón's project has the blessing of the author. Rendón encompasses and sublates important elements of both Andean and Spanish cultures, whereas Cisneros and Cabrejos are bent on destruction. Arguedas posited Rendón as the alternative that he hoped would be taken by Perú. To his dismay, however, he found in his ethnographic studies that Cisneros and Cabrejos as "types" were increasingly dominating the national scene. Theoretically, Arguedas understood Cisneros's project to be the destruction of two worlds and the creation of an alternative culture, affirming that the mestizo of the future would be a cuña, a wedge between two worlds. At a personal level, however, Arguedas felt excluded from the new nation that mestizos like Cisneros and Cabrejos were forming, and he feared their hatred.

Arguedas's last and incomplete novel, *El zorro de arriba y el zorro de abajo,* deals with these characters. In this book Arguedas writes about the impossibility of continuing to inscribe his self in a world in which he no longer belongs. These meditations turn into a carnivalesque babel of voices, abject in content and sexually obscene in language.[73] In *El zorro,* the description of moral and economic degradation and exploitation, of which there had been only glimpses in *Todas las sangres,* now predominates. Cisneros's sexual abjection (which mirrors his cultural ambiguity) becomes the symbol of modern-day Perú, a nation in process. Exploitation is presented in terms of its sexual manifestation and is evidenced in the appearance of prostitution in the Andean world. Modern sexuality, particularly when it is shaped by money, is systematically opposed to the "primitive," ritualistic, "good" sexuality of the native culture. The institution of market relations in the Andes is symbolically represented as the rape of both men and women. For Arguedas, however, only the men are ultimately degraded because they participate, in turn, in the degradation of others weaker than themselves (such as Kutu in the story "Warma Kuyay (Amor de niño)." In Arguedas's novels, women are the victims of male abuse and violence. At the same time, they are also the only ones who rebel and fight the system, as in the uprising of the *chicheras* in *Los ríos profundos;* the resistance of the squatters in *Todas las sangres* and the dance of the prostitutes in *El zorro de arriba y el zorro de abajo.*

In *Todas las sangres,* the tension between different kinds of conceptions of subjectivity and work is translated into the confrontation between Cabrejos and Rendón. Cabrejos embodies the veritable destruction of one world by another for the sake of what he mistakenly understands as his personal economic gain. Rendón sees through Cabrejos's divisory tactics. He realizes that the concept of "the individual" wielded by Cabrejos has begun to replace Western ways of manipulating native beliefs and superstitions. Rendón fights back by emphasizing and valorizing the communal understanding of the self, which has always been part of the Andean world. Thus, when the army arrives to rob the peasants of their lands, he asks them all to stand firm, not to run. Running leads to one individual scrambling over others, trying to save his or her own life. Standing firm confronts the enemy with a solid resistance, with a community. Rendón asks them: "¿Quién va a matar a todos?" [Who is going to kill everyone?].[74]

With the illuminating message that solidarity alone will save the Andean world, everyone in the novel—except the president of the U.S. company—

hears "un sonido de grandes torrentes que sacudían el subsuelo, *como que si las montañas empezaran a caminar*" [the sound of torrential waters shaking underground, *as if the mountains were beginning to walk*"] (emphasis added).[75] The same phenomenon—a precursor to the *yawar mayu* (rivers of blood), which foreshadow the Sendero Luminoso rebellion—is described by one character in this way: "Es como si un río subterráneo empezara su creciente" [It is as if an underground river were rising].[76] When the mountains begin to move, as they did in ancient times, the novel predicts a rebellion in the Andean world.[77] This irruption of mythical phenomena comes at the end of this most sociological of Arguedas's novels. It can only be understood as a culmination of the Andean cosmogony that was introduced by the narrator at the outset. In order to understand the novel's exorbitant turn towards the Andean and the magical, we will have to examine the crucial role that the narrator plays.

### Split Narrators/Split Subjectivities

The narrator of *Todas las sangres,* like Rendón and some of the other characters, manipulates two languages and two cultural codes, often mixing them in a single sentence. Because of this divided narrative stance, Ángel Rama claims that there are two narrators in Arguedas: the adult/ethnographer and the child protagonist.[78] I think that there is only one narrator, but—Rama was pointing in the right direction—he is divided culturally and linguistically and is therefore split as a subject. Arguedas's narrators not only speak a fictional Quechua-Spanish, they also offer both Western sociological and Andean animistic interpretations. That is, they explain the world to the reader according to two different and, at times, mutually exclusive paradigms. The appeal to two explanatory systems is evident from the first pages of *Todas las sangres* and culminates with the "walking" of the mountains at the end.

At the beginning of the novel, when the Indians are summoned to a meeting at don Bruno's house, the narrator provides a series of historical and economic reasons to explain the extreme poverty and hopelessness of the *colonos* (landless peasants):

La tierra del siervo es de la hacienda, por tanto el siervo es de la hacienda, a vida y muerte. En tiempos del rey español, la tierra era del rey español y también la vida, al menos en los escritos. Desde la República cada hacendado era un rey español. Ellos dictaban las leyes y la ley se cumplía únicamente en lo que al señor le convenía.

[The land of the serf belongs to the hacienda; because of that the serf belongs, from the moment he is born to his death, to the hacienda. During the time of the Spanish king, the land—and also the serf's life—belonged to the king, at least by law. Since the days of the Republic, each landowner was also a Spanish king. They dictated the laws and the law was only obeyed when it benefited the landowners.][79]

This schematic historical explanation of *gamonalismo* is then dramatized by don Bruno when he tells his serfs: "Los colonos no venden. ¡Los colonos no tienen nada . . . ! Todo es de mi pertenencia" [Serfs do not sell. They do not own anything . . . ! Everything belongs to me]. Addressing one of them, he emphasizes his feudal, god-like power, which has already been explained in socio-historical terms by the narrator: "¿No sabes que tu alma es también de mí, que yo respondo por ella ante Dios, nuestro Señor?" [Don't you know that your soul also belongs to me? That I am responsible for it before God?].[80] This incident serves to corroborate the narrator's explanation of gamonalismo. Bruno's assertion that the souls of his serfs belong to him adds another dimension, highlighting the role played by religion and evangelization in the subjection of the native population, which also served as Spain's ideological justification for the Conquest.[81]

These examples show how the artistic development of the novel is subjected to Arguedas's political agenda. If Arguedas had continued to mechanically illustrate the points made by his narrator, we would be discussing social realism and the subordination of the Andean world as described from a Western, sociological point of view. However, the narrator introduces as a third element Andean cosmogony—in particular, the Indians' relation to nature. This element sometimes subverts and at other times underlines the sociological thrust of the novel. Returning to the example of Bruno, not only does the narrator give us a history lesson and then, for better effect, its dramatic rendering, but he also witnesses how nature is affected by Bruno's harsh words. He writes: "Don Bruno concluyó de hablar. El *pisonay*, entonces, abrió sus flores que se habían opacado mientras él amenazaba" [Don Bruno stopped talking. The *pisonay*, then, displayed its flowers, which had dimmed while he spoke threateningly].[82] The relation between people and nature does not remain unilateral, for just as Bruno affects nature, so too does nature affect him. Towards the end of his exchange with the colonos, a lark flies to a branch of the pisonay and sings. Bruno hears its song. Imperceptibly, the narrator tells us, it soothes him:

La solitaria calandria voló del pisonay; la luz del nevado sonreía en sus plumas ama-
rillas y negras que aleteaban en el aire. Cubrió el patio, todos los cielos, con su canto
en que lloraban las más pequeñas flores y el torrente del río, el gran precipicio que
se elevaba en la otra banda, atento a todos los ruidos y voces de la tierra. Pero su
vuelo, lento, ante los ojos intranquilos del gran señor a quien le interrogaba un
indio, iluminó a la multitud. Ni el agua de los manantiales cristalinos, ni el lucero
del amanecer que alcanza con su luz el corazón de la gente, consuela tanto, ahonda
la armonía en el ser conturbado o atento del hombre. La calandria vuela y canta no
en el pisonay sino . . . en la frente insondable del patrón que repentinamente se
estremece.

[The solitary skylark flew from the pisonay; the light of the snow-covered mountain
smiled in its fluttering yellow and black feathers. It hovered over the patio, attentive
to all the sounds and voices of the earth and the heavens; in its song even the smallest
flowers, the torrential river, the abyss on the other side, could be heard crying. But
its slow flight, questioned by an Indian, passed before the worried eyes of the great
landowner and illuminated the multitude. Not even the water of crystalline springs,
nor the morning star which reaches the hearts of people with its light, consoles as
much and deepens the sense of harmony in those who are either attentive or per-
turbed. The skylark flies and sings not in the pisonay but . . . on the inscrutable
forehead of the landowner, who suddenly shudders.][83]

Just as nature has reacted to Bruno's angry words—the red blossoms of a
tree lost their brilliance—now nature, in turn, affects him and the crowd.
Appeased by the bird's song, Bruno behaves generously towards his colonos.
That is why, searching for signs of the outcome at the beginning of the
meeting, the colonos had raised their heads and studied the sky. Within an
Andean economy of meaning, when the lark sings, it also signals. The bird's
song shows that nature is still experienced—both by the Indians and by the
narrator—as alive and full of signs to be interpreted.[84]

In contrast to the narrator, Rendón, who has learned to read and write,
now interprets nature's signs in a different manner. Both he and a friend,
Anto, hear the same song. For Anto it signifies that all is well, but for Rendón it means something else. He tells Anto: "Igual vemos, distinto entendemos" [We see the same thing, but interpret things differently].[85] Anto,
who is illiterate, "reads" the signs of nature. Rendón, who has learned to
read and write in Lima, cannot read nature's signs because for him the back
of a hawk upon which the sun shines is merely that and nothing else. In
Lima, Rendón lost the experience of nature's immanence; he now relates to
it in a different way. Nature has lost its subject position and has become an
object, like any other. Where nature has acquired the status of a subject in
the novel, the narrator's stance is closer to Anto's than to Rendón's.

Arguedas explains the subject position of nature in Andean cosmogony when he writes that in the huaynos, "Una sola unidad forman el ser, el universo y el lenguaje" [Human beings, language, and the universe are one].[86] That is, nature is understood as a totality and as sheer immanence. As Arguedas writes elsewhere: "Nada hay, para quien aprendió a hablar en quechua, que no forme parte de uno mismo" [There is nothing, for those whose first language is Quechua, that is not a part of him or herself].[87] This cosmogony voiced by Indian huaynos is also part of the narrator's interpretive scheme. He situates himself on Rendón's side when he gives historical and ethnographic explanations that deconstruct the dominant ideology, and on Anto's side when he reads nature.

The narrator's adherence to two different explanatory systems gives rise to a new aesthetic sensibility. It can be seen in the following description of the *puku-puku,* a bird that sings at dusk:

Cuando por la noche salen a cantar estos puku-pukus, sus nidos se van como helando, mientras ellos emiten esa voz tristísima con la que el colono esclavo y todo hombre sufriente se compara en centenares de huaynos, (la canción más popular del Perú. Es de origen prehispánico), porque el puku-puku canta de hora en hora, como un péndulo que midiera y ahondara la desolación, allí en el lugar donde es mayor que en ningún otro sitio del mundo: la estepa y las cumbres de los Andes peruanos, donde llegan, a la luz nocturna, palpitando, la superficie y la hondura de los ríos y los mares de sangre (yawar mayu, yawar k'ocha) que guardan desde la primera lágrima humana hasta la última, y el llanto de los cóndores que fueron abandonados por sus parejas.

[When at night the puku-pukus come out to sing, their nests gradually begin to freeze, as they emit that extremely sad song, to which the colono slaves and all those who suffer compare themselves in hundreds of huaynos, (the most popular song of Perú. It is of pre-Hispanic origin), because the puku-pukus sing every hour, as if they were pendulums measuring desolation and making it deeper; there, where it is greatest in the world: in the steppes and the heights of the Peruvian Andes, where the surface and the depth of rivers and oceans of blood (yawar mayu, yawar k'ocha), repositories of the first as well as the last human tears, and the crying of condors that were abandoned by their partners, reach them in the night light, palpitating.][88]

The narrator's observation of the natural world is connected to the ethnographer's study of the huayno. The association of puku-puku, huayno, and sadness is incorporated into the narrator's interpretation. Like all Andean inhabitants, he perceives in the bird's song the sadness of the cold and desolate steppes. The narrator also sees in that song the reflection of rivers and seas that, like dams, have stored all the blood-tears of humans and condors alike. Thus, what begins as a description of nature is followed by an ethno-graphic association with the huayno and ends in an Andean poetic interpre-tation of lakes and rivers as seas of blood that reflect the suffering of the world. This paragraph is broken only by one period, which comes in the middle of the ethnographic parenthesis on the huayno as if to call attention to itself, to its exteriority, and to its artificiality in relation to a world that is being described in Andean poetic terms. For it is only from the perspective of coastal metropolitan cities and a certain Western-shaped worldview that the steppes and the great Andean heights can appear as sad and desolate. In this description of the puku-pukus, we glimpse a new aesthetic sensibility in the making: that of the Arguedian mestizo narrator. Like the mestizo huayno singers studied by Arguedas in the shantytowns of Lima, the narrator writes in Spanish to tell of an Andean world that he has left behind and recalls with nostalgia.

If, then, the question of transculturation as set out here is one of bodies and cultures in transition, and therefore of split subjectivities, one of the main fronts on which these battles are fought is language. As critics have repeatedly pointed out, for Arguedas language was the fundamental ques-tion, and the greatest fiction of all in Arguedian narratives is the "new" language that his narrators use.

## From Ethnography to Fiction via Language: Two Fictions?

Arguedas, like the mestizos he studied, could no longer assume any one language as his own.[89] Like the singer Gabriel Aragón, he finds that Quechua better expresses a world that is whole and a whole world. Opting to write for a Spanish-speaking audience about a Quechua-speaking world, Arguedas finds himself in a dilemma. He must write in a language that he does not consider his own, because Quechua "es idioma sin prestancia y sin valor universal" [is a language that is not admired and that lacks universal value]. Thus, a literature written in Quechua "es literatura estrecha y con-denada al olvido" [is narrow and condemned to be forgotten].[90] Yet if he and the mestizos speak pure Spanish, they find themselves in a bind. In Spanish, they are unable to express nature or their subjectivity, because Quechua still was their legitimate means of expression. In other words, in order to reach a wider audience, Arguedas feels that he must use a language that is alien to him and to the world that he writes about.[91] Yet, like all colonials, he is forced to use the master's tools to dismantle the master's house.[92]

Arguedas finds a partial solution to this dilemma by writing Spanish as it is spoken by the Indians who are becoming mestizos. That is, he transforms the language in order to describe more poignantly Andean life and the world of his childhood. He uses Spanish but modifies it through a technique of "sutiles desordenamientos" [subtle disorderings];[93] that is, Arguedas transculturates Spanish. This transformation of literary Spanish corresponds to his realization that when the mestizos learn Spanish well, they will nevertheless incorporate some Quechua syntax and "genius."[94] Arguedas explains his use of Spanish in the following terms:

¿Es que soy acaso un partidario de la "indigenización" del castellano? No. Mas existe un caso, un caso real en que el hombre de estas regiones, sintiéndose extraño ante el castellano heredado, se ve en la necesidad de tomarlo como un elemento primario al que debe modificar, quitar y poner, hasta convertirlo en un instrumento propio.

[Does that mean that I am in favor of indigenizing Spanish? No. But there is a case, a real case where the people of these regions, feeling themselves strange when speaking an inherited Spanish, find themselves in the position of having to adopt it as a primary element that has to be modified, taking and adding, until they make Spanish their own tool.][95]

What Arguedas is describing here is the inevitable transculturation of the foreign that takes place in the process of appropriating something and making it one's own. Although he denies it, Arguedas clearly indigenized Spanish, thus situating himself in the place of those who feel strange and estranged from a language that they have been forced to assume as their own.

Arguedas has described his linguistic struggle as "una pelea verdaderamente infernal con la lengua" [a truly infernal battle with language]. This battle began when he first wrote *Agua* in conventional literary Spanish and found that he had "disfrazado al mundo" [disguised the world]. He then wrote and rewrote the stories until he reached a satisfying compromise, which consisted of mixing "un poco la sintaxis quechua dentro del castellano" [a little Quechua syntax within Spanish].[96] The Spanish he writes and the Spanish spoken by the Indians in his novels is therefore a fiction, making the language of the novels the prime fiction in Arguedian narratives.[97]

Arguedas coded the Spanish he wrote as Quechua through various means. These have been analyzed by Alberto Escobar and include the use of Quechua words; the elimination of articles; the disregard of Spanish concordance; the use of sentence constructions favoring the gerund; the loss of the pronominal form of the personal pronoun; the proliferation of diminutives and their extension to adverbs and gerunds that normally do not take them; the phonetic confusion between *e* and *i* and between *o* and *u* and the indiscriminate use of formal and informal forms of address.[98] The result of this linguistic fiction is that Arguedas's readers know that they do not know or understand Quechua, and they also know that the Indian characters do not speak Spanish, yet they are led into believing that they are reading Quechua.[99] In other words, Quechua is made to reverberate in the "Spanish" of Arguedas's works, where it is invariably present yet seemingly absent.[100] The end for Arguedas was to create "en el castellano un estilo en que pudiera sentirse el quechua siendo al mismo tiempo castellano" [a style in Spanish in which Quechua could be felt, yet at the same time remain Spanish].[101]

Arguedas's narrators see their role as that of cultural and linguistic translators. They are always mestizos who change the Spanish they use according to the rhythms and syntax of their native tongue. In the process of negotiating between two languages and two different world views, they sometimes tell us that the characters are speaking Quechua, but the story continues in Spanish and we must assume that we are reading their translation. In these translations of spoken Quechua, the narrators give us a literal rendering of the Indians' speech and thereby rearrange Spanish syntax according to foreign speech patterns. The result is that Spanish changes and expands to incorporate the rhythms of another language. Through the artificiality of the language that they now manipulate, the narrators constantly remind the reader that Spanish is an imposed and foreign language. Therefore, although Arguedas realized that to become an acknowledged writer he had to write in Spanish, by indigenizing Spanish he undermined the perceived superiority of Spanish to Quechua. Furthermore, translation now became transculturation, a two-way street in which each language was changed by the other. For, just as Spanish seems to have slipped into the Quechua that the characters appear to speak, so too has Quechua infiltrated Spanish.

In the Arguedian text, translation ceases to function as yet another means of colonization. It has become cultural translation and is the principal means by which Arguedas attempts to describe the rich diversity of the Andean world to readers who are exterior to that world. When Arguedian narrators explain the meanings of Quechua words to the Spanish-speaking reader, they point out the wealth of metonymic associations to which these words give rise. A well-known example will serve to illustrate this point. The narrator of *Los ríos profundos* tells that the *zumbayllu* (spinning top) represents the sound made by wings in flight because of its onomatopoeic ending, *yllu*. In turn, yllu is similar to the ending *illa*, which names both a certain kind of light and monsters that are born deformed by the light of the moon. The chain of associations is endless: yllu becomes a dancer, an insect, and an epic musical instrument that drives people into a frenzy. Furthermore,

Killa es la luna, e illapa el rayo. Illariy nombra al amanecer, la luz que brota por el filo del mundo, sin la presencia del sol. Illa no nombra la fija luz, la esplendente y sobrehumana luz solar. Denomina la luz menor: el claror, el relámpago, el rayo toda luz vibrante. Estas especies de luz no totalmente divinas con las que el hombre peruano antiguo cree tener aún relaciones profundas, entre su sangre y la materia fulgurante.

[*Killa* is the moon, and *illapa* lightning. *Illariy* names the dawn, the light that springs from the edge of the world without the presence of the sun. *Illa* does not name fixed light, the resplendent and superhuman light of the sun. It gives a name to minor light: brilliant light, lightning, a thunderbolt all vibrant light. These kinds of light—not completely divine—with which ancient Peruvians believe they still have a deep bond, a bond between their blood and shining matter.][102]

This passage not only shows that Arguedas can launch a linguistic tour de force using Quechua as a base, but also underlines the fact that Spanish is inadequate to describe the Andean world. While there are few words in Spanish that can be used to refer to different kinds of light, in Quechua there are many. In this sense, to the native speaker of Quechua, Spanish can only be viewed as a poor language.

## The War of the Worlds

Arguedas himself lived the cultural ambivalence and division that we have seen in the characters and narrator of *Todas las sangres*. The individual, as a unified self in whom the world and meaning are held together, is absent in his novels. He is replaced by the *hombre confuso*, the mestizo-in-process. This is already evident in the autobiographical "Warma kuyay (Amor de niño)," one of the stories in Arguedas's early collection *Agua*. In this story Arguedas writes of the dilemma of the mestizo who does not belong anywhere. The protagonist-narrator is a fourteen-year-old white boy who belongs to the landowning class but is in love with Justina, one of the Indian workers. She loves an Indian, Kutu. When the protagonist makes advances and addresses her using "Justinay," the Quechua diminutive for affection, she laughs and tells him off. The others who hear this exchange laugh too and form a circle to dance. The boy stands outside the circle, excluded physically and symbolically: "Yo me quedé fuera del círculo, avergonzado, vencido para siempre" [I was left outside the circle, ashamed, forever defeated].[103] Later, when Kutu leaves, the boy stays and enjoys life in the village for a while longer. Although Justina never reciprocates his feelings, he is happy until he is forced to go to Lima: "me arrancaron de mi querencia, para traerme a este bullicio, donde gentes que no quiero, que no comprendo" [they tore me from that place I loved and brought me to this bustling city, among people whom I do not love and do not understand].[104] At the end of the story there is a break in the narrative stance. The narrator, now an exiled adult, reflects on his position in the world and compares it to that of Kutu: "Kutu en un extremo y yo en el otro. El quizá habrá olvidado; está en su elemento; en un pueblecito tranquilo. . . . Mientras yo, aquí, vivo amargado y pálido, como un animal de los llanos fríos, llevado a la orilla del mar, sobre los arenales candentes y extraños" [Kutu in one extreme and I in another. Maybe he will have forgotten; he is in his element, in a quiet, little village. . . . Whereas I live here, bitter and pale, like an animal from the cold plains transplanted to the shores of the ocean and an incandescent and strange desert].[105]

This story, which Arguedas has said is an autobiographical account of his first love, shows how the author experienced his exclusion from two worlds. As an adult, he no longer belonged to the small Andean community in which he was raised and protected by the Indians. In Lima, although white, he felt like a misplaced Indian. The story also explores the emotional anguish and cultural split that Arguedas tried but failed to overcome. The mestizos are always excluded, because their position is ambivalent and on the margins of two cultures. They must struggle not only with two languages, but also with the two cultures from which they come but to which they, paradoxically, do not belong and cannot return.

In "Yo no soy un aculturado," the speech given in 1968, one year before he committed suicide, Arguedas looked back on his life and explained that his sole ambition as a writer had been to

volcar en la corriente de la sabiduría y el arte del Perú criollo el caudal del arte y la sabiduría de un pueblo al que se consideraba degenerado, debilitado o "extraño" e "impenetrable" pero que, en realidad, no era sino lo que llega a ser un gran pueblo, oprimido por el desprecio social, la dominación política y la explotación económica en el propio suelo donde realizó hazañas por las que la historia lo consideró como un gran pueblo: se había convertido en una nación acorralada.

[spill into the current of wisdom and Peruvian creole art, elements of the art and knowledge of a people considered degenerate, weak, or "strange" and "impenetrable." In reality, these characteristics were only the manifestations of what a great culture becomes when it is oppressed politically, exploited economically, and socially despised in its own land; a land where Inca culture had once realized great feats because of which history considered the Incas a great people: the Indians had become a caged nation in their own land.][106]

Through his ethnography and his fiction, Arguedas tried to incorporate one world into another—to transculturate. He wanted to expand the boundaries of nationality so that it would encompass the Andean world. He attempted to destroy the fence that had been built around Quechua culture from within the culture of the oppressors. As a child, Arguedas had been thrown over that fence, from the coast to the Andes. Later, he was thrown back over it again, from the Andes to the University of San Marcos in Lima. He was "contagiado para siempre de los cantos y los mitos" [infected forever with the songs and myths] of the Andean world. His life became a constant movement back and forth between one world and the other: "hablando de por vida el quechua, bien incorporado al mundo de los cercadores, visitante feliz de grandes ciudades extranjeras" [speaking Quechua for life, well incorporated into the world of the fence-builders and marginalizers, happy visitor of great foreign cities].[107] He speaks Quechua and therefore belongs to the world of the marginalized, yet he also belongs to the world of the coast and the big foreign cities.

Arguedas tried to write Quechua "orality" and thus to write what he was: "intenté convertir en lenguaje escrito lo que era como individuo: un vínculo vivo, fuerte, capaz de universalizarse, de la gran nación cercada y la parte generosa, humana, de los opresores" [I tried to write what I was as an individual: a living, strong bond, capable of universalizing myself, between the fenced nation and the generous, human side of the oppressors].[108] He lived his life as the living bond between two uneven entities, a suppressed culture and what he understood—perhaps somewhat naively—as the good side of the oppressing culture. Like the mestizos he studied, Arguedas wanted to be the living proof that transculturation was possible. In one of his happier moments he affirmed: "Yo no soy un aculturado. Yo soy un peruano que orgullosamente, como un demonio feliz habla en cristiano y en indio, en español y en quechua" [I am not acculturated. I am a Peruvian who, proudly like a happy demon, speaks in Christian and in Indian, in Spanish and in Quechua].[109]

Like his characters and narrators, he operated within two different and at times mutually exclusive belief systems, the Christian and the Andean, and spoke two languages, Quechua and Spanish. Arguedas's suicide is perhaps a sign of the inescapable anguish of trying to live between two waters. It points to the superhuman struggle and ultimate impossibility of being a happy demon in a world in which demons have no place.

### NOTES

1. See Cornejo Polar, *Los universos narrativos de José María Arguedas.*
2. Mario Vargas Llosa, "Novela primitiva y novela de creación en América Latina," 29.
3. Vargas Llosa, "Novela primitiva," 31.
4. Cornejo Polar, *Literatura y sociedad*, 68.
5. Vargas Llosa, *José María Arguedas, entre sapos y halcones*, 9.
6. Ana María Barrenechea, *Textos hispoamericanos: De Sarmiento a Sarduy;* Sara Castro Klarén, *El mundo mágico de José María Arguedas;* Alberto Escobar, *Arguedas o la utopía de la lengua;* Roland Forgues, *José María Arguedas: Del pensamiento dialéctico al pensamiento trágico;* Martin Lienhard, *Cultura andina y forma novelesca: Zorros y danzantes en la última novela de Arguedas;* Gladys C. Marin, *La experiencia americana de José María Arguedas;* Silverio Muñoz, *José María Arguedas y el mito de la salvación por la cultura;* Julio Ortega, *Texto, comunicación y cultura: Los ríos profundos de José María Arguedas;* William Rowe, *Mito e Ideología en la obra de José María Arguedas* and Antonio Urrello, *José María Arguedas, el nuevo rostro del indio: Una estructura mítico-poética.*
7. "Misti" is the Quechua name given to the "white" dominant class. In Quechua, the word means "white."
8. Arguedas, *Indios, mestizos y señores,* 134.
9. Dances, according to Arguedas, were an important medium to be studied because they were one of the privileged modes of expression in pre-Columbian times. Any changes evidenced in them would therefore point to wider social movements. See Arguedas, *Señores e indios: Acerca de la cultura quechua,* 56. The sijllas, Arguedas found, not only changed under the influence of Spanish domination, but also criticized that influence. They represent another instance of Andean cosmogony where the world is turned upside down; this time the reversal takes place in terms of parody and the carnivalesque mocking of imposed hierarchies. The dancers depict Spanish and republican "justice" by impersonating the judges and executioners. They wear masks that represent Spanish faces: faces full of hair, faces with idiotic expressions, grotesque faces that, as Arguedas writes, provoke "la risa violenta e irresistible de los tran-seúntes y de los espectadores" [the violent and irresistible laughter of the passers-by and of the spectators]. Arguedas, *Indios, mestizos y señores,* 110. The Indian dancers *become* Spanish judges and executioners and criticize the exploitative social relations and lack of justice instituted by the colony (108). Arguedas does not explain why the dancers wear ragged clothes, or why only their whips and masks are new. This might perhaps point to a much more self-reflective moment than simple parody and the inversion of social hierarchies. The body dressed in rags shows the ravages of the white mask and therefore a vision in which oppressor and oppressed are lived in one body, which is split.

For more recent studies of Andean dances, see Verger, *Fiestas y danzas.* For photographs of the sijllas and their costumes, see figures 66 and 67.

The parodic representation of conditions of domination is, apparently, a widespread phenomenon in colonized societies. During a visit to Nicaragua in 1986, Roger Lancaster observed the parody of American and European brigade workers: "Last year I attended the Carnival at Massaya. In the procession, I was confronted by a Morimbo youth who wore a mask that gave him red hair and blue eyes. Like myself, he was wearing a white T-shirt and a small backpack. When I reached for my camera to capture this event, he reached for his small, wooden facsimile of an Instamatic to take my picture." Lancaster concludes: "Carnival . . . reverses the usual gaze of colonial and class power: subject and object, Indian and Spaniard, peasant and landlord, powerless and powerful, the observer and the observed—all exchange places." Roger Lancaster, "Festival of Disguises," 40. On the role of carnivalesque reversal, see also Mikhail Bakhtin, *L'oeuvre de François Rabelais et la culture populaire au moyen âge et sous la renaissance*, 19.

10. Arguedas, *Formación*, 173. See also Pease, "El mito de Inkarrí y la visión de los vencidos"; Flores Galindo, *Buscando un Inca*, 53; Alejandro Ortiz Rescaniere, *De Adaneva a Inkarrí: Una visión indígena del Perú* and López-Baralt, *El retorno del Inca Rey*.

11. Arguedas, *Indios, mestizos y señores*, 56.

12. Arguedas, *Señores e indios*, 173.

13. Arguedas, *Señores e indios*, 171.

14. It is from this observation that Ángel Rama derives his theory of how big cities and ports are more readily Westernized than interior, rural areas.

15. Arguedas, *Señores e indios*, 174.

16. Arguedas, *Formación*, xviii.

17. Arguedas writes autobiographically that his father had remarried and was required by his work to travel continually. Arguedas was left with his stepmother, who disliked him. She relegated him to the kitchen and forced him to grow up with the household's Indian servants. They became Arguedas's true family and were the source of his lifelong identification with and love for Andean culture. In the series of stories *Amor mundo*, Arguedas also points to his mistreatment at the hands of his sexually perverse stepbrothers.

18. Arguedas, *Señores e indios*, 257.

19. James Clifford and George E. Marcus, eds., *Writing Culture: The Poetics and Politics of Ethnography*. See Clifford's article "On Ethnographic Allegory," 112–3.

It is interesting to note that at the beginning of the Industrial Revolution, the Romantics attempted to salvage folklore, fairy tales, and folk songs that were well on their way to becoming forgotten. The Romantics not only compiled these oral traditions, but also studied and incorporated them into their works. Ludwig Tieck's "Kunstmärchen" and E.T.A. Hoffmann's *Tales* can be seen in such a transculturating light.

20. Clifford and Marcus, *Writing Culture*, 115. Arguedas goes back, both as an adult and as an ethnographer, to the communities where he lived as a child. Paradoxically, he reproduces the gesture of Western ethnographers who go to "primitive" tribes in order to study the childhood of man. In this case, however, the childhood being studied is the ethnographer's own.

21. Arguedas, *Formación*, xxvi–xxvii.

22. Particularly *gamonalismo*, a system of landownership whereby the landowner had the powers of a feudal lord. He was the owner of lands and Indians and the administration was enfiefed to him.

23. Arguedas, "Evolución de las comunidades indígenas. El valle del Mantaro y la ciudad de Huancayo: Un caso de fusión de culturas no comprometida por la acción de las instituciones de origen colonial," in *Formación*, 91.

24. Arguedas, *Formación*, 105.

25. In Arguedas's novel *Todas las sangres*, for example, one of the landowners explains: "¿Quién convirtió a los indios en los brujos que ahora son? ¿Quién? ¿Quién dejó crecer árboles salvajes en esos andenes que seguramente lucían como huertos? ¡Nuestos abuelos! Convirtieron en brutos a los indios para que reináramos nosotros" [Who converted the Indians into the sorcerers that they have now become? Who? Who let trees grow wildly on these terraces that surely used to be beautiful orchards? Our grandfathers! They made brutes out of the Indians so that we could rule]. In other words, mechanisms of oppression produce and distort both the dominated and the dominant, making brutes out of the dominated and irrational and grotesque despots out of the landowners. Arguedas, *Todas las sangres*, 194.

26. As Ángel Rama writes, modernization and the roads "favorecían el proceso transculturante en el cual se instala quien es, en definitiva, el producto beneficiado: el mestizo" [favored the transculturating process which formed and definitely benefited the mestizo]. Arguedas, *Formación*, xx.

27. Arguedas, "La novela y el problema de la expresión literaria en el Perú," in Juan Larco, ed., *Recopilación de textos sobre José María Arguedas,* 400.

28. Arguedas, *Primer Encuentro de Narradores Peruanos,* 237.

29. For an excellent history of the mestizo in Mexico and Guatemala, see Wolf, *Sons of the Shaking Earth,* especially the last chapter, "The Power Seekers."

30. Arguedas, "Razón de ser del indigenismo," in *Recopilación de textos sobre José María Arguedas,* 61–2.

31. For an analysis of these changes, see Rama, *Transculturación.*

32. Arguedas, "La narrativa en el Perú contemporáneo," in *Recopilación,* 417.

33. Even if the sublation of Indian elements in the mestizo redeemed the latter, Arguedas nevertheless was unable to rid himself of his ambivalence towards the mestizos. They signaled the disappearance of a familiar world with which he strongly identified throughout his life, even though he too was a displaced mestizo.

34. See Linda Kintz, *The Subject's Tragedy.*

35. Arguedas, *Indios, mestizos y señores,* 59.

36. Arguedas, *Indios, mestizos y señores,* 6.

37. Arguedas, *Indios, mestizos y señores,* 66.

38. Arguedas, *Señores e indios,* 184–5.

39. Drama and comedy were highly developed forms in Indian culture. See Teodoro L. Meneses, ed., *Usca Paucar: Drama Quechua del siglo XVIII.* See also Jesús Lara, "El teatro en el Tawantinsuyu," 309–13.

40. Arguedas, *Indios, mestizos y señores,* 71.

41. Arguedas, *Señores e indios,* 172.

42. Arguedas, *Todas,* 121.

43. Arguedas, *Formación,* 177.

44. Frantz Fanon, analyzing a very different colonial situation, wrote of decolonization in these very terms. "'The last shall be first and the first last.' Decolonization," he explained, "is the putting into practice of this sentence." In a sense it cannot be otherwise, for just as colonies are implanted through raw force, so too the dream of decolonization is the reversal of those conditions through the very means used to achieve them: violence. Frantz Fanon, *The Wretched of the Earth,* 37.

45. The attempt to write a totality can better be understood if seen in the context of Fredric Jameson's concept of "mapping" as the "grasping of the social totality . . . structurally available to the dominated rather than the dominating classes." Arguedas's narrator, as a medium through which such a totality is articulated, aligns himself, paradoxically, with the dominated, although he employs a dominant medium. Many of the characters in the novel have an unexpected lucidity as to their ideological position in the world. This could be explained perhaps in terms of the novel's positing of them as pongos of foreign capital. Thus, they too are oppressed in a way that first-world dominant classes would not be. According to Jameson, third-world literature can be characterized by the fact that "the telling of the individual story and the individual experience cannot but ultimately involve the whole laborious telling of the experience of the collectivity itself." Furthermore, "Third-World texts, even those which are seemingly private and invested with a properly libidinal dynamic—necessarily project a political dimension in the form of national allegory: *the story of the private individual destiny is always an allegory of the embattled situation of the public Third-World culture and society.*" Fredric Jameson, "Third-World Literature in the Era of Multinational Capitalism," 88, 85–6, and 69. For an excellent analysis and critique of Jameson, see Aijaz Ahmad, "Jameson's Rhetoric of Otherness and the 'National Allegory.'"

46. Rama, *Transculturación.*

47. Nicolás Wey-Gómez makes a similar observation in relation to the writings of Inca Garcilaso de la Vega. He writes: "El (un) discurso transcultural se forja, por lo tanto, no solo al encontrarse las palabras y los conceptos para describir referentes culturales y materiales dispares y mutuamente contradictorios, sino principalmente, al encontrar un **sujeto** (del enunciado) capaz de recuperarlos y articularlos conjuntamente al nivel del discurso" [The [a] transcultural discourse is forged, here, not only by finding the nods of concepts to describe dissimilar—and mutually contradictory—cultural referents and materials, but rather by finding a **subject** (of the enunciation) who is able to recuperate and articulate them together at the level of discourse]. See Nicolás Wey-Gómez, "¿Dónde está Garcilaso?: La oscilación del sujeto colonial en la formación de un discurso transcultural," 13.

48. Arguedas, *Indios, mestizos y señores,* 16.

49. René Despestre makes the same point for the British and the French in the Caribbean. See his "Les aspects créateurs du métissage culturel aux Caraïbes," 61–5.

50. Arguedas, *Todas,* 11.

51. In his ethnographic works, Arguedas gives examples of such insults: "Tienes la cara solemne como la de un gato que está haciendo su 'necesidad'" [You have the solemn look of a cat taking a dump] (Arguedas, *Indios, mestizos y señores,* 157). He often incorporates this tradition into the discourse of his characters: one of them is insulted as "excremento del diablo" [excrement of the devil] (Arguedas, *Todas,* 60); another one has the face of "mierda triste" [sad shit] (Arguedas, *Todas,* 128).

52. Arguedas, *Todas,* 12.

53. Arguedas, *Todas,* 12.

54. Arguedas, *Todas,* 13.

55. Arguedas, *Todas,* 22.

56. Arguedas, *Todas,* 158.

57. Arguedas, *Todas,* 287.

58. Arguedas writes that when he came to Lima for the first time, he was chased in the streets by gangs who immediately recognized him as a *serrano* (inhabitant of the sierra). He was easily spotted: "En 1919, la primera vez que vine a Lima, fui perseguido en las calles como animal raro, por los "palomillas." Nos reconocían a los "serranos" por el modo de andar y de hablar, de tal modo la Cordillera de los Andes había separado al Perú, lo había partido y diferenciado" [In 1919, the first time I came to Lima, I was chased through the streets as if I were a strange animal by street "gangs." We were readily recognized as Andean by our way of walking and talking, which shows to what an extent the mountains had separated Perú, split and differentiated the country]. Arguedas, *Señores e indios,* 183. The first action of a culture is to inscribe bodies. For Deleuze and Guattari, "Cruelty has nothing to do with some ill-defined or natural violence that might be commissioned to explain the history of mankind; cruelty is the movement of culture that is realized in bodies and inscribed on them, belaboring them. . . . The sign is a position of desire; but the first signs are the territorial signs that plant their flags in bodies." Gilles Deleuze and Félix Guattari, *Anti-Oedipus: Capitalism and Schizophrenia,* 145.

59. José E. Limón argues that the same mechanism is at work in the United States. See his "Dancing With the Devil: Society, Gender, and the Political Unconscious in the Mexican-American South," 234.

60. Arguedas, *Todas,* 153–4.

61. Arguedas, *Indios, señores y mestizos,* 27.

62. Arguedas, *Todas,* 198.

63. Arguedas, *Todas,* 337. Using Mary Douglas's *Purity and Danger* as a basis, Julia Kristeva studies the mechanisms of exclusion and division, which establish the logic of the clean and proper in society. Everything that confuses borders is defined as dirty and abject. The categories of pure and impure evidence the harsh battle that Judaism fights in order to constitute itself and repress paganism and its maternal cults. These categories have the function of establishing a symbolic logic by which those allowed in the Temple also adhere to a specific, accepted logic. Kristeva shows that there is no opposition between material abomination and topological (holy place of the temple) or logical (holy law) reference. The one and the other are two aspects, semantic and logical, of the imposition of a strategy of identity, which is, in all strictness, that of monotheism. See Kristeva, *Powers of Horror,* 71.

64. As Kristeva suggests: "It is thus not lack of cleanliness or health that causes abjection but what disturbs identity, system, order. What does not respect borders, positions, rules. The in-between, the ambiguous, the composite." Kristeva, *Powers of Horror,* 4.

65. Arguedas, *Todos,* 162. *Cholo* is the derogatory term for mestizo.

66. Arguedas, *Todas,* 389.

67. Arguedas, *Todas,* 388.

68. Max Horkheimer and Theodor Adorno analyze how Enlightenment thinkers attempted to dispel myths in order to free men. Instead, however, the Enlightenment itself turned into oppression. Horkheimer and Adorno argue that the "program of the Enlightenment was the disenchantment of the world." Rendón Willka also attempts to disenchant the world in order to free his community. In the place of myth and animism he sets not only rationality, but also the belief and trust in the power of an age-old community and communitarian way of being in the world. In *Todas las sangres,* the disenchantment that Rendón effects is compensated for by the "enchantment" that the narrator introduces in the

unity of self, language, and nature. Rendón and the narrator's discourse are contrapuntal in this sense. Max Horkheimer and Theodor Adorno, *Dialectic of Enlightenment*, 3.

69. In passing, Rama makes a distinction between two kinds of heirs to tradition: the pious and the renegade. Rama, *Transculturación*, 201. This distinction is also made by the critic Efraín Barradas, who sees Nuyorican writers as either "herejes" or "mitificadores," writers who choose to act either as heretics or as mythmakers. Efraín Barradas and Rafael Rodríguez, *Herejes y mitificadores*, 11–30. This distinction will become important in my analysis of Chicano writers, particularly Gloria Anzaldúa, in chapter 7.

70. Arguedas, *Todas*, 118.

71. Arguedas, *Todas*, 388.

72. Arguedas, *Todas*, 412. In this sense he is the embodiment of the affinity that Mariátegui found between Marxism and Andean agrarian communism.

73. Kristeva writes that this is the gesture of much twentieth-century "abject" literature: "the sort that takes up where apocalypse and carnival left off" and that "did not realize that the narrative web is a thin film constantly threatening with bursting. For, when narrated identity is unbearable, when the boundary between subject and object is shaken, and when even the limit between inside and outside becomes uncertain, the narrative is what is challenged first. If it continues nevertheless, its makeup changes; its linearity is shattered, it proceeds by flashes, enigmas, short cuts, incompletion, tangles, and cuts. At a later stage, the unbearable identity of the narrator and the surroundings that are supposed to sustain him can no longer be *narrated* but *cries out* or is *described* with maximal stylistic intensity (language of violence, of obscenity, or of a rhetoric that relates the text to poetry)." Kristeva, *Powers of Horror*, 141.

74. Arguedas, *Todas*, 442.

75. Arguedas, *Todas*, 448.

76. Arguedas, *Todas*, 447–8.

77. It is interesting to note that this novel, written in 1964, foreshadows the uprising of the Sendero Luminoso. In fact, at the time of writing, Arguedas's second wife, Sybilla Arredondo, is in jail in Perú charged with terrorism.

78. Rama, *Transculturation*, 270–5.

79. Arguedas, *Todas*, 33–4.

80. Arguedas, *Todas*, 38.

81. Paulo Freire writes that a similar situation exists in Brazil: "Hay paternalismo. Condescendencia del 'adulto' hacia el 'menor'" [There is paternalism. The condescendence of the 'adult' towards the 'minor']. Paulo Freire, *La educación como práctica de la libertad*, 64.

82. Arguedas, *Todas*, 37–8.

83. Arguedas, *Todas*, 40.

84. See Ernest Robert Curtius's chapter "The Book of Nature" in his *European Literature and the Latin Middle Ages*, 319–26. Curtius traces the development of the concept of the book of nature from religious to secular, scientific, and poetic (pre-Romantic) discourse. In the beginning it was held that the work of God could be seen in every creature in the world. With Galileo, the book of nature became readable only in mathematical language.

In Arguedas, the signs of nature are not only there to be interpreted; they also affect human actions. There is a relationship established between people and nature characteristic of Andean culture, where man, nature, and language are equally important. Here nature is not Curtius's *object* of study. It is a *subject*, just like people and language.

85. Arguedas, *Todas*, 32.

86. Quoted in Rama, *Transculturación*, 245.

87. Arguedas, *Recopilación*, 351–2.

88. Arguedas, *Todas*, 202.

89. In an ethnographic essay he writes: "Yo no tuve necesidad de hablar el castellano hasta los siete años de edad. En una vastísima región en que pasé mi niñez y adolescencia no era imprescindible" [I had no need to speak Spanish until I was seven years old. In a very vast region where I spent my childhood and adolescence, it was not necessary]. Arguedas, *Señores e indios*, 175. The age at which Arguedas claims he learned Spanish varies; in another text he states "yo aprendí a hablar el castellano con cierta eficiencia después de los ocho años, hasta entonces sólo hablaba quechua" [I only learned to speak Spanish with a certain fluency after turning eight years. Until then, I had only spoken Quechua]. Arguedas, *Primer*, 41.

90. Arguedas, *Indios, mestizos y señores*, 37–8.

91. For a critique of the literacy (Spanish language instruction) programs in Perú and their ineffectiveness, see Arguedas, *Nosotros los maestros*.

92. See Audre Lorde, *Apartheid U.S.A.*, for an African-American perspective on this dilemma.

93. Arguedas, "La novela y el problema de la expresión literaria en el Perú," in his *Recopilación*, 403.

94. Arguedas, *Indios, mestizos y señores*, 38.

95. Arguedas, *Recopilación*, 401.

96. Arguedas, *Indios, mestizos y señores*, 41.

97. Arguedas, *Primer*, 73.

98. Alberto Escobar, *Arguedas*, 34.

99. Escobar, *Arguedas*, 72.

100. Escobar, *Arguedos*," 88.

101. Walter Benjamin's theory of translation matches Arguedas's praxis very closely. For Benjamin, a good translation is one that is "transparent; it does not cover the original, does not block its light." This effect may be achieved "above all, by a liberal rendering of the syntax which proves words rather than sentences to be the primary element of the translator." Quoting Rudolf Pannwitz, he concludes that good translators, in the case of German literature, "have extended the boundaries of the German language," because they deal with language as a fluid medium and do not fall into the trap of trying to turn "Hindi, Greek or English into German instead of turning German into Hindi, Greek, English." Benjamin, "Task of the Translator," 80.

102. Arguedas, *Los ríos profundos*, 72.

103. Arguedas, *Relatos completos*, 158.

104. Arguedas, *Relatos*, 163–4.

105. Arguedas, *Relatos*, 164.

106. Arguedas, "Yo no soy un aculturado," in his *El zorro*, 9.

107. Arguedas, *El zorro*, 9–10.

108. Arguedas, *El zorro*, 10.

109. Arguedas, *El zorro*, 10.

# 6 ≈
# THAT FAST RECEDING
# TOWARDS THE PAST THAT IS
# WOMEN'S FUTURE: "La culpa es de
# los Tlaxcaltecas."

*La memoria es la dueña del tiempo [Memory is the owner of time].*
— OLD PROVERB

*A people that negates itself is in the process of committing suicide.*
— FERNANDO ORTIZ

The common use of terms such as miscegenation or mestizaje to describe transcultural processes implicitly shows that any cultural contact is, before anything else, sexual. At the level of the body, transculturation has to do with the body of women. The "encounter" between two worlds that has given rise to today's uneasy mestizaje began as a sexual violation of the indigenous women by the Spaniards. Fernando Ortiz is heir to a metaphoric tradition when he describes cultural contact in Cuba as the *abrazo* (embrace) of different cultures. However, when he and other critics exclude women from their analyses, they tacitly identify culture as male. Not only are women generally absent from their discourse on culture, but if we are mentioned at all it is to inscribe us into history as traitors. A biblical logic that postulates the creation of culture out of the treacherousness of women is repeated tirelessly.

If culture is to become an inclusive category, it must embrace all the different components that have constituted it historically. Theories of transculturation therefore always entail the recuperation and rewriting of history. From the vantage point of the present and an assumed sense of homogeneity, we must reclaim history in all its racial, cultural, and linguistic diversity. This reclamation must also write women into history.

In her story "La culpa es de los Tlaxcaltecas," Elena Garro overlays the story of a middle-class woman in contemporary Mexico City with that of la Malinche, a portentous figure in Mexican history and myth. Garro's choice is neither accidental nor arbitrary, for the encounter between Spaniards and Aztecs was mediated by an Indian slave, a woman now known as la Malinche, who not only acted as translator between Cortés and various Indian tribes, but who was also his mistress and the mother of his son. This son, Martín Cortés, is considered the first mestizo and la Malinche—the "bad mother"—a traitor to the Indian world and hence the founder of the modern nation. In essence, Malinche's supposed betrayal of the Indian world is the original sin that gives rise to today's Mexico. The woman/translator has gone down in history and in the popular imagination as the traitor, in keeping with the well-known Italian saying *traduttore, traditore*. By extension, Malinche as Mexican Eve also becomes the sign under which all Mexican and Chicana women are born. "La culpa es de los Tlaxcaltecas" shows how women must assume their feminine identities as traitors. The nature of their betrayal becomes the point around which the story revolves.

Even though much has been written about la Malinche, we know surprisingly little about her. Bernal Díaz del Castillo's sixteenth-century chronicle of the New World, an attempt to tell the story of the common soldier absent in Cortés's account, is our main source of information.[1] From this account we learn that la Malinche was sold into slavery by her mother, who wanted to disinherit her in favor of her half-brother; the Mayans sold her to the Tabascans; the Tabascans gave her to Cortés, along with nineteen more women and other gifts; she served as Cortés's translator, mediator, and "lover"; and she was married off by Cortés to Juan Jaramillo. She was baptized Marina by the Spaniards and is now known as la Malinche, a hispanicized form of her Indian name, Malinalli.[2] Cortés himself mentions her by name only once. He writes about her briefly in letters two and five of his *Cartas de relación*. Although his quick subjection of the Aztecs is largely attributed to Malinche's role as translator, Cortés's suppression of her can be attributed not only to his notorious egocentrism, but also to the fact that the Indians called *him* Malinche (after her), a fact that made it imperative for him—in his account at least—to distance himself from her. In Nahua *códices*,[3] she appears as the axis along and through whom communication between Spaniards and Aztecs took place. As Rachel Philips points out,

Malinche is portrayed in the *códices* as a large, imposing figure standing in a position of strategic importance between Spaniards and Indians: "Often little speech balloons go out from her in both directions, showing that she was in fact a linguistic bridge between cultures."[4]

Because the official story relies on Spanish accounts of the Conquest and subsequent reinterpretations of those accounts, Malinche has become a symbol of Latin America's acculturation and her important transcultural function in native historiography is disregarded.[5] If she was a positive figure for Bernal Díaz because she was so "manly" and helped the Spaniards, she becomes a negative one during the period of independence precisely because of her alleged affinity for the Spaniards, which was interpreted as a betrayal of the nation. Thus, as Sandra Messinger Cypess writes, "the texts of newly independent Mexico show [that] many of the characteristics of Doña Marina considered positive by the Spaniards are reelaborated as negative elements"[6] in order to distance the new nation from Spanish influence, Spanish myths, and the Spanish imagination. Later, in the writings of the indigenistas, committed as they were to revalorizing Mexico's native heritage, la Malinche is again reviled for her allegiance to the Spaniards and her betrayal of the Indian world. Curiously, her evaluation changes over time and is used in close conjunction with the nation-forming needs of the moment. La Malinche, then, exists only insofar as she functions as a polysemous sign. Reinterpretations and reelaborations of that sign "signal the development of real structural changes in social relationships."[7]

That la Malinche continues to circulate as a coin whose value changes with the times can perhaps be accounted for by the fact that she—not Ariel[8] or Caliban[9]—best embodies native negotiations during the Conquest and colonization of America.[10] That critics continue to revert to Caliban as a symbol of Latin America's colonial and neocolonial situation—despite the fact that Caliban lost his language while many native languages survive— points to an implicit favoring of acculturation over transculturation. La Malinche has been made to embody the negative aspects of acculturation—the divisiveness, the split subjectivity, the hatred of the self, and the love of the foreign—that are instituted by colonization. That she is bypassed by theories of colonization, that she is adopted as the embodiment of the negative aspects of Latin America's colonial condition, derives from the fact that she is a woman and as such cannot represent the universal—men and women— as male symbols such as Ariel and Caliban supposedly do. Thus, male Latin American critics who want to theorize the colonial condition travel all the way to England—to Shakespeare—in order to find and reappropriate a symbol for Latin America.

Given Malinche's alleged crucial role in the Conquest, Latin American writers and Latino/a writers in the United States continually return to her, but their stakes in doing so are very different. Male reinterpretations of la Malinche revolve around the issue of nation formation during Mexican Independence and the revolutionary and post-revolutionary periods—that is, at key moments of crisis in national identity. Whether la Malinche is cast in a positive or a negative light depends on whether Spain, Mexico, or both are being valorized at that moment. Because of this tradition, Mexican and Chicana women writers, whose identities are constructed according to the conjunction of Eve/la Malinche, feel compelled to reclaim la Malinche in order to redefine themselves. To do so, they must first critique male interpretations of la Malinche and reappropriate her as either a victim or a positive figure. They thus resituate themselves both in terms of their own identities and in relation to Mexico's past and to the role of women therein. As a result, la Malinche is constantly reinterpreted in women's writings. She is la Malinche as betrayed by her mother, a hatred that operates within the paradigm of women's self-hatred;[11] la Malinche as prototype of all raped and victimized Indian women since the Conquest;[12] la Malinche as visionary who founded a new race and a new culture, just as the Chicanas are doing today;[13] la Malinche as the counterpoint to the Virgin of Guadalupe;[14] and so on.[15]

Garro's story engages two crucial texts in the formation of the Malinche myth. The first of these is Bernal Díaz del Castillo's chronicle, *Historia verdadera de la conquista de la Nueva España,* which Laura, the protagonist, begins to read obsessively. It is significant that Garro chooses this particular chronicle, because it is written by a common soldier in Cortés's army, a man who sought to vindicate the history of those like himself and to inscribe the heroism of the common man into history. It is an account that in turn engages Cortés's own account, as well as that of Francisco López de Gómara.[16] Gómara's history is continually criticized by Bernal Díaz because Gómara was not an eyewitness to the events he describes. "La culpa es de los Tlaxcaltecas" therefore reverberates within this doubly revindicatory frame. The second text is Octavio Paz's *El laberinto de la soledad,* an important precursor to Garro's feminist critique since Paz insisted on reinscribing the tradition of modernity's betrayal of the past onto the body of women. In his seminal essay "Los hijos de la Malinche," Paz wrote: "Si la Chingada es una representación de la Madre violada, no me parece forzado asociarla a la Conquista, que fue también una violación, no solamente en el sentido histórico, sino en la carne de la indias. El símbolo de la entrega es doña Malinche, la amante de Cortés" [If the *Chingada* (raped woman) is a representation of the raped Mother, it does not seem far-fetched to me to associate her with the Conquest, which was also a rape, not only in the historical sense but also in the very flesh of Indian women. The symbol of this surrendering-herself-to-the-Other is Malinche, the lover of Cortés].[17] The all-too-easy slippage from "rape" to "entrega" (surrender herself) shows the extent to which interpretations of la Malinche are male projections.[18] Insisting on the same fiction in which rape is interpreted as voluntary surrender and gendering culture as male, Paz added: "el pueblo mexicano no perdona su traición a la Malinche. Ella encarna lo abierto, lo chingado" [the Mexican people do not forgive Malinche for her betrayal. She embodies openness, that which can be fucked/raped].[19] In Paz's tautological and Eurocentric dialectic, where men who are "closed" rape or "open" women who already are open, the Spanish conquistador (the Other/the Stranger) is the paradigm of the absent father, the great Macho Chingón (the great raping/fucking macho), and la Malinche is the passive native woman forever open to the exterior.[20]

Paz was writing in the 1950s, when the crucial question for Mexico was whether to modernize under the influence of the West—to "open" itself passively and acculturate—or to reject modernization in favor of an autonomous national project. La Malinche, and hence *malinchismo,* became the embodiment of the evils and perils of acculturation, of selling out one's culture to another.[21] Paz, who was once married to Garro,[22] postulates malinchismo as the treacherous love for the foreign and betrayal of the native that contemporary Mexicans have inherited from la Malinche. Although such warnings about the perils of acculturation are articulated at the expense of women, they are nonetheless redeemable in that they stress the sexual component of the Conquest overlooked in most other accounts.

Paz's essay serves as subtext in "La culpa es de los Tlaxcaltecas" when Laura and her maid Nacha talk in the kitchen. In this conversation, which frames the story, the two feel a bond of solidarity when each defines herself as a traitor. They assume that treacherousness is an intrinsic component in the identities of all Mexican women, recalling the betrayal theorized by Paz as the basis of Mexican culture. The story thus expands Bernal Díaz's vindicatory frame while at the same time implicitly criticizing Paz's rearticulation of the myth of la Malinche.

In the story, the conjunction of myth and history emerges when Laura, a middle-class woman in Mexico City, begins to question her racial, sexual, and cultural origins. She has every reason not to do this, since she belongs to a privileged class that classifies her body as white, situating her within Mexico's hegemony. The cyclical time of myth disrupts the teleological time of the narrative and, returned to the days of the Conquest as a young Indian woman, Laura is forced to compare her past life with her present one. This leads her to realize, for the first time, that she is bored with her husband, her marriage, and her life. At the root of her discontent she sees Mexican machismo, defined as the violence of men against women. Absent in the utopian reconstruction of her past life, it is exemplified in the present by her husband's attitudes and violence towards her.

The whole issue of machismo revolves around and is complicated by the fact that Mexican women see themselves as traitors. Laura and Nacha assume this characterization unquestioningly, but as the story develops, it is shown to be a cultural construct based on the story of la Malinche. Laura turns this myth around, understanding the miscegenation of modern Mexico as the "traición permanente" [permanent betrayal] of Mexico's Indian past by its present.[23] The male tradition that Laura overturns incorporates not only a betrayal of the racial duality of the past—evidenced in the bodies of all mestizos—but also men's permanent betrayal of women in terms of their machismo as well as in the history and tradition that they write. That is, machismo is understood as both epistemic and physical violence against women. To Paz's cry "¡malinchismo!," Garro responds "¡machismo!"

## The Archaeological Dream of Mexico: The Flip Side of a Postcard, the Flip Side of History

"La culpa es de los Tlaxcaltecas" begins when Laura—who is married to Pablo, a great friend of the President's—travels from Mexico City to Guanajuato with her mother-in-law. In Cuitzeo, in the middle of a bridge, the car runs out of gas and comes to a standstill. Laura's mother-in-law goes in search of help while Laura stays behind on the bridge, looking down at the bottom of a dry lake. Suddenly there is a change in the atmosphere and everything begins to float in a very bright light. Laura concludes that time has taken a 180-degree turn "como cuando ves una tarjeta postal y la vuelves para ver lo que hay escrito detrás. Así llegué en el lago de

Cuitzeo, hasta la otra niña que fui" [as when you see a postcard and you turn it around to see what is written on the back side. That is how, in the lake of Cuitzeo, I returned to the other girl that I was].[24] Laura sees an Indian coming towards her and immediately recognizes him as her cousin/husband from the days of the Conquest. He is hurt and walks with the weight of defeat on his bare shoulders.[25] The first thing that Laura says to him is "la culpa es de los Tlaxcaltecas" [it is the fault of the Tlaxcaltecas].[26] He leaves her to continue fighting, but Laura is afraid to be alone amid the din of battle and does not wait for him. She then returns to the present, her dress dirty and full of blood. When her mother-in-law sees her in this state, she immediately assumes that one of the Indians—whom she fears and despises—has raped Laura.

These fluctuations between present and past take place two more times. When Laura goes to a café in Tacuba, a place she does not know and which was once an Aztec exit from the city of Tenochtitlán, she wears the same dirty and bloody dress that she wore in Cuitzeo. Upon arriving, the only thing she says of the café is that it is "very sad," thus indirectly referring to the Noche Triste of 1520 and entering into dialogue with Spanish accounts of the Conquest. Tired of waiting, she goes outside and again time revolves and there is no present, past, or future.[27] Her cousin/husband again comes towards her and suddenly she is in front of her house in the days of the Conquest. The house is in flames and Laura's parents and siblings are dead.

A night on which the Spaniards came very close to being defeated by the Aztecs is thus also a sad night for Laura. This could point to Garro's characterization of Laura as a Malinche in the male tradition, an Indian woman who first and foremost identifies with the Spanish point of view. Laura's sadness, however, can also be situated in the Mexico City of the present, and would thus stem from the realization that had the Spaniards been wiped out during that night, the Laura of the present would not exist. If this is the case, "La culpa es de los Tlaxcaltecas" seems to imply that the narrative "I" and, by extension, Mexican subjectivity are invariably torn between two perspectives and two cultures. In this respect, whether it is the Indian or the Spanish point of view that is assumed, the Mexican "I" invariably betrays the other side. Treacherousness is thus the crucial component of that colonized identity. It is perhaps with these reflections in mind that Garro, in a letter to José Bianco, writes: "Y los mexicanos somos traidores. Traidores. Traidores" [And we Mexicans are traitors. Traitors. Traitors].[28]

Time once again revolves to the past when Laura is in Chapultepec Park and escapes from the supervision of her mother-in-law, who by now thinks Laura has gone mad. When her cousin/husband arrives, they go to the Tacuba exit where, he tells her, there are many betrayals.[29] In Tacuba everything is burning and the canals are infested with the bodies of the dead. Left alone, Laura again returns to the present. On her way home, she notes that the highways that the taxi follows are the same Aztec canals.[30]

As the story continues, the distortions in time become progressively greater. What seem to Laura to be seconds or minutes become first hours, then days, and finally weeks. At the end of the story, Laura disappears forever with her cousin/husband, presumably into a utopian future that assumes the Indian side of Mexico's identity.

Garro's choice of Cuitzeo as the site of the first time distortion is not accidental, since it would make Laura's husband a Tarascan Indian.[31] Indeed, the Indian is referred to as a cousin/husband and the Tarascans had closely endogamous marriage customs.[32] Significantly, the Tarascans were never conquered by the Aztecs.[33] Moreover, they have successfully resisted acculturation and have managed to maintain their own culture relatively intact since the Conquest. Even today, as anthropologist Lucio Mendieta y Núñez writes, "No nos encontramos ante una raza indígena que degenera y se extingue como acontece con algunas otras del país, sino frente a un pueblo aborigen que, cuando menos desde el punto de vista numérico, se encuentra en plena evolución ascendente" [We do not find ourselves confronted by an indigenous race that has degenerated and become extinct but who, numerically at least, finds itself in plain expansion].[34] History has it that when the Spaniards invaded, Moctezuma II sent an ambassador to Tarascan King Zuanga, asking him to form an alliance with the Aztecs against the Spaniards. Zuanga agreed to help him but died soon thereafter. King Tzinzicha Tangaxoan, the son who succeeded him, refused to help the Aztecs and in fact allowed the Spaniards to enter his territory.[35] It would seem, then, that Garro's choice of a Tarascan Indian as Laura's husband refers to that one moment of possible Indian unity and solidarity as well as of Indian autonomy. The fact that Laura blames the Tlaxcaltecas—one of the first Indian tribes to ally themselves with Cortés against the Aztecs—shifts the responsibility for the Spaniards' victory away from la Malinche and all Mexican women. Treacherousness and betrayal are postulated to be at the root of modern Mexican subjectivity, whether male or female.[36] Given Mexico's history of miscegenation, betrayal also becomes a characteristic of modernity and modernity's relation to the past.

In "La culpa es de los Tlaxcaltecas," the past, the present, and the future coexist. The history of Mexico, inscribed in stones, revives and tells its story in the present. Hence Garro's insistence, not only in this story but also in her novel *Los recuerdos del porvenir,* that the words and actions of her protagonists are turned into stone and thereby engraved forever in time. As Laura tells Nacha: "Todo se olvida . . . pero se olvida sólo por un tiempo" [Everything is forgotten . . . but it is only forgotten for a time].[37] Hence too, Garro's insistence on—or obsession with—the past and the flip side of things: modern highways are the Aztec canals of the past; time is the flip side of a postcard; the life of a woman in Mexico City today is the other side of her life during the Conquest; and intellectuals (men) are the propagators not of enlightenment and reason, but of fear and darkness.[38]

Garro has written that, as a child, she was obsessed with the flip side of things.[39] She even learned to read backwards, thus creating a language that was understood only by her and her sister Deva.[40] At the end of "La culpa es de los Tlaxcaltecas," Laura and Nacha also speak a language that only they understand. Garro's insistence that she learned to read backwards can be seen as a feminist gesture to retrieve women's stories from the underside of history. Walter Benjamin called for a reading "against the grain" as a way of uncovering the history of those absent from history—history being the history of the victors and not the vanquished, of the ruling classes and not the proletariat.[41] In a similar way, Garro calls for a "reading backwards" as a way of inscribing women into history. Her obsession also characterizes Laura, who reads Bernal Díaz's chronicle backwards. In it she finds not the glorious and heroic history of the common soldier that Díaz attempted to write, but rather the history of men's multiple and endless betrayals.

The fact that there was for Garro a flip side of time and space coincides with the coexistence of different religions and cosmologies in the story. Garro explains that her idiosyncratic conception of time is based on the various systems of thought that were much discussed in her home, including the theory of relativity and Aztec time. Her father used to say that "como éramos ayer, éramos hoy, y éramos mañana, que es como un juego de espejos" [as we were yesterday, we were today, and we were tomorrow, which is like a play of mirrors].[42] The past condemns the present for its mestizaje, or permanent betrayal. At the same time, the present condemns the past for its long line of betrayals, which led to the defeat of one world by another, one race by another, and one gender by another.

Once Laura has relived the past, she views the present with new eyes.

Thus, after returning from her first encounter with her Tarascan cousin/ husband in Cuitzeo, she sees that a world—literally—separates her from her husband Pablo. She tells Nacha: "Este marido nuevo, no tiene memoria y no sabe más que las cosas de cada día" [This new husband has no memory and knows only about everyday affairs].[43] In this sense the story responds to Adrienne Rich's call for a "radical critique of literature" that not only shows how Mexican women have been forced to imagine themselves, but also points the way to "how we can begin to see and name—and therefore live—afresh."[44]

"La culpa es de los Tlaxcaltecas" also articulates the necessity of reclaiming history in order to correct the aberrations and meaninglessness of the present.[45] Pablo resembles Laura's Tarascan husband but is differentiated from him by the fact that he has no memory.[46] To repress the past, as the story implicitly claims is done by Pablo and all the men of Mexico City, is to live in the present with dead eyes, without memory, and with a physical and metaphysical violence towards others, especially women and marginalized cultures like the Indians of Mexico today.[47]

Within a colonial context, the erasure of cultural duality underlies every miscegenation.[48] It also entails a repression of the sexual, which is manifested in the violence of men against women. The myth of la Malinche reproduces this violence at a symbolic and discursive level. For women writers, the first task becomes the recuperation of history, because, as Elaine Showalter writes: "each generation of women writers has found itself, in a sense, without a history, forced to rediscover the past anew, forging again and again the consciousness of their sex."[49] If this is true for the European and North American women about whom Showalter writes, it is much more so for Mexican and Chicana women writers, because the alleged betrayal of la Malinche has become so entrenched in Mexico's cultural identity that it will not be erased, no matter how many times women rewrite that myth. That is, men's violence against women takes place not only physically, but also at the levels of tradition, history, and writing.

The establishment of a female tradition—particularly a literary tradition—necessarily entails the disruption—that is, the betrayal—of the male tradition.[50] As feminism has repeatedly shown, women can articulate their consciousness only through male discourse,[51] making women's writing a "double-voiced" discourse.[52] As Adriana Méndez Rodenas has pointed out, "*entre traición y tradición* se abre la letra femenina" [women's writing opens up a space for itself *between betrayal and tradition*] (emphasis added).[53]

Hence, Garro's feminist critique must be articulated by "reading backwards" and in turn "betraying" key Mexican texts such as *Historia verdadera* and *El laberinto de la soledad*.[54]


## The Betrayal of Tradition. ¡Qué pinche ser Malinche!

Two phrases serve as counterpoints in Garro's story. The first of these, "la culpa es de los Tlaxcaltecas," recurs with the second, "yo soy como ellos: traidora" [I am like them: treacherous]. Laura and Nacha agree on their common treacherousness, but the story assumes that Nacha is more in touch with her Indian past. This fact allows her to live a cultural and racial duality that the upper classes vehemently negate and actively repress. It is precisely this duality that Laura, in a gesture unusual for people of her class, is shown to be reclaiming.[55]

The moment of solidarity between the two women is rare in Garro's narratives, especially in her more recent novels and stories. More often, her women protagonists are isolated, lack goals, and have no identity other than that constructed for them by others. In *Las casa junto al río,* the narrator is in danger of losing her identity because her name has been appropriated by others in order to disinherit her. Her family is no longer her family, nor her name her name. This novel shows that identity is neither intrinsic nor ontological, but a social and cultural fabrication. In *Testimonios sobre Mariana,* the protagonist—like la Malinche—exists only through the discourse of others. This loss of identity is equated with death. Laura and Nacha parody and subvert such cultural constructs when they characterize themselves exclusively as traitors, underscoring the poverty and ridiculousness of this naming. Parody has been theorized as one of the sole weapons of the colonized, and sometimes their only possibility of expression.[56] In Garro's story, women must usurp male history from within.

The displacement of male discourse effected in "La culpa es de los Tlaxcaltecas" takes place at two levels. At the level of the colonized, the story imagines Mexico as a hybrid composite of cultures and races in which the native is given equal agency in the formation of modern Mexico.[57] The past repeats itself in the present with only slight variations, exemplified in the difference between Laura's skin color then and now. This cyclical and mythical conception of history contrasts with the prevailing one, in which the present functions as sheer negativity and negation of the past. As Octavio

Paz writes: "El mexicano condena en bloque toda su tradición, que es un conjunto de gestos, actitudes y tendencias en el que ya es difícil distinguir lo español de lo indio" [The Mexican condemns his tradition in its totality; a tradition which is constituted by gestures, attitudes, and tendencies wherein it has become impossible to distinguish the Spanish elements from the Indian].[58] This denial of origins is institutionalized in the nation's schools. Mexican novelist María Luisa Puga recalls:

Cuando en la escuela me enseñaban historia de México, yo después le preguntaba a mis padres: ¿Cómo llegaron ustedes aquí? ¿De España? ¿O son indios? Mi papá se enojaba. No hagas preguntas tontas me decía. ¿Qué no vos ves? Cómo vamos a ser indios. Pero yo quería saber. Qué éramos entonces, si no éramos indios ni españoles. ¿Quiénes éramos? Mexicanos decía mi papá, qué otra cosa vamos a ser. Pero ¿de dónde vienen los mexicanos? ¿Qué pasó con los indios? Lo más que logré entender fue que los indios eran los pobres y los españoles los ricos. . . . Y así hice la primaria, sin entender mucho.

[When they taught me Mexican history in school I would ask my parents: Where did you come from? From Spain? Or are you Indians? My father would get angry. Don't ask silly questions, he used to say. Don't you see us? How could we be Indians? But I wanted to know. What were we then if we were neither Indians nor Spaniards. Who were we? Mexicans, my father used to say, what else. But, where do the Mexicans come from? What happened to the Indians? The only thing that I managed to understand was that Indians were the poor and Spaniards the rich. . . . That is how I got through grade school, without understanding much.][59]

Laura fights against this denial of origins learned by all Mexicans. At the center of her fight is a feminist project to reclaim la Malinche and thus Mexico's Indo-Hispanic history. La Malinche, like Laura, becomes a woman who escapes from the past in order to survive in the present. As such, she is a symbol of transculturation and the numerous adaptations, translations, and mediations between the two cultures that were necessary before Mexico could exist as it does today.

In the male myth of origins, la Malinche is the traitor, the bad mother who gives birth to Mexico, a nation of bastards.[60] In the female version, betrayal and guilt are generalized and la Malinche becomes a victim of rape and violence. She does not like it, as Paz's slippage from "violación" to "entrega" would have us believe. The insistence on distorting Mexico's primordial scene[61] by blaming the victims shows that there is a break at the origin of contemporary Mexican culture. According to the logic of this split, everything Indian is despised, hated, feared, and repressed, while everything Hispanic is valorized. This disparagement of the indigenous is internalized by both women and men, and leads to self-condemnation and to paralysis.[62] The story postulates another kind of guilt, that of the present towards the past, whereby all those living in the present have somehow betrayed the past in order to survive. Laura's betrayal, like Malinche's, lies precisely in the fact that she escapes into the present and survives. The miscegenation of contemporary Mexico, according to this scheme, insists on forgetting a divided past and stubbornly affirms a Mexican national identity out of the repression and distortion of the Indian and female elements at its origin.

## Reading/Writing Backwards

Garro's use of time makes "La culpa es de los Tlaxcaltecas" a story that can be read in two different ways. A linear reading corresponds with the way in which Pablo and his mother perceive events. Laura's mother-in-law first interprets Laura's actions as the result of too much sun, then as unfaithfulness, and finally as madness. This last characterization of Laura is in keeping with a way of reading the story that emphasizes the irrationality of its plot. The conclusion that Laura has gone mad is backed by the story itself, which, if read linearly and teleologically, makes no sense at all. The second reading is the mythical one espoused by both Laura and Nacha. This interpretation understands the present to be a palimpsest of both the past and the future.[63] It can be traced in the grammatical and syntactical organization of the narration. Since past and future coincide, they increasingly disrupt the fluidity of the present. For example, when Laura is about to escape into the future with her Tarascan husband, the narration almost comes apart or, as one might say in Spanish, Garro desgarra.[64] Logic and syntax become irrational, as when the narrator says of Pablo's mother: "Margarita se quedó muy asombrada al oír lo del indio, porque ella no lo había visto en el Lago de Cuitzeo, sólo había visto la sangre como la que *podíamos ver todos*" [Margarita was astonished to hear about the Indian because she had not seen him at the lake in Cuitzeo, she had only seen the blood which *we could all see*] (emphasis added).[65] The sudden appearance of a "we" out of nowhere is not due to editorial mistakes, as one critic argues,[66] but instead is consistent with a mode of narration in which women's double-voiced discourse disrupts the flow of traditional male narratives.

These changes become very clear at the end of the story, when Laura and Nacha talk in the kitchen. In this last magical moment of intimacy before the arrival of Laura's Tarascan cousin/husband, the two women communicate in a new language.

Nachita se sirvió sal sobre el dorso de la mano y la comió golosa.
—¡Cuánto coyote! ¡Anda muy alborotada la coyotada! —dijo con la voz llena de sal. Laura se quedó escuchando unos instantes.
—Malditos animales, los hubieras visto hoy en la tarde—dijo.
—Con tal de que no estorben el paso del señor, o que le equivoquen el camino— comentó Nacha con miedo.
—Si nunca los temió ¿por qué había de temerlos esta noche?—preguntó Laura molesta.
Nacha se aproximó a su patrona para estrechar la intimidad súbita que se había establecido entre ellas.
—Son más canijos que los tlaxcaltecas—le dijo en voz muy baja.
[Nachita put salt on the back of her hand and licked it hungrily.
"So many coyotes! The pack is all excited," she said, her mouth full of salt. Laura listened for a few minutes.
"Damned animals, you should have seen them this afternoon," she said.
"As long as they don't stand in the way of the Señor, or lead him astray" Nacha said, fearfully.
"He was never afraid of them. Why should he be afraid tonight?," Laura asked annoyed.
Nacha got closer to her mistress, so that distance would not disturb the sudden intimacy that they had established.
"They're more treacherous than the Tlaxcaltecas," she said in a low voice.][67]

This exchange is only comprehensible if the reader takes into account that the two women have entered a new reality, one in which a pre-Hispanic conception of the world—coyotes as treacherous beings that lead people astray—is textualized in the present of the narration. This tearing away of narrative logic shows us a way of writing that evades the rules of male discourse.[68] It also puts into evidence a new understanding of the subject that leaves traces of its liminal, bicultural situation in the incomprehensibility of a new language.[69] With this story, Garro makes it easy for feminists to argue for the distinctiveness of women's writing. As Françoise Lionnet writes, women, "use linguistic and rhetorical structures that allow their plural selves to speak from within the straitjackets of borrowed discourses."[70] Thus women's discourse constitutes itself by subverting hegemonic and historiographical discourses.[71]

Nacha and Laura's use of a new language not only points to transcendence of class barriers, but also situates their story within a much larger literary phenomenon. In their most progressive and experimental stages, movements such as regionalism and indigenismo also "regionalized," "Quechuaized," or "latinamericanized" the Spanish language. With its invention of language, "La culpa es de los Tlaxcaltecas" forces these movements to expand and include women's voices and women's writing in the linguistic registers of the literary. In this sense, Garro's story not only thematizes transculturation as the merging of Indian and Spaniard, past and present, and teleological and mythical time, but also forces us to expand our concept of transculturation to encompass women's writing and women's language.

Feminism is a matter of imagining another future by reinterpreting the past. In a poem that reinterprets la Malinche for Chicana women today, Carmen Tafolla writes:

And you came.
My dear Hernan Cortés, to share your "civilization"—to play god . . . and I began to dream . . .
    I saw,
        and I acted!

  I saw our world
    And I saw yours
      And I saw—
          another.[72]

## NOTES

1. Díaz del Castillo, *Historia verdadera de la conquista de la Nueva España*.

2. For the source of this information and an excellent history and analysis of the role of la Malinche in Mexican literature, see Sandra Messinger Cypess, "The Figure of la Malinche in the Texts of Elena Garro," and by the same author, *La Malinche in Mexican Literature: From History to Myth*.

3. See Georges Baudor and Tzvetan Todorov, "The Códice Florentino."

4. Rachel Philips, "Marina/Malinche: Masks and Shadows." See also Baudor and Todorov, "Códice Florentino."

5. Nicolás Wey-Gómez, in his analysis of the transculturated writings of the Inca Garcilaso de la Vega, situates the story of la Malinche as the fundamental paradigm for the importance of translation in the formation of Latin America. Transculturation and translation function as technologies of acculturation when it comes to his interpretation of la Malinche. He writes: "Es decir, que el sujeto que produce el discurso (el discurso adoptado) es un sujeto descentrado: La Malinche, ausente de sí misma, habla a través de Doña Marina, se ve a sí misma a través de Doña Marina la cristiana, sierva y esposa del español, antes adoradora de 'ídolos'" [That is to say, that the subject that produces the discourse (the adopted discourse) is a decentered subject: La Malinche, absent to herself, speaks through Doña Marina, sees herself through Doña Marina the Christian, the servant and spouse of the Spaniard, as past "idol" worshiper]. See Wey-Gómez, "¿Dónde está Garcilaso?," 7–31, 12.

Statements such as these assume that la Malinche was merely a tabula rasa upon whom Spanish culture inscribed itself. She is presented as having lost herself in translation as well as having lost the ability to read Spanish culture with indigenous eyes, thus becoming again a symbol of acculturation or the one-way imposition of Spanish culture.

6. Messinger Cypess, *La Malinche in Mexican Literature*, 9.

7. Messinger Cypess, *La Malinche in Mexican Literature*, 13.

8. The seminal essay on Ariel as symbol for Latin America is José Enrique Rodó's *Ariel*.

9. Roberto Fernández Retamar, *Calibán: Apuntes sobre la cultura de nuestra América*. For more recent discussions of Caliban, see José David Saldívar, *The Dialectics of Our America: Genealogy, Cultural Critique, and Literary History*, and *Nuevo Texto Crítico* 5, which reopens the debate concerning Caliban and Latin American culture.

10. Eliana Ortega makes the same argument and adopts Anacaona, Indian woman poet and rebel autochthonous mother, as symbol for the Latin American colonial condition and loss of the motherland and mother tongue. See her "Poetic Discourse of the Puerto Rican Woman in the U.S.: New Voices of Anacaonian Liberation," in Asunción Horno-Delgado, Eliana Ortega, Nina M. Scott, and Nancy Saporta Sternbach, eds., *Breaking Boundaries: Latina Writings and Critical Readings*.

11. See Rosario Castellanos, "Malinche." For a Chicana interpretation along the same lines, see Norma Alarcón, "Chicana's Feminist Literature: A Re-vision through Malintzín, Or, Malintzín: Putting Flesh Back on the Object."

12. Luis Leal writes that in the work of Rosario Castellanos, "Marina se convierte en el prototipo de la concubina indígena" [Marina becomes the prototype of the Indian concubine]. Luis Leal, *Aztlán y México: Perfiles literarios e históricos*, 169. See also Castellanos, *Balún Canán*.

13. See Carmen Tafolla, *To Split a Human: Mitos, Machos y la Mujer Chicana*, 16–7.

14 See Alarcón, "Traduttora, Traditora: A Paradigmatic Figure of Chicana Feminism."

15. For further bibliography on women's reelaborations of la Malinche, see Alarcón, "Chicana's Feminist Literature"; Cherríe Moraga, "A Long Line of Vendidas," in her *Loving in the War Years;* Elizabeth J. Ordóñez, "The Concept of Cultural Identity in Chicana Poetry" and "Sexual Politics and the Theme of Sexuality in Chicana Poetry"; Yvonne Yarbo-Bejarano, "The Female Subject in Chicano Theatre: Sexuality, 'Race,' and Class"; and Philips, "Marina/Malinche." For an excellent overview of Chicana struggle and Chicana literary production, see Angie Chabram, "I Throw Punches for My Race, but I Don't Want to Be a Man: Writing Us—Chica-nos (Girl, Us)/Chicanas—into the Movement Script."

16. Francisco López de Gómara, *La conquista de México*.

17. Octavio Paz, *El laberinto de la soledad. Posdata. Vuelta al laberinto de la soledad*, 90. For an English translation, see *The Labyrinth of Solitude: Life and Thought in Mexico*, 86. Again, I have not used Kemp's translation in the interests of a more literal if less elegant version and because English translations of Spanish texts seem to evade the sexual connotations of the original in favor of more puritan versions. Thus Kemp translates "violación" as "violation" and "entrega" as "violation," which twists Paz's argument. Kemp's translation reads as follows: "If the *Chingada* is a representation of the violated Mother, it is appropriate to associate her with the Conquest, which was also a violation, not only in the historical sense but also in the very flesh of Indian women. The symbol of this *violation* is doña Malinche, mistress of Cortés" (emphasis added).

18. Even though Paz assumes la Malinche and her "betrayal" as the original scene at the base of Mexican identity, his paradigm is actually quite Eurocentric. As Helen Carr writes: "colonialist, racist and sexist discourse have continually reinforced, naturalized and legitimized each other during the process of European colonization. From the first contact with the New World, the model of the power relationship between men and women has been used to structure and articulate the relationship of the European to the New World inhabitants." Helen Carr, "Woman/Indian: 'The American' and His Others," 46.

19. Paz, *El laberinto*, 90.

20. Paz, *El laberinto*, 85. Paz's dialectic of the "closed" and the "open," even if written in the interests of an autonomous Mexican national project, is well in line with Eurocentric colonial discourse that has always associated the colonized with the female. See Carr, "Woman/Indian," 46.

21. Paz, *El laberinto*, 91.

22. Significantly, in the pages dealing with la Malinche, Paz employs the verb "desgarrar" no less than seven times. See my discussion of "Garro desgarra" later in this chapter.

23. Elena Garro, "La culpa es de los Tlaxcaltecas," 29.

24. Garro, "La culpa," 11. For an English translation, see Alberto Manguel, ed. and trans., *Other Fires: Short Fiction by Latin American Women*. Although Manguel's introduction to the story is excellent, I have not used his translation very often in the interest of a more literal if less elegant rendering. Manguel translates this passage as "And there, on Lake Cuitzeo, I became a child again," avoiding Garro's ungrammatical juxtaposition of the past with the present while incurring considerable semantic loss (161). He also translates "traidora" as "unfaithful," again losing the nuance of Garro's prose.

25. Garro, "La culpa," 12.

26. Garro, "La culpa," 11.

27. Garro, "La culpa," 22.

28. Garro to Bianco, Monday, August 27, 1962, José Bianco Correspondence, Princeton University Firestone Library.

29. Garro, "La culpa," 30.

30. Garro, "La culpa," 32.

31. I thank Armando Morales, fellow student at the University of Oregon, for pointing this out in one of our discussions of this story many years ago.

32. See Lucio Mendieta y Nuñez, *Los Tarascos: Monografía histórica, etnográfica y económica*, 37.

33. The Tarascan independence is assumed due to the fact that they maintained their own language. As Lucio Mendieta y Nuñez writes in his history of the Tarascans: "Ni siquiera es posible suponer una larga convivencia de vencedores y vencidos, porque tal convivencia habría dejado profundas huellas en el lenguaje. O los tarascos rechazaron toda conquista o conquistaron destruyendo al pueblo conquistado; sólo así pudieron conservar la integridad de su idioma" [It is not even possible to assume a lengthy period of coexistence of victors and vanquished because such a cohabitation would have left profound marks in the language. Either the Tarascans rejected all attempts to conquer them or they conquered and completely destroyed the people they had conquered; only in this way would they have maintained the integrity of their language]. Mendieta y Nuñez, *Los Tarascos*, xx.

34. Mendieta y Nuñez, *Los Tarascos*, xxvii.

35. Mendieta y Nuñez, *Los Tarascos*, xxiii.

36. Fray Toribio de Benavente Motolinía, corroborating the view that the Tlaxcaltecas' alliance with the Spaniards was instrumental in the conquest of Mexico, writes: "Este día [Corpus Christi, 1538] fue el primero que estos tlaxcaltecas sacaron sus armas, que el Emperador les dio cuando a este pueblo hizo ciudad; la cual merced aún no se ha hecho con otro ninguno de indios, sino con éste, que lo merece bien porque ayudaron mucho cuando éste se ganó toda la tierra, a don Hernando Cortés, por su Majestad" [This day (Corpus Christi, 1538) was the first time that the Tlaxcaltecas took out the weapons which the Emperor had given them when he made that people a city. This honor has only been granted to the Tlaxcaltecas and no one else because they helped Cortés in conquering all the land in the name of his majesty]. Motolinía, *Historia de los indios de la Nueva España*, 124.

37. Garro, "La culpa," 11.

38. For an analysis of this concept, see Lady Rojas-Trempe's article "El estado en 'Las cabezas bien pensantes' de Elena Garro."

39. Garro, "A mí me ha ocurrido todo al revés."

40. Emmanuel Carballido, *Protagonistas de la literatura mexicana*, 498.

41. Benjamin, "Task of the Translator," 257.

42. "Entrevista con Elena Garro," in Beth Miller and Alfonso González, eds., *26 autoras del México actual*, 205.

43. Garro, "La culpa," 17.

44. Adrienne Rich, *On Lies, Secrets, and Silence: Selected Prose 1966–1978*, 35.

45. As Lois Parkinson Zamora writes, history, particularly the history of one's origins, haunts Latin American literature in a way quite unlike that of the West, which does not find it necessary to continually justify and redefine "the nation." See Zamora's article "The Usable Past: The Idea of History in Modern U.S. and Latin American Fiction."

46. Here I completely disagree with Messinger Cypess's interpretation, in which she argues that the

two men are competing for Laura and that the Indian in the end wins. Messinger Cypess, *La Malinche in Mexican Literature,* 165.

47. In the story, the present also affects and changes the past. The first time that Laura meets her cousin/husband, she has lost all respect for men and kisses him. The third time she sees him, she has forgotten how she despises the men of Mexico City and now waits for his words with respect. Garro, "La culpa," 30.

48. For an excellent analysis of this point, see Guillermo Bonfil Batalla, *México profundo: Una civilización negada.*

49. Elaine Showalter, *A Literature of Their Own: British Women Novelists from Brontë to Lessing,* 11–2.

50. Adriana Méndez Rodenas, "Tradition and Women's Writing: Towards a Poetics of Difference."

51. Showalter, "Feminist Criticism in the Wilderness," 200. Showalter bases her essay on the studies of the anthropologists Shirley and Edwin Ardener.

52. Showalter, "Feminist Criticism," 201.

53. Rodenas, "Tiempo femenino, tiempo ficticio: *Los recuerdos del porvenir* de Elena Garro," 843–51.

54. Françoise Lionnet argues that "Since history and memory have to be reclaimed either in the absence of hard copy or in full knowledge of the ideological distortions that have colored whatever written documents and archival materials do exist, contemporary women writers especially have been interested in reappropriating the past so as to transform our understanding of ourselves." Lionnett, *Autobiographical Voices,* 4–5.

55. For a critique of Mexican women writers' manipulation of such codes and women's exploitation of women, see Cynthia Steele, "The Other Within: Class and Ethnicity as Difference in Mexican Women's Literature."

56. See especially the essays by Homi K. Bhabha, "Signs Taken for Wonders: Questions of Ambivalence and Authority under a Tree outside Delhi, May 1817," and "The Other Question: Stereotype and Colonial Discourse."

57. For Guillermo Bonfil Batalla, there are two different Mexicos. The first is an imaginary construct that excludes the Meso-American civilization. The second, "México profundo" as he calls it, comprises the negated Indian cultures. See Bonfil Batalla, *México profundo,* 10–1.

58. Paz, *El laberinto,* 91.

59. María Luisa Puga, *Pánico o peligro,* 11.

60. Leopoldo Zea, theorizing about the colonial condition of Latin America, writes: "El americano es sólo el hijo natural, el bastardo de su descubridor, conquistador y colonizador, y su existencia un simple hecho etnológico ajeno a toda calificación cultural. Hijo natural, bastardo, de una cultura que nunca podrá considerar como plenamente suya. . . . Bastardía que averguenza porque impide al mestizo acceder al mundo del padre" [The American male is only the natural child, the bastard of his discoverer, conqueror and colonizer, and his existence is a simple ethnographical given that is beyond any kind of cultural qualification. Natural son, bastard, of a culture that he will never be able to consider completely his. . . . A bastardness that makes him ashamed because the mestizo will never be able to gain full access to the world of the father]. Leopoldo Zea, "Búsqueda de la identidad latinoamericana," 174.

61. I borrow this expression from Antonio Cornejo Polar, who uses it to describe the encounter between Atahualpa and Father Valverde in Perú. See Cornejo Polar, "Heterogeneidad y contradicción en la literatura andina. (Tres incidentes en la contienda entre oralidad y escritura)," 104.

62. Hence Cynthia Duncan's assertion that this story is a mythopoeia which, through the creation of a new myth, tries to exorcise the rupture with the past. This article is important, even though it never mentions Malinche. See Cynthia Duncan, "La culpa es de los Tlaxcaltecas: A Reevaluation of Mexico's Past through Myth," 118.

63. There is yet another possible reading, although it is one with which I do not agree. Beth Miller and Alfonso González argue that "La culpa es de los Tlaxcaltecas" deals with "una dama azteca que no pudiendo soportar la destrucción de su pueblo, se transporta mágicamente al México de nuestros días" [an Aztec lady who, not being able to bear the destruction of her people, transports herself magically to present-day Mexico]. This interpretation seems faulty, since the movement of the story is from the present to the past, and not vice versa. See Miller and González, *26 autoras,* 203.

64. It is surprising how often Paz insists on "degarrar," or tearing apart, as the verb which accompanies "chingar." That is, if tautologically the male Chingón only "opens" the already open (women), he does so in order to tear apart, to "desgarrar."

65. Garro, "La culpa," 20.

66. See Carmen Salazar Parr, "Narrative Technique in the Prose Fiction of Elena Garro," 157.

67. Garro, "La culpa," 32.

68. For an excellent critique of this tearing of language in the theater of Garro, see Messinger Cypess, "Visual and Verbal Distances in Mexican Theatre: The Plays of Elena Garro."

69. For a theorization of this point, see the work of Julia Kristeva, particularly her *Revolution in Poetic Language,* 37. Susan Rubin Suleiman writes that Kristeva, along with Barthes, Derrida, and Bataille, argues that "the transgression of rules of discourse implies the transgression of law in general" and, citing Barthes, that "the transgression of values, which is the declared principle of eroticism, has its counterpart—perhaps even its foundation—in a technical transgression of the forms of language.'" See Susan Rubin Suleiman, "Pornography, Transgression, and the Avant-Garde: Bataille's *Story of the Eye,*" 119.

70. Lionnet, *Autobiographical Voices,* 19.

71. For an analysis of the fictional bases of historiography, see White, "Historical Text."

72. Tafolla, *To Split a Human,* 17. Elizabeth Ordóñez, in her article on Chicana appropriations and revisions of la Malinche, cites this poem as an example of la Malinche seen as visionary of another race, another culture, and another future. See her "Sexual Politics," 339.

## 7 ≈
# BY WAY OF CONCLUSION:
## The New Mestiza Writes

*When Álvar Núñez [Cabeza de Vaca] made his trip from Florida to Texas in the sixteenth century, he was somehow laying the foundation of a future American literature written in Spanish north of the Río Grande.*
— ROLANDO HINOJOSA

*Like the border graffiti says: "Simulacra stops here" (at the border).*
— GUILLERMO GÓMEZ-PEÑA

The first version of this chapter, drafted six years ago, consisted of a long introduction to Mexican-American literature and an analysis of Gloria Anzaldúa's *Borderlands/La Frontera: The New Mestiza Writes* (1987), which had recently appeared. Since then, so much has been written and theorized from "the borderlands" as to make this introduction obsolete. Works such as Héctor Calderón and José David Saldívar's *Criticism in the Borderlands: Studies in Chicano Literature, Culture, and Ideology* (1991) have revolutionized Latino studies in the United States.[1] The boom in multiculturalism has also contributed to this trend, since Latino writings are increasingly being incorporated into critical journals, literary collections, and school curricula.

On the downside, there are problems with this trend. The main one is that the politics and poetics of multiculturalism tend to erase differences between minorities, so that "everything becomes everything else."[2] As Gloria Anzaldúa writes, multiculturalism is a "euphemism for the imperializing and now defunct 'melting pot.'"[3] Guillermo Gómez-Peña, mourning the increasing appropriation and depoliticization of "the border" in the mainstream, corroborates her assertion: "The border as metaphor," he writes, "has become hollow. Border aesthetics have been gentrified and border culture as a utopian model for dialog is temporarily bankrupt."[4] What both Anzaldúa and Gómez-Peña are saying is that the specificity of Mexican-American literature and the Mexican-American experience is lost when appropriated by proponents of multiculturalism. This is not to say that theorizing from the borderlands is not a valid position, particularly in light of the fact that as academics teaching in Spanish, English, and Comparative Literature departments, we often have been displaced from our originating cultures and hence participate in the increasing transnationalization of today's world.

Another problem concerns the fact that even though the discourse of Latino literature and criticism is increasingly being mobilized, it is adopted only superficially. That is, it has not brought about structural changes in the way that we apply criticism. The problem is the same as that addressed by Norma Alarcón with regard to the relationship between Cherríe Moraga and Gloria Anzaldúa's now seminal *This Bridge Called My Back: Writings by Radical Women of Color* (1983) and Anglo-American feminism. "Notwithstanding the power of *Bridge* to affect the personal lives of its readers," writes Alarcón, "*Bridge*'s challenge to the Anglo-American subject of feminism has yet to effect a newer discourse."[5]

This observation can also be applied to the lack of a structural revision as to just what constitutes the literary canon of the United States. As Mexican-American critics argue, a literature in Spanish north of the Río Grande has existed since the United States' annexation of Texas, New Mexico, and California in 1848. Fundamental to the creation of a Mexican-American people is the Treaty of Guadalupe Hidalgo, whereby Mexicans living in the borderlands became citizens of the United States.[6] More radically, other Mexican-American scholars have criticized mainstream literary histories that set the beginning of literature in the United States with the foundation of Jamestown and an English colonial period. They argue that a Spanish colonial period, which would antedate Jamestown by a century, should be included. Instead, Mexican-American literature tends to be studied in Latin American and Spanish departments and not in English or American literature departments.[7] Books such as *Do the Americas Have a Common Literature?* (1990)[8] are trying to correct this slanted version of what constitutes the literary canon by establishing connections with a "greater" America. As with

Arguedas's works, however, Latino literature still poses a special problem for critics and literary historians who are reluctant to analyze non-canonic forms. For them, a literature with its origins in the borderlands poses particular problems that their critical apparatus is ill-equipped to study.

Throughout this book, I have tried to show how an understanding of the intercultural and transcultural dynamics of Latin American narratives can lead to a different way of reading and analyzing texts. This way of reading takes into account—as Antonio Cornejo Polar put it—the radical heterogeneity of those narratives. Crucial to this project is Gloria Anzaldúa's *Borderlands/La Frontera: The New Mestiza Writes*. Anzaldúa adopts the historical Spanish borderlands as a point of departure for the conceptualization of the Mexican-American experience today. Thus, a historical continuity can be established between the chronicle of Cabeza de Vaca and contemporary Latino writings.

## The Space of Writing in the Borderlands

*Borderlands* is difficult, if not impossible, to classify. It is autobiography (Anzaldúa describes her life in the Río Grande valley and her search for meaning); it is Aztec and personal mythology (like all Chicanos,[9] she assumes Aztec history and mythology and changes them to conform to the present as well as to establish continuity in the Southwest); it is history (the history of the United States' appropriation of the greater part of Mexico); it is philology (the history of the origins and development of the Chicano language); it is a novel (the development of all these themes as the story of a life, a bildungsroman); and it is a collection of poems and an archive of popular culture (*corridos* [Mexican songs][10] form an integral part of her work and serve to voice a popular, oral history that runs counter to mainstream Anglo-American history).

Anzaldúa describes her method of writing as creating an inventory of all the different legacies and traditions that have influenced and shaped her. The process is artisanal and emphasizes manual labor: "*Despojando, desgranando, quitando paja*" [Stripping, thrashing, getting rid of straw]. In determining the source of these influences, it is difficult to differentiate between "lo heredado, lo adquirido, lo impuesto" [the inherited, the acquired, the imposed]. She therefore "puts history through a sieve, winnows out the lies. . . . *Luego bota lo que no vale* [throws away whatever is useless]. . . . This step is a conscious rupture with all oppressive traditions of all cultures and religions. She communicates that rupture, documents the struggle. She reinterprets history and, using new symbols, she shapes new myths."[11]

Just as Anzaldúa continually shapes and reshapes herself, selecting the valuable and useful elements of diverse traditions, so too does she write. If there were a simple means of describing the process, it would be that of a constant deconstruction and reconstruction of history, tradition, culture, and language, all sieved through and tested by her own life and experiences. The movement of *Borderlands* is therefore a continual interplay between the general and the particular, the public and the private, and the historic and the personal.

In the section titled "Movimientos de rebeldía y las culturas que traicionan" [Movements of rebellion and the cultures that betray], for example, the movement back and forth between the particular and the general, evidenced throughout the book, is at work already in the first line. "Esos movimientos de rebeldía que tenemos en la sangre nosotros los mexicanos," she writes, "surgen como ríos desbocanados en mis venas" [Those movements of rebellion that we Mexicans have in our blood arise like rivers that burst their banks in my veins].[12] After meditating on how she has come to terms with her own need to rebel, Anzaldúa goes on to examine how culture tyrannizes people. In the section "Intimate Terrorism: Life in the Borderlands," she analyzes how this has affected her personally. The movement is similar in the section "Entering into the Serpent," in which she elaborates the history of the goddess Coatlalopeuh. In the first paragraph Anzaldúa recollects how her "*mamagrande Ramona*" had always had an altar with candles lit for the Virgin of Guadalupe. The suggestion that Guadalupe is in fact Coatlalopeuh serves as the transition point for the elaboration, in the next paragraph, of the history of the Aztec goddess and the palimpsest between her and Guadalupe.

The transitions from the particular to the general are often achieved by the incorporation of corridos and other songs. As popular "truths," these represent the point of view of "everyone" and thus embody both the particular and the general. The section "*El destierro*/The Lost Land," which describes how the Mexicans lost most of their territory to the United States, begins with Violeta Parra singing about the Arauco Indians who lost their land: "Entonces corre la sangre/no sabe el indio que hacer,/le van a quitar su tierra,/la tiene que defender" [The blood flows/the Indian does not know what to do,/they are going to take away his land,/he has to defend it].[13] Parra's song, set at the beginning of Anzaldúa's historicization of Mexico's loss of land, shows that this experience was common to both North and South America. After Anzaldúa describes how General Santa Anna lost Texas, a Mexican corrido presents the popular version of history:

> *Ya la mitad del terreno*
> *les vendió el traidor Santa Anna*
> *con lo que se ha hecho muy rica*
> *la nación americana.*
>
> *¿Qué acaso no se conforman*
> *con el oro de las minas?*
> *Ustedes muy elegantes*
> *y aquí nosotros en ruinas.*
>
> [Already half the land
> traitor Santa Anna sold them
> enriching
> the United States
>
> And they are still not happy
> with the gold from the mines
> You over there very elegant
> and us here in ruins.][14]

In this instance, the corrido represents the popular viewpoint, the underside of history. The Anglo-American point of view is also presented in the form of a poem, although it is in fact a historical text justifying and praising the North American appropriation of Texas. William H. Wharton wrote this eulogy of North American imperialism in the mid nineteenth century:

> The justice and benevolence of God
> will forbid that . . . Texas should again
> become a howling wilderness
> trod only by savages, or . . . benighted
> by the ignorance and superstition,
> the anarchy and rapine of Mexican misrule.
> The Anglo-American race are destined
> to be forever the proprietors of
> this land of promise and fulfillment.

This speech is presented as a corrido and thus as the popular version of North American history. In its form, it also resembles an "Our Father." The speech ends most appropriately when Wharton writes: "The wilderness of Texas has been redeemed/by Anglo-American blood & enterprise."[15] Wharton's version of history is thus made to parody itself. The movement back to the particular and the personal comes immediately after Wharton is cited and shows the direct and palpable effect of opinions like his: "*Con el destierro y el exilio fuimos desuñados, destroncados, destripados*—we were jerked out by the roots, truncated, disemboweled, dispossessed, and separated from our identity and our history."[16]

As Rumel Fuentes, a writer of Chicano corridos, explains, the corrido is about social values, customs, culture, and injustices. It tells of these things in a simple form that is accessible to anyone who cares to listen. Fuentes understands the corrido "*como un medio de exponer males e injusticias y de relatar la verdad acerca de las cosas que están pasando hoy en día. . . . El corrido es el lado chicano de la historia. El lado gringo de la historia está, en muchos casos, falseado y perverso*" [as a means of exposing the evils and injustices of society and of telling the truth about things that are happening today. . . . The corrido is the Chicano side of history. The gringo side of history is, in many cases, falsified and perverted].[17]

Corridos are political songs and songs of protest that tell of the "*pleito eterno entre el que tiene y que no tiene*" [eternal struggle between those who have and those who do not have].[18] In the corridos, however, the have nots become the protagonists. The corrido consists of many short verses, the number of which increases continually as the singers improvise. Since the corrido is never a closed and finished form, it makes of the singer the agent once again. Anzaldúa's *Borderlands* not only incorporates corridos to help explain events, but the book itself has the loose and open structure of a corrido. There is no necessity to the form other than that of incorporating as much as possible. As Anzaldúa writes:

The new *mestiza* copes by developing a tolerance for contradictions, a tolerance for ambiguity. She learns to be an Indian in Mexican culture, to be Mexican from an Anglo point of view. She learns to juggle cultures. She has a plural personality, she operates in a pluralistic mode—nothing is thrust out, the good the bad and the ugly, nothing rejected, nothing abandoned. Not only does she sustain contradictions, she turns the ambivalence into something new.[19]

This only superficially contradicts her previous claim that she picks and chooses from each culture. Both statements point to the incredible tension that accompanies transcultural living, especially in the metropolis. When the colony is situated within the "belly of the beast," the freedom to choose is greatly circumscribed by the sheer force of the acultural impetus.

The incorporation of eclectic materials and varied sources and genres into *Borderlands* situates it as open, in process, and on the margins of several dif-

ferent genres, languages, and cultures. *Borderlands* refuses to respect the established purity of language, of literary genres, and of sexual genders. In
other words, Anzaldúa does not respect boundaries or borders. For her a
borderland

is a vague and undetermined place created by the emotional residue of an unnatural
boundary. It is in a constant state of transition. The prohibited and forbidden are its
inhabitants. *Los atravesados* live here: the squint-eyed, the perverse, the queer, the
troublesome, the mongrel, the mulato [sic], the half-breed, the half dead; in short,
those that cross over, pass over, or go through the confines of the 'moral.'[20]

Instead, she makes the border a new point of departure. This perspective
can clearly be seen in the layout of the title. *Borderlands* appears in English
and in capital letters in the superior position, with *La frontera* below and in
cursive. This disposition signals the social hierarchy that dominates the life
of the author and to which she gives a new configuration and new meaning.
The dividing line suggests that the border that confronts the writer is both
physical and psychic. The subtitle *The New Mestiza* begins to redistribute
the elements by incorporating a Spanish word into English. The slash that
divides *Borderlands* from *La frontera* is also the fence of barbwire that divides
Mexico from the United States, as well as the line that separates the linguistic
signifier from the signified. But, by giving the signifier *Borderlands* the signified *La frontera,* Anzaldúa forces the semiotic disposition of the title to
cross borders in an unorthodox manner, as she herself proceeds to do in the
table of contents. In the two main divisions of the book, Spanish comes first:
"Atravesando fronteras/Crossing Borders" and "Un agitado viento/Ehécatl,
The Wind." If English and Anglo-American culture dominate the exterior
and public sphere, then Spanish and Nahuatl mythology dominate the interior and private sphere, mirroring Anzaldúa's own cultural split and borderland subjectivity.[21]


Linguistic Terrorism

*Borderlands* is written primarily in English with a sprinkling of
Spanish. Corridos are often used to introduce or close chapters. The Spanish
that is used reflects private situations in the home and in the Chicano community, where it stems from a predominantly oral tradition in which few
people learned the language formally. In many cases, Anzaldúa writes Spanish as she hears and speaks it: "Hija negra de la noche, carnala, ¿Porqué me

sacas las tripas, porqué cardas mis entrañas? Este hilvanando palabras con tripas me está matando. Jija de la noche ¡vete a la chingada!" [Dark Daughter of the night, sister, why do you pull out my guts? Why do you card my innards? This basting together of words with guts is killing me. Dark daughter of the night, go to hell!].[22]

These transcriptions of the spoken are similar to the linguistic fiction that Arguedas created for his novels, which any Peruvian reader would immediately recognize as the language of a Quechua speaker who had just recently learned to speak Spanish. Some of the linguistic changes effected by Chicano Spanish are similar to Arguedas's literary language: the change in stress (*maíz/maiz*), the omission of consonants (*lado/lao*), the *f* pronounced as *j* (*fue/jue*), the use of archaisms that are remnants of Spanish colonization in the sixteenth century (*traje/truje, haya/haiga, nadie/naiden*), the omission of initial or final syllables (*estar/tar, para/pa*), and the intervocalic *y* or *ll* replaced by an *i* (*tortilla/tortia*).[23]

Yet another predominant characteristic of Chicano Spanish is the prevalent use of anglicisms or *pochismos,* as they are called contemptuously in Mexico. Since Spanish is suppressed in the public schools and in the universities, it is not surprising that like so many Mexican-Americans, Anzaldúa, when she does use Spanish, often translates very literally from English: "En unas pocas centurias . . ."[24] Other examples of pochismos include *cookiar,* from to cook; *watchar,* to watch; and *parkiar,* to park. In other words, an English word or verb is used with a Spanish ending and conjugated as such: *yo watcho, tu watchas, él watcha.* Important precursors to this restructuring of language were the zoot suiters or *pachucos* of the 1940s, who created a coded language that others found difficult to understand: *pónte águila,* or watch out. It is interesting to note that the pachucos' new language was accompanied by an awareness of their identity as being outside mainstream Anglo-American culture.[25] The anglicization of Spanish also corresponds to Arguedas's Quechuaization of Spanish. The Spanish Anzaldúa writes stems from her home and the terms of endearment that she heard as a child. It serves as what I will call—for lack of a better word—a "marker" of the Mexican side of her American identity. Spanish words and phrases are inserted into a predominantly English narrative so as not to let the reader forget that this is a Chicana writing.

This increasing linguistic acculturation forces Anzaldúa to conclude that by the end of this century, "English, and not Spanish, will be the mother tongue of most Chicanos and Latinos."[26] Elsewhere, however, she argues that Chicano Spanish is constantly renewing itself because of the steady flow of Mexicans back and forth across the border and because of the proximity of the two countries. In this sense, the Chicano community is different from other minorities, for whom distance plays an important role in the rate of acculturation.

Anzaldúa, in her manifesto-like preface to *Borderlands,* explains her language not in terms of loss, but as a borderland language: "The switching of 'codes' in this book from English to Castilian Spanish to the North Mexican dialect to Tex-Mex to a sprinkling of Nahuatl to a mixture of all of these, reflects my language, a new language—the language of the Borderlands."[27] Fernando Peñalosa, in an essay dealing with the issue of the Chicano language and the establishment of a bilingual and bicultural education, writes that the distinctions made between languages and dialects are not linguistic but sociopolitical. He thus concludes that "one would prefer to avoid the spurious language-dialect distinction and use the more neutral term 'code.'"[28] Peñalosa argues that it is difficult to determine exactly what makes up the Chicano language. He finds that most Chicanos speak several different codes: Standard Mexican Spanish as spoken by the educated in Mexico; rural, lower-class Mexican Spanish as spoken by the uneducated in Mexico and in the Southwest; pachuco, or a youth argot; Spanish infiltrated by pochismos or anglicisms; and colloquial and standard English.

Anzaldúa herself writes:

And because we are a complex, heterogeneous people, we speak many languages. Some of the languages we speak are:
 1. Standard English
 2. Working class and slang English
 3. Standard Spanish
 4. Standard Mexican Spanish
 5. North Mexican Spanish dialect
 6. Chicano Spanish (Texas, New Mexico, Arizona and California have regional variations)
 7. Tex-Mex
 8. *Pachuco* (called *caló*)

And she adds, evaluating the list: "My home tongues are the languages I speak with my sister and brothers, with my friends. They are the last five listed, with 6 and 7 being closest to my heart."[29] Peñalosa finds that it is difficult to tell which of all these is the "mother tongue" of the Chicanos and whether the prevalent use of anglicisms is "Spanish with English interference, English with Spanish interference, simple code switching, all of these, or a separate code that can properly be said to act as 'mother tongue.'"[30] He concludes that the case of the Chicano community is a case of "multiglossia and multilingualism, with very complex relationships among the half-dozen codes in use among Chicanos."[31]

Juan Bruce-Novoa breaks down the distinction between languages and dialects and argues that Chicanos speak neither Spanish nor English. Nor are they bilingual: "We do not go from one to the other, nor do we keep them separate. The two are in dynamic tension creating a new, interlingual 'language.'" He expands on Ricardo Sánchez's concept of a tertiary principle by which both Spanish and English fragment into types of Spanish and English, so that "what the Chicano speaks is the product of many fragments."[32] Bruce-Novoa's linguistic argument fits well into his theorization of the Chicano literary space as neither Mexican nor American, but the hyphen between Mexican and American. Chicano literature stems from "the intercultural nothing of that space"; it is constantly pushing and expanding that space apart while creating its own reality and at the same time creating strong bonds of "interlocking tension that hold the two in relationship."[33]

To end the discussion of Chicano language is impossible, since this matter is often debated and no one is in the position to say the last word on it. It is still evolving into new configurations that are difficult or impossible to theorize. However, one thing is certain: the choice of a language, for Chicano writers, is always problematic. As Cherríe Moraga, in her poem "It's the Poverty," writes:

> . . . But it's the poverty
> the poverty of my imagination, we agree.
> *I lack imagination* you say.
> *No.* I lack language.

She concludes in terms very reminiscent of Arguedas's "batalla infernal con la lengua": "Words are a war to me."[34]

## Linguistic Terrorism/English Only

Anzaldúa, living in the borderlands, writes to reaffirm her language—and by extension her subjectivity—and to defend it against attacks from both sides of the border. A greaser on this side of the border, Spanish is under siege: it is literally beaten out of her in school, it is gently prodded out by her family, it becomes uncomfortable with friends, and it is criticized as incorrect by Spanish speakers. She describes this process in "How To Tame a Wild Tongue": "I remember being caught speaking Spanish at recess—that was good for three licks on the knuckles with a sharp ruler. I remember being sent to the corner of the classroom for 'talking back' to the Anglo teacher when all I was trying to do was tell her how to pronounce my name."[35]

At home, the process is gentler and is intended to help her succeed in a society that marginalizes those who do not acculturate: "Pa' hallar buen trabajo," her mother tells her, "tienes que saber hablar el inglés bien. Qué vale toda tu educación si todavía hablas inglés con un 'accent'" [In order to find good work, you have to know how to speak English well. Of what use is all your education if you still speak English with an "accent"].[36] Other Spanish speakers, especially those who are recent immigrants to the U.S., consider her Spanish deficient and incorrect. Anzaldúa retorts: "Their language was not outlawed in their countries."[37] A pocho, attacked for her anglicisms and her acculturation to North American society, Anzaldúa describes herself as living in a situation of linguistic terrorism: "*Deslenguadas. Somos los del español deficiente.* We are your linguistic nightmare, your linguistic aberration."[38]

Anzaldúa understands attacks on her language as attacks on her self. "If a person . . . has a low estimation of my native tongue, she also has a low estimation of me. . . . So if you really want to hurt me, talk badly about my language. Ethnic identity is twin skin to linguistic identity—I am my language." She continues:

Until I can take pride in my language, I cannot take pride in myself. Until I can accept as legitimate Chicano Texas Spanish, Tex-Mex and all the other languages I speak, I cannot accept the legitimacy of myself. Until I am free to write bilingually and to switch codes without having always to translate, while I still speak English or Spanish when I would rather speak Spanglish, and as long as I have to accommodate the English speakers rather than having them accommodate me, my tongue will be illegitimate.[39]

Anzaldúa experiences in her body what has been theorized by semiotics and psychoanalysis as subjectivity; that is, subjectivity understood as socially and discursively structured, constructed in and through language. As Emile Benveniste puts it, "Language is . . . the possibility of subjectivity because it always contains the linguistic forms appropriate to the expression of subjectivity." Or, as Lacan more cryptically writes, "A signifier represents a subject to another signifier."[40] That is, we exist within signification. When the linguistic "I" is attacked or denigrated, the self is also attacked.

*Borderlands* is Anzaldúa's attempt not only to defend her language, but also to write a subjectivity that is at least bilingual and bicultural. As such, it exists on the margins of the two cultures from which it derives, in the hyphen between Mexican and American that Bruce-Novoa sees as an "intercultural nothing." It is in this respect a borderland subjectivity that has yet to be theorized.[41] Anzaldúa's home is the edge of barbwire that separates the two cultures, the border that Ronald Reagan called "a war zone."[42]

## Hijas de la Chingada

In *This Bridge Called My Back: Writings by Radical Women of Color,* the anthology that she coedited with Cherríe Moraga, Anzaldúa continually hears an inner voice that asks as she writes: "Who am I, a poor Chicanita from the sticks, to think I could write?"[43] She elaborates on the origins of this voice as exterior to herself and to the other minority women in the United States: "How hard it is for us to *think* we can choose to become writers, much less *feel* and *believe* that we can."[44] Having grown up sixth-generation Chicana in the Río Grande valley, it is extremely difficult for her to conceive of an existence other than that of field worker. The first in her family to leave the valley and get an education, she cannot rid herself of the voices of acculturation that persist in her mind, even as she counters them by writing.

Anzaldúa is socially defined only in negative and stereotypical terms that depend upon the color of her skin and the movements of her body. These misrepresent her to herself and to others as "DUMB, HYSTERICAL, PASSIVE PUTA, PERVERT."[45] The problem is magnified in the mirror of reflexivity: "To be close to another Chicana is like looking into the mirror. We are afraid of what we'll see there. *Pena.* Shame. Low estimation of self."[46] In *Making Face, Making Soul: Haciendo Caras,* Anzaldúa reiterates that the masks worn by women of color are "steeped with self-hatred and other internalized oppressions."[47] As a woman defined by patriarchy as lacking, as a minority defined solely by reductive and racist stereotypes, and later as a lesbian, Anzaldúa is pure negativity. She therefore conceives of her writing as a way of imposing her own image of herself: "I write to record what others erase when I speak, to rewrite the stories others have miswritten about me. . . . To discover myself, to preserve myself, to make myself, to achieve self-autonomy."[48] The act of writing, then, becomes a utopian moment of reconciliation. In *This Bridge Called My Back,* the tiger that rides Anzaldúa's back and does not leave her alone is a metaphor for the imperative to write. This imperative takes the form of a voice that obsesses her relentlessly. If one voice constantly asks "Who am I a poor Chicanita . . . ?," thereby attempting to silence her, this other voice asks "Why aren't you riding, writing, writing?" If the first voice promises silence and negativity, the second, more urgent, forces her to constantly write and move forward away from negativity.

In *Borderlands,* Anzaldúa's remaking, re-creating, and rewriting of herself is likened to the desire to chisel her own face. "When I write it feels like I am carving bone. It feels like I'm creating my own face, my own heart—a Nahuatl concept."[49] She writes with hands that were destined for coarser work: "to hold the quill [with] hands broadened and calloused."[50] Bruce-Novoa has pointed out that the insistence on the hands in Chicano writing is socially overdetermined, since they function "as a symbol [that] fit[s] well into the ideology of making one's world and the emphasis on the working class. In radical terms, to control one's hand movements is to control the basic human needs of production."[51]

More recently—and perhaps as a reflection of her incorporation into mainstream criticism—Anzaldúa's focus has shifted from the hands to the face as the privileged space of cultural inscription. In *Making Face, Making Soul,* her writing becomes a means by which women of color

strip off the *máscaras* others have imposed on us, see through the disguises we hide behind and drop our *personas* so that we become subjects in our discourses. We rip out the stitches, expose the multi-layered "inner faces," attempting to confront and oust the internalized oppressions embedded in them, and remake anew both inner and outer faces. We begin to displace the white and colored male typographers and become, ourselves, typographers, printing our own words on the surfaces, the plates, of our bodies. We begin to acquire the agency of making our own *caras.* "Making faces" is my metaphor for constructing one's identity.[52]

From a territory of contradictions and a landscape of hatred, Anzaldúa defines herself as a new mestiza in whose flesh "revolution works out the clash of cultures."[53] For her, as for Arguedas, *nepantla,* or the space of the borderlands, is anything but a comfortable space to inhabit. Hands intended for field labor must become typographical hands that can reinscribe a Chicana beyond the paralyzing effects of mainstream negative stereotyping. As a woman writer, Anzaldúa combines the elements of two or more cultures and two or more languages. In this sense her back is both the bridge of *This Bridge Called My Back* and the bridge between two worlds.

In living on the borders of two cultures, Anzaldúa experiences not only abuse, but also a certain sense of freedom. This freedom allows her to negotiate her way between the two cultures. In true transculturating fashion, she adopts the role of the mediator, appropriating and discarding from each culture whatever she wants and thus shaping herself as a bricolage. She thus becomes what Efraín Barradas has called a "heretic" or "mythmaker," according to the circumstances.[54] As a mythmaker, Anzaldúa takes what she finds valuable from Chicano culture: the closeness to the land, Aztec myths, the past, and the emphasis on writing fostered by the Chicano Movement. As a heretic, she iconoclastically and almost joyfully discards the family, believing it to be oppressive to Latinas. In so doing, she positions herself against the mainstream of Chicano writing, which is concerned with and fearful of the disintegration of the family. When Anzaldúa rejects the family, the heterosexuality on which it is based also flies out the window and she chooses to become a lesbian. Applying the mistake made by one of her students, who defined homophobia as "fear of going home after a residency," Anzaldúa describes her own position as characterized by the fear of going home "and of not being taken in"; fearful of "being abandoned by the mother, the culture, la Raza, for being unacceptable, faulty, damaged."[55]

Homosexuality, in part, plays such a central role in Anzaldúa's work because it is "the ultimate rebellion" that any Chicana "can make against her native culture."[56] In a traditional, Catholic, rural community isolated in its *mexicanismo,* there are few accepted or acceptable possibilities from which to choose. Typically, a woman can become a nun, a prostitute, or a mother; sexuality is taboo. Anzaldúa chooses to study, to leave the valley of the Río Grande, and to become a lesbian: "Gané mi camino y me largué" [I found my way and left], she writes; but she is followed by the voices and prejudices from home: "Muy andariega mi hija [Very streetwise my daughter]. Because I left of my own accord me dicen, '¿Cómo te gusta la mala vida?'" [they tell me: "How do you like the bad life?"][57] Upon her return visits she is asked "'¿Y cuándo te casas, Gloria?'... Y yo les digo 'Pos si me caso, no va a ser con un hombre.'... Sí, soy hija de la Chingada" ["And when are you getting married, Gloria?"... And I tell them: "If I marry it is not going to be to a man."... Yes, I am the daughter of the Chingada].[58]

Like Garro, Anzaldúa assumes and rewrites the myth of la Malinche in order to redefine herself. Like Garro too, Anzaldúa realizes that it is not she who betrayed her culture with her lifestyle and her choice of sexuality, but rather that (male) culture betrays women. In Anzaldúa's case, her culture betrayed her—as it betrays all its women—by transforming them into "lowly *burras* [donkeys]," turning their strengths against them, deeming their highest virtue the ability to serve men, and making "macho caricatures of its men." Mexican culture creates a new verb for women: "[to] abnegate."[59]

Anzaldúa's project, like Garro's, is to turn the statement "Sí, soy hija de la Chingada" on its head and into something positive.[60] Malinche has become la chingada, the swear word that "passes a dozen times a day from the lips of Chicanos. Whore, prostitute, the woman who sold out her people to the Spaniards." Anzaldúa contends that the "worst kind of betrayal lies in making us believe that the Indian woman in us is the betrayer."[61] Her project is to rewrite and reinterpret history by negotiating a position for the borderland subject between the racism of middle-class feminism in the United States and the machismo of the Chicano Movement. Unlike most feminist theorists, Anzaldúa emphasizes the Indian past and points to the middle-class nature of feminism, calling on Chicanas to "forget the room of one's own."[62] Unlike the postulates of the Chicano Movement, her personal pantheon is peopled solely with female figures. Anzaldúa starts out from Aztlán, a symbol of the Chicanos' mythical homeland "somewhere" in the Southwest.[63] She finds that women played an important role in the tribes from which the Aztecs derived, but that their status was subverted when the Aztecs created an empire. Her emphasis, then, lies on the era before the Aztec consolidation of power and before the era favored by Chicanos. However, her critique remains well within the context and parameters of both the Chicano Movement and North American feminism and it has been readily appropriated by mainstream literary critics.

Anzaldúa's feminist writing is dominated by three major female figures: the Aztec goddess Coatlicue, la Malinche, and la Llorona. Like her use of Spanish, these three serve as markers for Anzaldúa's specifically Mexican-American identity. Coatlicue, or "serpent skirt," whose huge stone effigy is in the Museum of Anthropology of Mexico City, is symbolized by a necklace of human hearts and a skirt of twisted serpents and taloned feet. A goddess of fertility and earth and the mother of Huitzilopochtli (the Aztec god of war), she embodied the dualities male/female, light/dark, upper/underworld, and life/death. Anzaldúa traces the process whereby that duality was split apart and replaced by deities that embodied only one aspect of Coatlicue. This process took place at the same time that the Aztecs, under Huitzilopochtli, consolidated into a militaristic state in which patrilinearity replaced early Toltec and Aztec matrilinearity.[64] During the three hundred years that saw the development and consolidation of Aztec power, another great shift took place. The egalitarian traditions of a wandering tribe were replaced by the class society of a "predatory state."[65] This point is emphasized by Anzaldúa, because it sheds new light on Mexican history and mythology. For Garro, the Tlaxcaltecas were to blame for the Spaniards' defeat of the Aztecs, but for Anzaldúa the Aztecs were themselves responsible. They were conquered so easily not because Malinche translated for them and betrayed her tribe, but because they created rigid and hierarchical social divisions that separated the nobility from the *mazehual* class,[66] subjected conquered peoples to extreme taxation, and practiced human sacrifice. The Aztecs thus alienated so many people that they could not muster enough forces to defend Tenochtitlán.[67]

After the Conquest, the Aztec goddess Tonantsi (a deity derived from the desexualized part of Coatlicue) and the Virgin of Guadalupe merged to form a divine and cultural palimpsest. According to tradition, Guadalupe appeared to a poor Indian, Juan Diego, on December 9, 1531, at the site on which a temple to Tonantsi had once stood. She told him that her name was María Coatlalopeuh (*coatl,* meaning serpent in Nahuatl, and *lopeuh,* meaning the one who has dominion over serpents).[68] However, Coatlalopeuh, or the sexual part of her identity, was taken out of her and her name was understood as "Guadalupe" by the Spaniards. She became the Virgin Mother, a dark parallel to the Virgin Mary, and patron saint of Mexicans and Chicanos alike. La Malinche or la Chingada, the bad woman, became her opposite and is considered mother of all Mexicans. La Llorona, Anzaldúa's third female figure, is derived from both Guadalupe and la Chingada. She is the ghost of a woman who cries in the night for her lost children.[69]

For Anzaldúa, the destruction and splitting of the duality that these deities originally embodied is a patriarchical attempt to subvert their significance and power. Thus, Guadalupe functions to make Mexicans docile and enduring, la Chingada to make them ashamed of their Indian heritage, and la Llorona to make them a long-suffering people. Anzaldúa rereads the role of these figures and lends them new significance:

Today, *la virgen de Guadalupe* is the single most potent religious, political and cultural image of the Chicano/*mexicano.* She, like my race, is a synthesis of the old world and the new, of the religion and culture of the two races in our psyche, the conquerors and the conquered. She is the symbol of the *mestizo* true to his or her Indian values.[70]

Anzaldúa sees Guadalupe and Malinche's main function as that of mediators between Spanish and Indian cultures. Guadalupe also symbolizes tolerance for ambiguity, which "Chicanos-*mexicanos,* people of mixed race, people who have Indian blood, people who cross cultures, by necessity possess."[71] It is within this long (female) tradition of mediation between cultures that Anzaldúa situates her own work.

Anzaldúa's choice of lesbian sexuality plays a crucial role in this context, because through it she attempts to embody the dualities inherent in pre-Aztec female deities. In other words, her lesbianism serves to undo the work of patriarchy and return to a conception of the self as capable of embodying the whole world at once and not just single and fragmented aspects of it. As Anzaldúa explains:

half and halfs [homosexuals] are not suffering from a confusion of sexual identity, or even from a confusion of gender. What we are suffering from is an absolute despot duality that says we are able to be only one or the other. . . . But I, like other queer people, am two in one body, both male and female. I am the embodiment of *hieros gamos:* the coming together of opposite qualities within.[72]

If Anzaldúa, as a lesbian, embodies both the male and the female, her writing incorporates every possible discourse at once. Given the multiplicity of being that she celebrates in her work, together with her persistent attempts to cross sexual, linguistic, and cultural borders, it is not surprising that *Borderlands* is such a hybrid text. The book implicitly questions the notion of a pure genre and a pure gender, subverting the idea of one dominant language and culture. By mixing modes—languages, cultures, and sexualities—Anzaldúa creates a new literary form as well as a new space from which to write.

I have referred to Anzaldúa's mobilization of a pre-Hispanic pantheon as a marker for the Mexican side of her American identity. This was a way of voicing a concern that made me uncomfortable with *Borderlands:* namely, what connection does a Chicana from the Río Grande have (really) to pre-Hispanic Mexican deities? In a highly contradictory article recently published in *Nacla,* Anzaldúa asks herself the same question after visiting a quincentenary exhibition on Aztec art and culture at the Denver Museum of Natural History. She writes:

Something about who and what I am and the 200 "artifacts" I have just seen does not feel right. . . . Yes, cultural roots are important, *but I was not born at Tenochtitlán in the ancient past nor in an Aztec village in modern times. I was born and live in that in-between space,* nepantla, *the borderlands.* Hay muchas razas *running in my veins,* mescladas dentro de mi, otras culturas *that my body lives in and out of.* Mi cuerpo vive dentro y fuera de otras culturas *and a white man who constantly whispers inside my skull. For me, being Chicana is not enough. It is only one of my multiple identities.*[73]

With this statement she is renouncing the label "Chicana" as the exclusive delimitation of her identity, thereby perhaps pointing to a new development in Latino consciousness.[74] Like mainstream critics who are now theorizing from the borderlands, Anzaldúa has begun to transnationalize the border to form (utopian?)[75] alliances of the displaced. As she writes: "The multi-subjectivity and split-subjectivity of the border artist creating various counter arts will continue, but with a parallel movement where a polarized us/them, insiders/outsiders culture clash is not the main struggle, where a refusal to be split will be a given." And, recalling Cabeza de Vaca's ambiguous "nostros," she concludes: "We are both *nos* (us) and *otras* (others)—*nos/otras*."[76] This last statement can be read as a passing moment evidencing border fatigue and a relinquishing to the desire for reconciliation. Beyond that—and more importantly—what we are seeing is the development of two distinct yet at times overlapping modes of conceptualizing the border. The first of these is oppositional, explosive, and politically engaged. It sees the border as a war zone in which dancing the mambo together will not erase the racism, xenophobia, and ethnocentrism of our time.[77] The second mode corresponds to the internationalization of the border and systematizes the consciousness of displacement. Here, as Guillermo Gómez-Peña writes, any encounter between people of different cultures constitutes a "border experience."[78]

NOTES

1. For a recent study on the politics of labeling, see Suzanne Oboler, "The Politics of Labeling: Latino/a Cultural Identities of Self and Others," and her book *Labeling the "Other Hispanics": Latin American Immigrants and the Dynamics of Race, Class, Language, and National Origins*. For the genesis of the term "Hispanic" and the U.S. government's politics of labeling, see Jack D. Forbes, "The Hispanic Spin: Party Politics and Governmental Manipulation of Ethnic Identity."

2. Guillermo Gómez-Peña, "The Multicultural Paradigm: An Open Letter to the National Arts Community."

3. Gloria Anzaldúa, ed., *Making Face, Making Soul: Haciendo Caras*, xxii.

4. Gómez-Peña, "Death on the Border: A Eulogy to Border Art," 9.

5. Norma Alarcón, "*This Bridge Called My Back* and Anglo-American Feminism," 31.

6. According to the treaty, Mexicans were allowed to keep their property, language, culture, and traditions. Needless to say, this was disregarded. In the sixties Chicanos rallied behind Reies López Tijerina, waging a legal battle for the restitution of land to Chicanos who still held land grants issued by the Spanish. The aim of domination, then as now, was not that of integrating Mexican Americans into the political and social life of the United States, but of accepting them as "fuerza de trabajo, pero manteniéndolos al margen de las decisiones que afectan el desarrollo del país como totalidad" [a work force, while keeping them marginal to the decisions that affect the development of the country as a totality]. See Juan Epple, "Literatura Chicana y crítica literaria," 153.

7. Philip D. Ortego, "Redefinición de la literatura norteamericana," 190.

8. Pérez Firmat, ed. *Do the Americas Have a Common Literature?*

9. The term "Chicano" was coined in the 1960s from the sixteenth-century pronunciation of "Mexicano" as "Mechicano" to denote a new political consciousness. It was assumed by those who experienced "a growing pride in their Mexican ethnicity" and who at the same time realized that they were different from Mexicans living in Mexico. See Bruce-Novoa, *La literatura chicana a través de sus autores,* 21. Part of the problem of putting the whole Mexican-American community under one term stems from the fact that such labeling erases important class and linguistic differences within the community. Many Mexicans have been in the United States for generations, others are first generation, and still others arrived only recently; they all have a different relationship with and response to domination. A further division consists of those who speak English and those who do not, regardless of how long they have been here. For a discussion of this problem, see Aída Hurtado and Carlos H. Arce, "Mexicans, Chicanos, Mexican Americans, or Pochos . . . ¿Qué somos? The Impact of Language and Nativity on Ethnic Labeling."

10. For a history of the corrido, see María Herrera-Sobek, *The Mexican Corrido: A Feminist Analysis.*

11. Anzaldúa, *Borderlands,* 82.

12. Anzaldúa, *Borderlands,* 15.

13. Anzaldúa, *Borderlands,* 6.

14. Anzaldúa, *Borderlands,* 6.

15. Anzaldúa, *Borderlands,* 7.

16. Anzaldúa, *Borderlands,* 7–8.

17. Rumel Fuentes, "Corridos de Rumel," 5.

18. Fuentes, "Corridos," 6.

19. Anzaldúa, *Borderlands,* 77.

20. Anzaldúa, *Borderlands,* 3. It is interesting to note how closely Anzaldúa's definition of the borderland is in concordance with Julia Kristeva's psychoanalytic definition of abjection as that which "disturbs identity, system, order. What does not respect borders, positions, rules. The in-between, the ambiguous, the composite." Kristeva, *Powers of Horror,* 4. However, whereas Kristeva's list of the abject consists mainly of criminals, rapists, traitors, and liars, Anzaldúa's is restricted to those who undermine cultural, linguistic, racial, sexual, and generic boundaries.

21. In her play *Coser y cantar: A One Act Bilingual Fantasy for Two Women,* the Cuban-American playwright Dolores Prida depicts the cultural division and split subjectivity that characterize Latinos living in the United States. The play's protagonist is a woman represented by two characters, Ella and She. The dialogue between the two women shows the tension and crisis as well as the strengths and the singular viewpoint derived from a bicultural existence. For an excellent article about this play, see Alberto Sandoval, "Dolores Prida's *Coser y cantar:* Mapping the Dialectics of Ethnic Identity and Assimilation."

22. Anzaldúa, *Borderlands,* 72.

23. Anzaldúa, *Borderlands,* 57–8.

24. Anzaldúa, *Borderlands,* 80.

25. The pachucos are considered forerunners of the Chicano Movement with their understanding of themselves as Other in the United States. They dramatically lived and staged this understanding in everyday life. The pachucos stood out not only because of their singular language, but also by breaking with accepted modes of behavior and dress. In effect, they rebelled and rejected both North American and Mexican culture. As Octavio Paz writes, "el hibridismo de su lenguaje y de su porte me parecen indudable reflejo de una oscilación psíquica entre dos mundos irreductibles y que vanamente quiere conciliar y superar: el norteamericano y el mexicano" [his hybrid language and behavior reflect a psychic oscillation between two irreducible worlds—the North American and the Mexican—which he vainly hopes to reconcile and conquer. He does not want to become either a Mexican or a Yankee]. Paz, "The Pachuco and Other Extremes," in *Labyrinth of Solitude,* n. 18.

26. Anzaldúa, *Borderlands,* 59.

27. Anzaldúa, *Borderlands,* preface.

28. Fernando Peñalosa, "Chicano Multilingualism and Multiglossia," 218.

29. Anzaldúa, *Borderlands,* 55–6.

30. Peñalosa, *Chicano,* 219–20.

31. Peñalosa, *Chicano,* 220.

32. Bruce-Novoa, "The Space of Chicano Literature," 28. At the Modern Language Association

Convention held in New Orleans in 1988, Bruce-Novoa reiterated that Chicano literature was increasingly and apparently being written in English. However, he asked "Is it really English?"

33. Bruce-Novoa, "Space of Chicano Literature," 27.
34. Moraga, "It's the Poverty," in Moraga, ed., *Loving in the War Years*, 62.
35. Anzaldúa, *Borderlands*, 53.
36. Anzaldúa, *Borderlands*, 53–4.
37. Anzaldúa, *Borderlands*, 58.
38. Anzaldúa, *Borderlands*, 58. This problem does not affect Chicanos alone. The Puerto Rican poet Luz María Umpierre expresses the same frustration as Anzaldúa in her collection of poems titled *En el país de las maravillas*. "Pointing Marginals" very graphically addresses the dilemma of the poet whose language is attacked by both Spanish and English speakers:

ANGLICISMO
COCHE NOT CARRO
PUERTORRIQUEÑISMO
CENA NOT COMIDA
REGIONALISMO
MISCONCEPTION
LOOK THIS UP IN A DICTIONARY!
MISPELLED
WRONG
YOU OBVIOUSLY DON'T UNDERSTAND THE CONCEPT
X
IGNORANCE OF TERMINOLOGY
ARCHAISM!
FAMILIARIZE YOURSELF WITH THE CASTILLIAN WORD!
I DON'T UNDERSTAND WHAT YOU ARE TRYING TO SAY!
UF!
    (mierda!)
    (bullshit!)

Luz María Umpierre, *En el país de las maravillas*, 8.
39. Anzaldúa, *Borderlands*, 58–9.
40. Quoted in Kaja Silverman, *The Subject of Semiotics*, 45.
41. As Kaja Silverman writes, the subjectivity that has been theorized by psychoanalysis is implicitly applicable to any cultural situation, but "must be understood as applying to the strict sense only of the dominant Western model." Silverman, *Semiotics*, 131. Crucial in this context is Gayatri Spivak's effort to write the post-colonial subject within feminism, Marxism, and deconstruction in her *In Other Worlds: Essays in Cultural Politics*.
42. Anzaldúa, *Borderlands*, 11.
43. Anzaldúa, "Speaking in Tongues: A Letter to 3rd World Women Writers," 166.
44. Anzaldúa, "Speaking in Tongues," 166.
45. Anzaldúa, "Speaking in Tongues," 167.
46. Anzaldúa, *Borderlands*, 58. Later on she quotes George Kaufman's definition of shame: "Shame is a wound felt from the inside, dividing us both from ourselves and from one another." Anzaldúa, *Borderlands*, 42. In Anzaldúa's case, the mirror does not show her an undivided, whole self; rather, it reflects back a wound, a split self, and a culture that is split.
47. Anzaldúa, ed., *Making Face*, xv.
48. Anzaldúa, "Speaking in Tongues," 169.
49. Anzaldúa, *Borderlands*, 73.
50. Anzaldúa, "Speaking in Tongues," 166.
51. Bruce-Novoa, "One More Rosary for Doña Marina," 84.
52. Anzaldúa, ed., *Making Face*, xvi.
53. Anzaldúa, *Borderlands*, 81.
54. Efraín Barradas theorized this concept for Puerto Rican literature in the United States. However, it can be extended to Chicano literature, where the same move is evident. Barradas, *Herejes y mitificadores*.

Anzaldúa herself changed from the outright rejection of her culture to a more measured response: "Fuí muy hocicona. Era indiferente a muchos valores de mi cultura. No me deje de los hombres. No fuí buena ni obediente. . . . Pero he crecido. Yo na soló paso toda mi vida botando las costumbres y los valores de mi cultura que me traicionan. También recojo las costumbres de respeto a las mujeres" [I was very outspoken. I was indifferent to the values of my culture. . . . But I have grown up. I no longer spend my life throwing away all the customs and values of my culture which betray me. I also gather the customs which have been proven by time as well as the customs of respect for women]. Anzaldúa, *Borderlands*, 15.

55. Anzaldúa, *Borderlands*, 20.

56. Anzaldúa, *Borderlands*, 19.

57. Cherríe Moraga, also a writer and a lesbian, finds it impossible to determine what it was that actually isolated her from her family and community: her lesbianism or her writing. Moraga, *Loving in the War Years*, iv.

58. Anzaldúa, *Borderlands*, 16.

59. Anzaldúa, *Borderlands*, 21.

60. Anzaldúa, *Borderlands*, 22.

61. For a survey of poetic rewritings and redefinitions of the significance of Malinche, see Ordóñez, "Cultural Identity in Chicana Poetry," 75–82.

62. Anzaldúa, "Speaking in Tongues." *This Bridge Called My Back,* in which this essay appears, is a landmark in North American feminism in that it points to that kind of feminism's white, middle-class, and racist nature. It also forms an unprecedented alliance between Black, Asian, and Hispanic women that is based on the theorization of a third-world feminism in the United States, where all minority women classify as "women of color."

63. The Aztec myth of origins became particularly important to Chicano self-understanding in the 1960s. This myth has it that the predecessors of the Aztecs wandered south and settled the valley of Mexico, or Anáhuac, from "somewhere in the north." That mythical land—the precise location of which is a matter of debate for archaeologists and historians alike—is taken to be the Southwest. As one critic puts it, the exact location is irrelevant; it is important as a symbol "in that it provides Chicanos with a deeper and more intimate sense of cultural continuity." See Raymond A. Paredes, "The Evolution of Chicano Literature," 61. Chicanos feel they have a double connection to the Southwest: as point of origin and as point of return. They resettled the Southwest during the Spanish colonization of this area in the sixteenth century and are continuing to do so today. Armando B.Rendón, in the *Chicano Manifesto* (1971), poeticizes Aztlán as interiorized psychic landscape. He writes: "We are the people of Aztlán, true descendants of the Fifth Sun, el Quinto Sol. In the early morning light of a day thousands of years old now, my forebears set out from Aztlán a region of deserts, mountains, rivers, and forests, to seek a new home. Where they came from originally is hidden in the sands and riverbeds, and only hinted at by the cast of an eye and skin which we, their sons, now bear. . . . My people have come in fulfillment of a cosmic cycle from ancient Aztlán, the seed ground of the great civilizations of Anáhuac, to modern Aztlán, characterized by the progeny of our Indian, Mexican, and Spanish ancestors. We have rediscovered Aztlán in ourselves." See Armando B. Rendón, "The People of Aztlán," 28, 30. Rendón stresses an identity that is fluid between borders and cultures and conforms to the cyclical pattern of migration back and forth across the Río Grande. Ancient Aztec elements provide the Chicano subject with a symbolic continuity and wholeness that the present constantly erodes.

64. Anzaldúa, *Borderlands*, 33.

65. Anzaldúa bases much of her argument on the studies of the anthropologist June Nash. See June Nash, "The Aztecs and the Ideology of Male Dominance."

66. The mazehual class was the lowest and poorest in Aztec society. Juan Diego, the Indian who saw the Virgin of Guadalupe, belonged to this class. Thus Guadalupe becomes the patron saint of the destitute.

67. Anzaldúa, *Borderlands*, 33.

68. Anzaldúa, *Borderlands*, 33.

69. In this figure, Anzaldúa finds an echo of Aztec women's wailing as their husbands and sons went to the Aztec wars of conquest, the "flowery wars." Anzaldúa, *Borderlands*, 33.

70. Anzaldúa, *Borderlands*, 30.

71. Anzaldúa, *Borderlands*, 30.

72. Anzaldúa, *Borderlands,* 19.

73. Anzaldúa, "Chicana Artists: Exploring *nepantla,* el lugar de la frontera," 42.

74. Richard Rodríguez, in a recent National Public Radio interview, also stated that he considers himself first gay and then Hispanic.

75. Guillermo Gómez-Peña also writes of the border in these utopian terms: "Border culture can help dismantle the mechanisms of fear. Border culture can guide us back to common ground and improve our negotiating skills. Border culture is a process of negotiation towards utopia, but in this case, utopia means peaceful coexistence and fruitful cooperation. The border is all we share." See Gómez-Peña, "Multicultural Paradigm," 21.

76. Anzaldúa, "Chicana Artists," 42.

77. See Gómez-Peña, "From Art-Maggedon to Gringo-Stroika," 23.

78. Gómez-Peña, "Multicultural Paradigm," 20.

# Bibliography

Acosta, Antonio. "Francisco de Avila: Cusco 1573(?)–Lima 1647." In *Ritos y tradiciones de Huarochirí del siglo XVII,* edited and translated by Gerald Taylor. Lima: Instituto de Estudios Peruanos, 1987.

Adorno, Rolena. "La *ciudad letrada* y los discursos coloniales." *Hispamérica* 16, no. 48 (December 1987).

———. *Cronista y Príncipe: La obra de don Felipe Guamán Poma de Ayala.* Lima: Fondo Editorial, 1989.

———. *Guaman Poma: Writing and Resistance in Colonial Peru.* Austin: University of Texas Press, 1988.

———. "The Negotiation of Fear in Cabeza de Vaca's *Naufragios.*" *Representations* 33 (winter 1991).

Ahmad, Aijaz. "Jameson's Rhetoric of Otherness and the 'National Allegory.'" *Social Text* 17 (fall 1987).

Alarcón, Norma. "Chicana's Feminist Literature: A Re-vision through Malintzín, Or, Malintzín: Putting Flesh Back on the Object." In *This Bridge Called My Back: Writings by Radical Women of Color,* edited by Cherríe Moraga and Gloria Anzaldúa. Watertown: Persephone Press, 1981.

———. "*This Bridge Called My Back* and Anglo-American Feminism." In *Criticism in the Borderlands: Studies in Chicano Literature, Culture, and Ideology,* edited by Héctor Calderón and José David Saldívar. Durham: Duke University Press, 1991.

———. "Traduttora, Traditora: A Paradigmatic Figure of Chicana Feminism." *Cultural Critique* 13 (1990).

*America: Bride of the Sun.* Antwerp: Imschoot, 1991.

Anzaldúa, Gloria. *Borderlands/La Frontera: The New Mestiza.* San Francisco: spinsters/aunt lute, 1987.

———. "Chicana Artists: Exploring *nepantla,* el lugar de la frontera." *Nacla* 27, no. 1 (July/August 1993).

————. "Speaking in Tongues: A Letter to 3rd World Women Writers." In *This Bridge Called My Back: Writings by Radical Women of Color,* edited by Cherríe Moraga and Gloria Anzaldúa. Watertown: Persephone Press, 1981.

————, ed. *Making Face, Making Soul: Haciendo Caras.* San Francisco: aunt lute, 1990.

Aparicio, Frances R. "Salsa, Maracas, and Baile: Latin Popular Music in the Poetry of Victor Hernández Cruz." *MELUS: The Journal of the Society for the Study of the Multi-Ethnic Literature of the United States* 16, no. 1 (spring 1989–90).

————. "La Vida Es un Spanglish Disparatero: Bilingualism in Nuyorican Poetry." In *European Perspectives on Hispanic Literature of the United States,* edited by Geneviève Fabre. Houston: Arte Público Press, 1988.

Apel, Willi, and Ralph T. Daniel. *The Harvard Brief Dictionary of Music.* New York: Pocket Books, 1960.

Arguedas, José María. *Deep Rivers.* Translated by Frances Horning Barraclough. Austin and London: University of Texas Press, 1958.

————. *Formación de una cultura nacional indoamericana.* Edited by Ángel Rama. Mexico City: Siglo Veintiuno, 1975.

————. *Indios, mestizos y señores.* Lima: Editorial Horizonte, 1985.

————. *Katatay.* Lima: Editorial Horizonte, 1984.

————. *Nosotros los maestros.* Edited by Wilfredo Kapsoli. Lima: Editorial Horizonte, 1986.

————. *Poesía Quechua.* Buenos Aires: Editorial Universitaria, 1965.

————. *Recopilación de textos sobre José María Arguedas.* Edited by Juan Larco. Havana: Casa de las Américas, 1986.

————. *Relatos completos.* Buenos Aires: Editorial Losada, 1967.

————. *Los ríos profundos.* Lima: Editorial Horizonte, 1980.

————. *Señores e indios: Acerca de la cultura quechua.* Edited by Ángel Rama. Buenos Aires: Arca Editorial, 1976.

————. *Todas las sangres.* Buenos Aires: Editorial Losada, 1973.

————. *El zorro de arriba y el zorro de abajo.* Lima: Editorial Horizonte, 1983.

Arriaga, Father Pablo Joseph de. *The Extirpation of Idolatry in Peru.* Edited and translated by L. Clark Keating. Lexington, Kentucky: University of Kentucky Press, [1616] 1968.

Arroyo, Leonardo, ed. *A Carta de Pero Vaz de Caminha: Ensaio de Informaçao á Procura de Constantes Válidas de Método.* São Paolo: Ediçoes Melhoramentos, 1976.

Ávila, Father Francisco de. *Ritos y tradiciones de Huarochirí,* 1608.

Bakhtin, Mikhail. *L'oeuvre de François Rabelais et la culture populaire au moyen âge et sous la renaissance.* Translated by André Robel. Paris: Gallimard, 1970.

Bandelier, Adolph F. *The Islands of Titicaca and Koati.* New York: Hispanic Society of America, 1910.

Barata, Mario. "Épocas y estilos." In *América Latina en sus artes,* edited by Damián Bayón. Mexico City: Siglo Veintiuno, 1974.

Barker, Francis, et al., eds. *Europe and Its Others.* Colchester: University of Essex, 1985.

Barnstone, Willis. *The Poetics of Translation: History, Theory, Practice.* New Haven: Yale University Press, 1993.

Barradas, Efraín, and Rafael Rodríguez. *Herejes y mitificadores.* Río Piedras: Ediciones Huracán, 1980.

Barrenechea, Ana María. *Textos hispoamericanos: De Sarmiento a Sarduy.* Caracas: Monte Ávila Editores, 1978.

Bassnett, Susan, and André Lefevere, eds. *Translation, History and Culture.* London: Pinter Publishers, 1990.

Baudor, Georges, and Tzvetan Todorov. "The Codice Florentino." In *Relatos aztecas de la conquista,* translated by Guillermina Cuevas. Mexico City: Grijalbo, 1983.

Bendezú Aybar, Edmundo. *Literatura Quechua.* Caracas: Biblioteca Ayacucho, 1980.

Benítez Rojo, Antonio. *La isla que se repite: El Caribe y la perspectiva postmoderna.* Hanover: Ediciones del Norte, 1989.

———. *The Repeating Island: The Caribbean and the Postmodern Perspective.* Translated by James Maraniss. Durham: Duke University Press, 1992.

Benjamin, Walter. "The Task of the Translator." In *Illuminations,* edited by Hannah Arendt and translated by Harry Zohn. New York: Schocken, [1969] 1978.

Bhabha, Homi K. "The Other Question: Stereotype and Colonial Discourse." *Screen,* November 1983.

———. "Signs Taken for Wonders: Questions of Ambivalence and Authority under a Tree outside Delhi, May 1817." In *Europe and Its Others,* edited by Francis Baker, et al. Colchester: University of Essex, 1985.

Bianco, José. Correspondence. Princeton University Firestone Library.

Bocanegra, Iván Pérez. *Ritual formulario e institución de curas, para administrar a los naturales de este Reyno los santos Sacramentos del Baptismo, Confirmación, Eucaristía, y Viático, Penitencia, Extremaución, y Matrimonio, Con advertencias muy necesarias.* Lima: Gerónymo de Contreras, 1631.

Bonavia, Duccio. *Ricchata Quellcani: Pinturas murales prehispánicas.* Lima, 1974.

Bonet Correa, Antonio. "Integración de la cultura indígena en el arte hispanoamericano." *Boletín del Centro de Investigaciones Históricas y Estéticas* (Caracas: Universidad Central de Venezuela) 12 (November 1971).

Bonfil Batalla, Guillermo. *México profundo: Una civilización negada.* Mexico City: Grijalbo, 1990.

Brett, Guy. "Being Drawn to an Image." *The Oxford Art Journal* 14, no. 1 (1991).

Brown Ruoff, A. LaVonne, and Jerry W. Ward, Jr., eds. *Redefining American Literary History.* New York: Modern Language Association, 1990.

Bruce-Novoa, Juan. *Chicano Authors: Inquiry by Interview.* Austin: University of Texas Press, 1980.

———. "El deslinde del espacio literario chicano." *Aztlán* 11, no. 2 (fall 1980).

———. *La literatura chicana a través de sus autores.* Translated by Stella Mastrangelo. Mexico City: Siglo Veintiuno, 1983.

———. "Naufragios en los mares de la significación." *Plural* 19–25, no. 221 (February 1990).

———. "One More Rosary for Doña Marina." *Confluencia* 1, no. 2 (1986).

———. "*Pocho* as Literature. *Aztlán* 7, no. 1 (spring 1976).

———. "The Space of Chicano Literature." *De Colores* 1, no. 4 (winter 1975).

————. "Una cuestión de identidad: ¿Qué significa un nombre?" In *Chicanos y riqueños: Imágenes e identidades: El puertorriqueño en la literatura,* edited by Asela Rodríguez de Laguna. Río Piedras: Ediciones Huracán, 1985.

Buschiazzo, Mario. "El problema del arte mestizo." *Anales del Instituto de Arte Americano e Investigaciones Estéticas* 22 (1969).

Cabeza de Vaca, Álvar Núñez. *Naufragios.* Edited by John Estruch. Barcelona: Editorial Fontamara, 1982.

Calderón, Héctor, and José David Saldívar, eds. *Criticism in the Borderlands: Studies in Chicano Literature, Culture, and Ideology.* Durham: Duke University Press, 1991.

Cali, François. *The Spanish Arts of Latin America.* Translated by Bryan Rhys. New York: Viking Press, 1961.

Carballido, Emmanuel. *Protagonistas de la literatura mexicana.* Mexico City: Editora del Ermitaño, [1965] 1986.

Carr, Helen. "Woman/Indian: 'The American' and His Others." In *Europe and Its Others,* vol. 2, edited by Francis Barker, et al. Colchester: University of Essex Press, 1985.

Carreño, Antonio. "*Naufragios,* de Álvar Núñez Cabeza de Vaca: Una retórica de la crónica colonial." In *Revista Iberoamericana* 140 (July–September, 1987).

Casaseca Casaseca, Antonio. *Pintura cuzqueña en el Museo de Salamanca.* Salamanca: Monografías del Museo de Salamanca, 1989.

Castedo, Leopoldo. *The Cuzco Circle.* New York: Center for Inter-American Relations and American Federation of Arts, 1976.

————. *Sobre el arte "mestizo" hispanoamericano.* Austin and Mexico City: Investigaciones Contemporáneas sobre Historia de México, 1971.

Castellanos, Rosario. *Balún Canán.* Mexico City: Fondo de Cultura Económica, [1957] 1984.

————. "Malinche." In *Poesía no eres tú* (Mexico City: Fondo de Cultura Económica, [1972] 1985.

Castillo, Debra A. *Talking Back: Toward a Latin American Feminist Literary Criticism.* Ithaca: Cornell University Press, 1992.

Castro Klarén, Sara. *El mundo mágico de José María Arguedas.* Lima: Instituto de Estudios Peruanos, 1973.

Chabram, Angie. "I Throw Punches for My Race, but I Don't Want to Be a Man: Writing Us—Chica-nos (Girl, Us)/Chicanas—into the Movement Script." In *Cultural Studies,* edited by Lawrence Grossberg, Cary Nelson, and Paula Treichler. New York: Routledge, 1992.

Chang-Rodríquez, Raquel. *La apropiación del signo: Tres cronistas indígenas del Perú.* Pempe, Arizona: Center for Latin American Studies, 1988.

————. *El discurso disidente: Ensayos de literatura colonial peruana.* Lima: Fondo Editorial de la Pontificia Universidad Católica del Perú, 1991.

————. *Violencia y subversión en la prosa colonial hispanoamericana, siglos XVI y XVII.* Madrid: Studia Humanitatis, 1982.

Child, Heather, and Dorothy Colles. *Christian Symbols.* London: G. Bell and Sons, 1971.

Clifford, James. *The Predicament of Culture: Twentieth-Century Ethnography, Literature, and Art.* Cambridge: Harvard University Press, 1988.

Clifford, James, and George E. Marcus, eds. *Writing Culture: The Poetics and Politics of Ethnography.* Berkeley: University of California Press, 1986.

Cobo, Father Bernabé. *Inca Religion and Customs.* Edited and translated by Roland Hamilton. Austin: University of Texas Press, 1990.

Community Gallery of Art, The. *Cuzco and Before: An Exhibition of Latin American Colonial Art, February 28–April 17.* Exh. cat. Gainesville, Florida: Santa Fe Community College, 1983.

Cornejo Polar, Antonio. *La formación de la tradición literaria en el Perú.* Lima: Centro de Estudios y Publicaciones, 1989.

————. "Heterogeneidad y contradicción en la literatura andina. (Tres incidentes en la contienda entre oralidad y escritura.)" In *Nuevo Texto Crítico* 5, no. 9/10 (1992).

————. *Literatura y sociedad en el Perú: La novela indigenista.* Lima: Lasontay, 1980.

————. *La Novela Peruana.* Lima: Editorial Horizonte, 1989.

————. *Sobre literatura y crítica latinoamericanas.* Caracas: Ediciones de la Facultad de Humanidades y Educación, Universidad Central de Venezuela, 1982.

————. *Los universos narrativos de José María Arguedas.* Buenos Aires: Editorial Losada, 1973.

————. *Vigencia y universalidad de José María Arguedas.* The publication of a roundtable in which Antonio Cornejo Polar, Alberto Escobar, Martin Lienhard, and William Rowe took part. (Lima: Editorial Horizonte, 1984).

Cortés, Hernán. *Cartas de relación.* Edited by Mario Hernández. Madrid: Historia 16, 1985.

Cossio del Pomar, Felipe. *Peruvian Colonial Art: The Cuzco School of Painting.* Translated by Genaro Arbaiza. New York: Wittenborn, 1964.

Covarrubias, Sebastián de. *Tesoro de la lengua Castellana, o Española.* Madrid, 1674.

Curtius, Ernest Robert. *European Literature and the Latin Middle Ages.* Translated by Willard R. Trask. New York: Pantheon, 1953.

Damian, Carol. "The Survival of Inca Symbolism in Representations of the Virgin in Colonial Perú." *Athanor* 7 (1988).

de Campos, Haroldo. "Tradición, traducción, transculturación: Historiografía y excentricidad." Translated by Néstor Perlongher. *Filología* 22, no. 2 (1987).

de Ceballos, Rodríguez G. "Las *Imágenes de la historia evangélica* del P. Jerónimo Nadal en el marco del jesuitismo y la Contrarreforma." In *Imágenes de la historia evangélica,* by P. Jerónimo Nadal. Barcelona: Ediciones El Albir, 1975.

de Estete, Miguel. *El descubrimiento y la conquista del Perú.* Quito: Universidad Central, 1918.

de Herrera, Antonio. *Historia General de los Hechos de los Castellanos.* Madrid: 1728.

de Lavalle, José Antonio, and Werner Lang, eds. *Pintura Virreynal.* Lima: Banco de Crédito del Perú, 1973.

de Mesa, José, and Teresa Gisbert. *Historia de la pintura cuzqueña.* Lima: Fundación Augusto N. Wiese, 1982.

————. "Lo indígena en al arte hispanoamericano." *Boletín del Centro de Investigaciones Históricas y Estéticas* (Caracas: Universidad Central de Venezuela) 12 (November 1971).

Deleuze, Gilles, and Félix Guattari. *Anti-Oedipus: Capitalism and Schizophrenia.* Translated by Robert Hurley, Mark Seem, and Helen R. Lane. Minneapolis: Minnesota University Press, [1972] 1986.

Depestre, René. "Les aspects créateurs du métissage culturel aux Caraïbes." *Notre Librairie,* April–June 1984.

Díaz del Castillo, Bernal. *Historia verdadera de la conquista de la Nueva España.* Edited by Joaquín Ramírez Cabañas. Mexico City: Porrúa, 1966.

————. *Para una teoria de la literatura hispanoamericana y otras aproximaciones.* Havana: Casa de las Américas, 1975.

Didron, Adolphe Napoleon. *Christian Iconography: The History of Christian Art in the Middle Ages.* Translated by E. J. Millington. New York: Frederick Ungar, 1968.

Douglas, Mary. *Purity and Danger: An Analysis of the Concepts of Pollution and Taboo.* London: Ark, [1966] 1985.

Duncan, Barbara. "Statue Paintings of the Virgin." In *Gloria in Excelsis: The Virgin and the Angels in Viceregal Painting of Peru and Bolivia.* New York: Center for Inter-American Relations, 1986.

Duncan, Cynthia. "La culpa es de los Tlaxcaltecas: A Reevaluation of Mexico's Past through Myth." *Crítica Hispánica* 2, no. 2 (1985).

Duviols, Pierre. *La lutte contre les religions autochtones dans le Pérou colonial: L'extirpation de l'idolatrie entre 1532 et 1660.* Lima: Institut Français d'Etudes Andines, 1971.

Echevarría, Roberto González. *Alejo Carpentier: The Pilgrim at Home.* Austin: University of Texas Press, 1977.

Eliade, Mircea. *Shamanism: Archaic Techniques of Ecstasy.* Translated by Willard R. Trask. New Jersey: Princeton University Press, [1951] 1974.

Epple, Juan. "Literatura Chicana y crítica literaria." *Ideologies and Literature* 16 (1983).

Escobar, Alberto. *Arguedas o la utopía de la lengua.* Lima: Instituto de Estudios Peruanos, 1984.

Fanon, Frantz. *The Wretched of the Earth.* Translated by Constance Farrington. New York: Grove Press, [1961] 1968.

Flores, Juan. *Divided Borders: Essays on Puerto Rican Identity.* Houston: Arte Público Press, 1993.

Flores Galindo, Alberto. *Buscando un Inca: Identidad y utopía en los Andes.* Lima: Ediciones Horizonte, 1988.

Forbes, Jack D. "The Hispanic Spin: Party Politics and Governmental Manipulation of Ethnic Identity." *Latin American Perspectives* 75, vol. 19, no. 4 (fall 1992).

Forgues, Roland. *José María Arguedas: Del pensamiento dialéctico al pensamiento trágico.* Lima: Editorial Horizonte, 1989.

Foucault, Michel. *The Order of Things.* New York: Vintage, 1973.

————. *Power/Knowledge.* Edited and translated by Colin Gordon. New York: Pantheon Books, [1972] 1980.

Franco, Jean. *A Literary History of Spain: Spanish American Literature Since Independence.* New York: Barnes and Noble Books, 1973.

———. "The Nation as Imagined Community." In *The New Historicism,* edited by H. Aram Veeser. New York: Routledge, 1989.

———. *Plotting Women.* New York: Columbia University Press, 1989.

Freire, Paulo. *La educación como práctica de la libertad.* Mexico City: Siglo Veintiuno, [1969] 1986.

Fuentes, Rumel. "Corridos de Rumel." *El Grito* 3 (spring 1973).

Galarza, Joaquín. *Lienzos de Chiepetlán.* Mexico City: Mission Archeologique et Ethnologique Française au Méxique, 1972.

García Canclini, Néstor. *Las culturas populares en el capitalismo.* Havana: Casa de las Américas, 1982.

———. "Escenas sin territorio: Estética de las migraciones e identidades en transición." *Revista de Crítica Cultural* 1, no. 1 (May 1990).

Garcilaso de la Vega, Inca. *Comentarios reales.* Caracas: Biblioteca Ayacucho, 1985.

Garro, Elena. *La casa junto al río.* Barcelona: Editorial Grijalbo, 1983.

———. "La culpa es de los Tlaxcaltecas." In *La semana de colores.* Xalapa, Mexico: Universidad Veracruzana, 1964.

———. "A mí me ha ocurrido todo al revés." *Cuadernos Hispanoamericanos* 346 (April 1979).

———. *Los recuerdos del porvenir.* Mexico City: Mortiz, 1977.

———. *Testimonios sobre Mariana.* Mexico City: Editorial Grijalbo, 1981.

Gasparini, Graziano. "La ciudad colonial como centro de irradiación de las escuelas arquitectónicas y pictóricas." *Boletín del Centro de Investigaciones Históricas y Estéticas* (Caracas: Universidad Central de Venezuela) 14 (September 1972).

———. "Opiniones sobre pintura colonial." *Boletín del Centro de Investigaciones Históricas y Estéticas* (Caracas: Universidad Central de Venezuela) 8 (October 1967).

———. "Los techos con armadura de pares y nudillos en las construcciones coloniales venezolanas." *Boletín del Centro de Investigaciones Históricas y Estéticas* (Caracas: Universidad Central de Venezuela) 1 (1964).

Gisbert, Teresa. "The Andean Gods throughout Christianity." In *Temples of Gold, Crowns of Silver: Reflections of Majesty in the Viceregal Americas,* exh. cat., curated by Barbara von Barghahn. Washington, D.C.: Art Museum of the Americas, 1991.

———. *Gloria in Excelsis: The Virgin and the Angels in Viceregal Painting in Peru and Bolivia.* New York: Center for Inter-American Relations, 1986.

———. *Iconografía y mitos indígenas en el arte.* La Paz: Gisbert y Cía, 1980.

Gómez-Peña, Guillermo. "Death on the Border: A Eulogy to Border Art." *High Performance* 53 (spring 1991).

———. "From Art-Maggedon to Gringo-Stroika." *High Performance* 55 (fall 1991).

———. "The Multicultural Paradigm: An Open Letter to the National Arts Community." *High Performance* 47 (fall 1989).

González S., Beatriz. "Narrativa de la 'estabilización' colonial: *Peregrinación de Bartolomé Lorenzo* (1586) de José de Acosta, *Infortunios de Alonso Ramírez* (1960) de Carlos Sigüenza y Góngora." *Ideologies and Literature* 2, no. 1 (spring 1987).

Grizzard, Mary. "Four Eighteenth-Century *Mestizo* Paintings from Cuzco." *University of New Mexico Art Museum Bulletin* 13 (1980–81).

Gruzinski, Serge. *L'Amérique de la conquête: Peinté par les Indiens du Méxique*. Paris: Unesco/Flammarion, 1991.

Guillén, Nicolás. *Sóngoro Consongo. Motivos de son. West Indies ltd. España, poema en cuatro angustias y una esperanza*. Buenos Aires: Losada, 1975.

Hall, Stuart. "Cultural Identity and Diaspora." In *Identity, Community, Culture, Difference*, edited by J. Rutherford. London: Lawrence and Wishart, 1990.

Harrison, Regina. *Signs, Songs, and Memory in the Andes: Translating Quechua Language and Literature*. Houston: University of Texas Press, 1989.

Harth-Terré, Emilio. *Las figuras parlantes en la arquitectura mestiza de arequipeña*. Lima: Editorial Universitaria, 1974.

————. *Por una arquitectura contemporánea que sea nuestra*. Lima: VI Congreso Panamericano de Arquitectos, 1947.

————. "Resumen histórico de la arquitectura peruana." In *La arquitectura peruana a través de los siglos. Circulación internacional* (Lima: Publicaciones Emisa), October 1964.

Herrera-Sobek, María. *The Mexican Corrido: A Feminist Analysis*. Bloomington and Indianapolis: Indiana University Press, 1990.

Horkheimer, Max, and Theodor Adorno. *Dialectic of Enlightenment*. Translated by John Cumming. New York: Seabury, [1944] 1972.

Horno-Delgado, Asunción, Eliana Ortega, Nina M. Scott, and Nancy Saporta Sternbach, eds. *Breaking Boundaries: Latina Writings and Critical Readings*. Amherst: University of Massachusetts Press, 1989.

Howes, Graham. "Religious Art and Religious Belief." *New Blackfriars* 17 (April–May, 1986).

Hunter, David, ed. *Encyclopedia of Anthropology*. New York: Harper and Row, 1976.

Hurtado, Aída, and Carlos H. Arce. "Mexicans, Chicanos, Mexican Americans, or Pochos . . . ¿Qué somos? The Impact of Language and Nativity on Ethnic Labeling." *Aztlán* 17, no. 1 (1987).

*International Dictionary of Regional European Ethnology and Folklore*. Vol. 1. Copenhagen: Rosenkilde and Bagger, 1960.

Jákfalvi-Leiva, Susana. *Traducción, escritura y violencia colonizadora: Un estudio de la obra del Inca Garcilaso*. Syracuse: Maxwell School of Citizenship and Public Affairs, 1984.

Jameson, Fredric. "Third-World Literature in the Era of Multinational Capitalism." *Social Text* 15 (fall 1986).

Jara, René, and Nicholas Spadaccini, eds. *1492–1992: Re/Discovering Colonial Writing*. Minneapolis: Prisma Institute, 1989.

Keleman, Pál. *Art of the Americas, Ancient and Hispanic*. New York: Thomas Y. Crowell, 1969.

Kintz, Linda. *The Subject's Tragedy*. Ann Arbor: University of Michigan Press, 1992.

Kristeva, Julia. *The Powers of Horror: An Essay on Abjection*. Translated by Leon S. Roudiez. New York: Columbia University Press, 1982.

————. *Revolution in Poetic Language*. Translated by Margaret Waller. New York: Columbia University Press, 1984.

Kubler, George. "Indianismo y mestizaje como tradiciones americanas medievales y clásicas." Translated by Jacinto Quirarte. *Boletín del Centro de Investigaciones Históricas y Estéticas* (Caracas: Universidad Central de Venezuela) 4 (1965).

Lancaster, Roger. "Festival of Disguises." *Inscriptions* (Santa Cruz, California: Group for the Critical Study of Colonial Discourse at the University of California at Santa Cruz) 2 (1986).

Lara, Jesús. "El teatro en el Tawantinsuyu." In *Literatura de la Emancipación Hispanoamericana y otros ensayos*. Lima: Universidad Nacional Mayor de San Marcos, 1972.

Larco, Juan, ed. *Recopilación de textos sobre José María Arguedas*. Havana: Casa de las Américas, 1986.

Leal, Luis. *Aztlán y México: Perfiles literarios e históricos*. Binghamton: Bilingual Press, 1985.

Leonard, Irving A. *Books of the Brave*. Cambridge: Harvard University Press, 1949.

Lienhard, Martin. *Cultura andina y forma novelesca: Zorros y danzantes en la última novela de Arguedas*. Lima: Editorial Horizonte, 1990.

Limón, José E. "Dancing with the Devil: Society, Gender, and the Political Unconscious in the Mexican-American South." In *Criticism in the Borderlands: Studies in Chicano Literature, Culture, and Ideology*, edited by Héctor Calderón and José David Saldívar. Durham: Duke University Press, 1991.

Lionnet, Françoise. *Autobiographical Voices: Race, Gender, Self-Portraiture*. Ithaca: Cornell University Press, 1989.

Liungman, Carl G. *Dictionary of Symbols*. Santa Barbara: ABC-CLIO, 1991.

Llubera, González, ed. *Gramática de la lengua castellana, o española*. London: Oxford University Press, 1926.

Lopez de Gómara, Francisco. *La conquista de México*. Edited by José Luis de Rojas. Madrid: Historia 16, 1987.

López-Baralt, Mercedes. *Icono y conquista: Guamán Poma de Ayala*. Madrid: Hiperión, 1988.

———. *El retorno del Inca Rey*. La Paz: HISBOL, 1989.

Lorde, Audre. *Apartheid U.S.A.* New York: Kitchen Table Press, Women of Color Press, 1986.

Lucio, Oscar Colchado. *Cordillera Negra*. Lima: Lluvia Editores, 1985.

———. *Hacia el janaq pacha*. Lima: Lluvia Editores, 1988.

MacCormack, Sabine. "Children of the Sun and Reason of State: Myths, Ceremonies, and Conflicts in Inca Peru." In *1992 Lecture Series: Working Papers No. 6*. College Park, Maryland: University of Maryland, Department of Spanish and Portuguese, 1992.

———. "Demons, Imagination, and the Incas," *Representations* 33 (winter 1991).

Malinowski, Bronislaw. Introduction to *Contrapunteo cubano del tabaco y el azúcar,* by Fernando Ortiz. Havana: J. Montero, 1940.

Manguel, Alberto, ed. and trans. *Other Fires: Short Fiction by Latin American Women*. New York: Clarkson N. Potter, Inc., 1986.

Mariátegui, José Carlos. *7 ensayos de interpretación de la realidad peruana*. Lima: Amauta, 1981.

————. *Seven Interpretive Essays on Peruvian Reality.* Translated by Marjory Urquidi. Austin: University of Texas Press, 1971.

Mariátegui Oliva, Ricardo. *Pintura cuzqueña del siglo XVII: Los maravillosos lienzos del Corpus existentes en la Iglesia de Santa Ana del Cuzco.* Lima: Alma Mater, 1951.

————. *Pintura cuzqueña del siglo XVII en Chile.* Lima: Alma Mater, 1954.

Marin, Gladys C. *La experiencia americana de José María Arguedas.* Buenos Aires: F. García Cambeiro, 1973.

Martínez Amador, Emilio M. *Standard English-Spanish and Spanish-English Dictionary.* Barcelona: Editorial Sopena, 1958.

Marzal, Manuel M. *El sincretismo iberoamericano.* Lima: Pontificia Universidad Católica del Perú, 1988.

Mendieta y Nuñez, Lucio. *Los Tarascos: Monografía histórica, etnográfica y económica.* Mexico City: Imprenta Universitaria, 1940.

Meneses, Teodoro L., ed. *Usca Paucar: Drama Quechua del siglo XVIII.* Lima: Biblioteca de la Sociedad Peruana de Historia, 1951.

Messinger Cypess, Sandra. "The Figure of La Malinche in the Texts of Elena Garro." In *A Different Reality: Studies on the Work of Elena Garro,* edited by Anita K. Stoll. Lewisburg: Bucknell University Press, 1990.

————. *La Malinche in Mexican Literature: From History to Myth.* Austin: University of Texas Press, 1991.

————. "Visual and Verbal Distances in Mexican Theatre: The Plays of Elena Garro." In *Woman as Myth and Metaphor in Latin American Literature,* edited by Carmelo Virgillo and Naomi Lindstrom. Columbia: University of Missouri Press, 1985.

Mignolo, Walter. "Cartas, crónicas y relaciones del descubrimiento y la conquista." In *Historia de la literatura hispanoamericana: Epoca colonial, Tomo I,* edited by Luis Iñigo Madrigal. Madrid: Ediciones Cátedra, 1982.

————. "Literacy and Colonization: The New World Experience." In *1492–1992: Re/Discovering Colonial Writing,* edited by René Jara and Nicholas Spadaccini. Minneapolis: Prisma Institute, 1989.

Miles, Margaret R. *Image as Insight: Visual Understanding in Western Christianity and Secular Culture.* Boston: Beacon Press, 1985.

Miller, Beth, and Alfonso González, eds. *26 autoras del México actual.* Mexico City: Costa-Amic, 1978.

Minc, Rose S., ed. *Literatures in Transition: The Many Voices of the Caribbean Area.* Gaithersburg, Maryland: Hispamerica and Monclair State College, 1982.

Mint Museum of Art. *Splendors of the New World.* Exh. cat. Curated by Charles L. Mo. Charlotte: Mint Museum of Art, 1992.

Moraga, Cherríe, ed. *Loving in the War Years: Lo que nunca pasó por sus labios.* Boston: South End Press, 1983.

Moraga, Cherríe, and Gloria Anzaldúa, eds. *This Bridge Called My Back: Writings by Radical Women of Color.* Watertown: Persephone Press, 1981.

Morejón, Nancy. *Nación y Mestizaje en Nicolás Guillén.* Havana: Ediciones Unión, 1982.

Motolinía, Fray Toribio de Benavente. *Historia de los indios de la Nueva España.* Edited by Giuseppe Bellini. Madrid: Alianza Editorial, 1988.

Muñoz, Silverio. *José María Arguedas y el mito de la salvación por la cultura.* Minneapolis: Instituto para el Estudio de Ideologías y Literatura, 1980.

Murúa, Fray Martín de. *Historia general del Perú, origen y descendencia de los Incas . . .* Edited by Manuel Ballesteros-Gaibrois. Madrid: Instituto Gonzalo Fernández de Oviedo, 1962.

Nash, June. "The Aztecs and the Ideology of Male Dominance." *Signs: Journal of Women in Culture and Society* 4, no. 2 (1978).

Newcomb, W. W., Jr. "Karankawa." In *Handbook of North American Indians,* edited by William C. Sturtevant. *Southwest,* edited by Alfonso Ortiz. Washington: Smithsonian Institution, 1983.

*Nuevo Texto Crítico* 5, no. 9/10, "Caliban en Sassari" issue (1992).

O'Gorman, Edmundo. *La invención, el universalismo de la cultura de occidente.* Mexico City: Fondo de Cultura Económica, 1958.

———. *The Invention of America: An Inquiry into the Historical Nature of the New World and the Meaning of Its History.* Westport: Greenwood, 1961.

Oboler, Suzanne. *Labeling the "Other Hispanics": Latin American Immigrants and the Dynamics of Race, Class, Language, and National Origins.* Minnesota: University of Minnesota Press, 1995.

———. "The Politics of Labeling: Latino/a Cultural Identities of Self and Others." *Latin American Perspectives* 75, vol. 19, no. 4 (fall 1992).

Ordóñez, Elizabeth J. "The Concept of Cultural Identity in Chicana Poetry." *Third Woman* 2, no. 1 (1984).

———. "Sexual Politics and the Theme of Sexuality in Chicana Poetry." In *Women in Hispanic Literature: Icons and Idols,* edited by Beth Miller. Berkeley: University of California Press, 1983.

Ortega, Julio. "Discurso del suicidio." *Anthropos: Revista de Documentación Científica de la Cultura* 128 (January 1992).

———. *La imaginación crítica: Ensayos sobre la modernidad en el Perú.* Lima: Ediciones PEISA, 1974.

———. "Postmodernism in Latin America." In *Postmodern Fiction in Europe and the Americas,* edited by Theo D'haen and Hans Bertens. Amsterdam: Rodopi, 1988.

———. *Texto, comunicación y cultura:* Los ríos profundos *de José María Arguedas.* Lima: Centro de Estudios para el Desarrollo y la Participación (cedep), 1982.

Ortego, Philip D. "Redefinición de la literatura norteamericana." In *Aztlán: Historia contemporánea del pueblo chicano,* edited by David Maciel and Patricia Bueno. Mexico City: Sep/Setentas, 1976.

Ortiz, Fernando. *Contrapunteo cubano del tabaco y el azúcar.* Havana: J. Montero, 1940.

———. *Cuban Counterpoint: Tobacco and Sugar.* Translated by Harriet de Onis. New York: A. A. Knopf, 1947.

Ossio, Juan M., ed. *Ideología mesiánica del mundo andino.* Lima: Edición de Ignacio Prado Pastor, 1973.

Pacheco, Carlos. "Trastierra y oralidad en la ficción de los transculturadores." *Revista de Crítica Literaria Latinoamericana* 15, no. 29 (1989).

Palm, Erwin Walter. "La ciudad colonial como centro de irradiación de la escuelas arquitectónicas y pictoricas." *Boletín del Centro de Investigaciones Históricas y Estéticas* (Caracas: Universidad Central de Venezuela) 14 (September 1972).

Pané, Fray Ramón. *Relación acerca de las antigüedades de los indios.* Edited by José Juan Arrom. Mexico City: Siglo Veintiuno, 1988.

Paredes, Raymond A. "The Evolution of Chicano Literature." In *Three American Literatures,* edited by Houston A. Baker, Jr. New York: MLA, 1982.

Park, Willard E. *Shamanism in Western North America: A Study in Cultural Relationships.* Evanston: Northwestern University, 1938.

Pastor, Beatriz. *The Armature of Conquest: Spanish Accounts of the Discovery of America, 1492–1589.* Translated by Lydia Longstreth Hunt. Stanford: Stanford University Press, 1992.

———. *Discursos narrativos de la conquista: Mitificación y emergencia.* Hanover: Ediciones del Norte, [1983] 1988.

Paz, Octavio. *El laberinto de la soledad. Posdata. Vuelta al laberinto de la soledad.* Mexico City: Fondo de Cultura Económica, 1981.

———. *The Labyrinth of Solitude: Life and Thought in Mexico.* Translated by Lysander Kemp. New York: Grove Press, Inc., 1961.

Pease, Franklin. "El mito de Inkarrí y la visión de los vencidos." In *Ideología mesiánica del mundo andino,* edited by Juan M. Ossio. Lima: Edición de Ignacio Prado Pastor, 1973.

———. *Los últimos Incas del Cuzco.* Lima: P. L. Villanueva, [1972] 1981.

Peñalosa, Fernando. "Chicano Multilingualism and Multiglossia." *Aztlán* 3, no. 2 (1972).

Pérez Firmat, Gustavo. *The Cuban Condition: Translation and Identity in Modern Cuban Literature.* Cambridge: Cambridge University Press, 1989.

———. "From Ajiaco to Tropical Soup: Fernando Ortiz and the Definition of Cuban Culture." Paper published as Dialogue #93. Miami: Latin American and Caribbean Center, Florida International University, 1987.

———. "Life on the Hyphen." Lecture delivered at Pomona College, November 1992.

———. "Transcending Exile: Cuban-American Literature Today." Paper published as Dialogue #92. Miami: Latin American and Caribbean Center, Florida International University, 1987.

———, ed. *Do the Americas Have a Common Literature?* Durham: Duke University Press, 1990.

Philips, Rachel. "Marina/Malinche: Masks and Shadows." In *Women in Hispanic Literature: Icons and Idols,* edited by Beth Miller. Berkeley: University of California Press, 1983.

Platt, Tristan. "The Andean Soldiers of Christ: Confraternity Organization, the Mass of the Sun, and Regenerative Warfare in Rural Potosí (18th–20th Centuries)." *Journal de la Société des Américanistes* 73 (1987).

Podestá, Guido A. "La deconstrucción de Lima." *Ideologies and Literature* 3, no. 1 (spring 1988).

Polo de Ondegardo. *Informaciones acerca de la religión y gobierno de los Incas*. Lima: Sanmartí y Ca., [1571] 1916.

———. *Narratives of the Rites and Laws of the Incas*. Translated by Sir Robert Clements Markham. London: Hakluyt Society, 1873.

———. *Tratado y averiguación*. Lima, 1584.

Poma de Ayala, Felipe Guamán. *Nueva corónica y buen gobierno*. Edited by Rolena Adorno and Jorge L. Urioste. Madrid: Historia 16, 1987.

———. *Nueva corónica y buen gobierno*. Edited and translated by Franklin Pease. Caracas: Biblioteca Ayacucho, 1980.

Portilla, Miguel León. *Literaturas de Mesoamerica*. Mexico City: Secretaría de Educación Pública, 1984.

———. *El reverso de la conquista*, Mexico City: Editorial Jaquín Mortiz, [1964] 1989.

*Primer Encuentro de Narradores Peruanos*. Casa de la Cultura del Perú. Lima: Latinoamericana Editores, 1986.

Puga, María Luisa. *Pánica o peligro*. Mexico City: Siglo Veintiuno, 1983.

Pupo-Walker, Enrique. "Pesquisas para una nueva lectura de los *Naufragios*, de Álvar Núñez Cabeza de Vaca." *Revista Iberoamericana* 140 (1987).

Rama, Angel. *La ciudad letrada*. Hanover: Ediciones del Norte, 1984.

———. *Transculturación narrativa en América Latina*. Mexico City: Siglo Veintiuno, [1982] 1985.

Réau, Louis. *Iconographie de l'Art Chrétien*. Paris: Presses Universitaires de France, 1955.

Rendón, Armando B. "The People of Aztlán." In *Introduction to Chicano Studies*, edited by Livie Isauro Durán and H. Russell Bernard. New York: Macmillan, 1973.

Rescaniere, Alejandro Ortiz. *De Adaneva a Inkarrí: Una visión indígena del Perú*. Lima: Ediciones Retablo de Papel, 1973.

Retamar, Roberto Fernández. *Calibán: Apuntes sobre la cultura de nuestra América*. Buenos Aires: Editorial La Pleyade, 1973.

Reyes, Alfonso. "Los autos sacramentales en España y América." In *Capítulos de literatura española*, by Alfonso Reyes. Mexico City: El Colegio de México, 1945.

Rich, Adrienne. *On Lies, Secrets, and Silence: Selected Prose 1966–1978*. New York: Norton, 1979.

Ripa, Cesare. *Baroque and Rococo Pictorial Imagery: The 1758–60 Hertel Edition of Ripa's "Iconologia" with 200 Engraved Illustrations*. Edited by Edward A. Maser. New York: Dover Publications, 1971.

Robles, Martha. *La Sombra Fugitiva: Escritoras en la Cultura Nacional*. Mexico City: Editorial Diana, 1989.

Rodenas, Adriana Méndez. "Tiempo femenino, tiempo ficticio: *Los recuerdos del porvenir* de Elena Garro." *Revista Iberoamericana* 51, no. 132–3 (1985).

———. "Tradition and Women's Writing: Towards a Poetics of Difference." In *Engendering the Word: Feminist Essays in Psychosexual Poetics*, edited by Temma F. Berg. Urbana: University of Illinois Press, 1989.

Rodó, José Enrique. *Ariel*. Madrid: Espasa-Calpe, [1948] 1975.

Rojas-Trempe, Lady. "El estado en 'Las cabezas bien pensantes' de Elena Garro."

In *Coloquio de estudios de la mujer: Encuentro de talleres.* Mexico City: El Colegio de México, 1987.

Rostworowski, María. "Presentación." In *Ritos y tradiciones de Huarochirí del siglo XVII,* edited and translated by Gerald Taylor. Lima: Instituto de Estudios Peruanos and Instituto Francés de Estudios Andinos, 1987.

———. *Señoríos indígenas de Lima y Canta.* Lima: Instituto de Estudios Peruanos, 1978.

Rotsman, Ruth Gubler. "La labor misional en Yucatán en el siglo XVI." In *Identidad y transformación de las Américas,* compiled by Elizabeth Reichel. Publication of the 45th International Congress of Americanists. Bogotá: Ediciones Uniandes, 1988.

Rowe, John Howland. "Colonial Portraits of Inca Nobles." In *Civilizations of Ancient America: Selected Papers of the XXIX International Congress of Americanists,* edited by Sol Tax. New York: Cooper Square, 1967.

Rowe, William. *Mito e Ideología en la obra de José María Arguedas.* Lima: Instituto Nacional de Cultura, 1979.

Rowe, William, and Vivian Schelling. *Memory and Modernity: Popular Culture in Latin America.* London: Verso, 1991.

Salazar Parr, Carmen. "Narrative Technique in the Prose Fiction of Elena Garro." Ph.D. diss., University of Southern California, 1978.

Saldívar, José David. *The Dialectics of Our America: Genealogy, Cultural Critique, and Literary History.* Durham: Duke University Press, 1991.

Sallnow, Michael J. *Pilgrims of the Andes: Regional Cults in Cusco.* Washington, D.C.: Smithsonian Institution, [1949] 1987.

Sandoval, Alberto. "A Chorus Line: Not Such a 'One, Singular Sensation' for Puerto Rican Crossovers." *Ollantay* 1, no. 1 (January, 1993).

———. "Dolores Prida's *Coser y cantar:* Mapping the Dialectics of Ethnic Identity and Assimilation." In *Breaking Boundaries: Latina Writings and Critical Readings,* edited by Asunción Horno-Delgado, Eliana Ortega, Nina M. Scott, and Nancy Saporta Sternbach. Amherst: University of Massachusetts Press, 1989.

———. "Una lectura puertorriqueña de la America de West Side Story. *Cupey: Revista de la Universidad Metropolitana* 7, no. 1 (January–December 1990).

Sarmiento de Gamboa, Pedro. *Historia de los Incas.* Madrid: Miraguano Ediciones and Ediciones Polifemo, 1988.

Showalter, Elaine. "Feminist Criticism in the Wilderness." *Critical Inquiry* 8, no. 2 (1981).

———. *A Literature of Their Own: British Women Novelists from Brontë to Lessing.* Princeton: Princeton University Press, 1977.

Silverblatt, Irene. "Political Memories and Colonizing Symbols: Santiago and the Mountain Gods of Colonial Peru." In *Rethinking History and Myth: Indigenous South American Perspectives on the Past,* edited by Jonathan D. Hill. Urbana: University of Illinois Press, 1988.

Silverman, Kaja. *The Subject of Semiotics.* New York: Oxford University Press, 1983.

Skidmore, Thomas E. "Racial Issues and Social Policy in Brazil, 1870–1940." In *The Idea of Race in Latin America, 1870–1940,* edited by Richard Graham. Austin: University of Texas Press, 1990.

Sommer, Doris. "Not Just a Personal Story: Women's *Testimonios* and the Plural Self." In *Life/Lines: Theoretical Essays on Women's Autobiography,* edited by Celeste Schenk and Bella Brodski. Ithaca: Cornell University Press, 1989.

Sommers, Joseph, and Tomás Ybarra-Frausto. *Modern Chicano Writers: A Collection of Critical Essays.* Englewood Cliffs, New Jersey: Prentice Hall, 1979.

Sosnowski, Saúl, ed. *Augusto Roa Bastos y la producción cultural americana.* Buenos Aires: Ediciones de la Flor, 1986.

————. "Crítica literaria hispanoamericana en Estados Unidos: Visiones desde la periferia." *Revista de Crítica Literaria Latinoamericana* 16, no. 31–32 (1990).

————. "Sobre la crítica de la literatura hispanoamericana: Balance y perspectivas." *Cuadernos Hispanoamericanos: Revista Mensual de Cultura Hispánica,* May 1987.

Spalding, Karen. *Huarochirí: An Andean Society under Inca and Spanish Rule.* Stanford: Stanford University Press, 1984.

Spivak, Gayatri. *In Other Worlds: Essays in Cultural Politics.* New York: Methuen, 1987.

Stastny, Francisco. "¿Un arte mestizo?" In *América Latina en sus artes,* edited by Damián Bayón. Mexico City: Siglo Veintiuno, 1974.

————. "The Cuzco School of Painting: A Gothic Revival." *Connoisseur,* May 1975.

————. *El Manierismo en la pintura colonial latinoamericana.* Lima: Universidad Nacional Mayor de San Marcos, 1981.

Steele, Cynthia. "Entrevista con Elena Poniatowska." *Hispamérica* 53–54 (1989).

————. "Indigenismo y postmodernidad: Narrativa indigenista, testimonio, teatro campesino y video en el Chiapas finisecular. *Revista de Crítica Literaria Latinoamericana* 19, no. 30 (1993).

————. "The Other Within: Class and Ethnicity as Difference in Mexican Women's Literature." In *Cultural and Historical Grounding for Hispanic and Luso-Brazilian Feminist Literary Criticism,* edited by Hernán Vidal. Minneapolis: Institute for the Study of Ideologies and Literature, 1989.

————. *Politics, Gender, and the Mexican Novel, 1969–1988: Beyond the Pyramid.* Austin: University of Texas Press, 1992.

————. "Testimonio y autoridad en *Hasta no verte Jesus mío* de Elena Poniatowska." *Revista de Crítica Literaria Latinoamericana* 18, no. 36 (1992).

Suleiman, Susan Rubin. "Pornography, Transgression, and the Avant-Garde: Bataille's *Story of the Eye.*" In *The Poetics of Gender,* edited by Nancy Miller. New York: Columbia University Press, 1986.

Tafolla, Carmen. *To Split a Human: Mitos, Machos y la Mujer Chicana.* Texas: Mexican American Cultural Center, 1985.

Taussig, Michael. *Shamanism, Colonialism, and the Wild Man: A Study in Terror and Healing.* Chicago: University of Chicago Press, 1987.

Todorov, Tzvetan. *La conquête de l'Amérique: La Question de l'Autre.* Paris: Seuil, 1982.

Tord, Luis Enrique. "La pintura virreinato en el Cusco." In *Pintura en el virreinato del Perú,* by Luis Enrique Tord. Lima: Banco de Crédito del Perú, 1989.

Toro Montalvo, César. *Historia de la literatura peruana.* Lima: Editorial San Marcos, 1991.

————. *Literatura Peruana: Inca y Colonial.* Lima: Editorial San Marcos, 1989.

Triviños Araneda, Gilberto. "Los relatos colombinos." *Ideologies and Literature* 3 (1988).

Umpierre, Luz María. "La ansiedad de la influencia en Sandra María Esteves y Marjorie Agosin." *Revista Chicano-Riqueña* 3–4, vol. 11 (1983).

———. *En el país de las maravillas.* Bloomington: Third Woman Press, 1982.

University of Iowa Museum of Art. *The Art of the Shaman: Northwest Indians.* Exh. cat. Iowa City: University of Iowa Museum of Art, 1973.

Urrello, Antonio. *José María Arguedas, el nuevo rostro del indio: Una estructura mítico-poética.* Lima: Librería Editorial J. Mejía Baca, 1974.

Valdez, Luis, and Stan Steiner, eds. *Aztlán: An Anthology of Mexican American Literature.* New York: Alfred Knopf, 1973.

Vargas Llosa, Mario. *José María Arguedas, entre sapos y halcones.* Madrid: Ediciones Cultura Hispánica del Centro Iberoamericano de Cooperación, 1978.

———. "Novela primitiva y novela de creación en América Latina." *Revista de la Universidad Nacional Autónoma de México* 23, no. 10 (June 1969): 29–36.

Verger, Pierre. *Fiestas y danzas en el Cuzco y en los Andes.* Buenos Aires: Editorial Sudamericana, 1945.

Vidal, Hernán. *Socio-historia de la literatura colonial hispanoamericana: Tres lecturas orgánicas.* Minneapolis: Institute for the Study of Ideologies and Literature, 1985.

Viola, Herman J., and Carolyn Margolis, eds. *Seeds of Change: Five Hundred Years Since Columbus.* Washington: Smithsonian Institution Press, 1991.

Wachtel, Nathan. *La vision des vaincus: Les Indiens du Pérou devant la Conquête espagnole 1530–1570.* Paris: Gallimard, 1971.

Weddle, Robert S. *Spanish Sea: The Gulf of Mexico in North American Discovery, 1500–1685.* College Station: Texas A&M University Press, 1985.

Wey-Gómez, Nicolás. "¿Dónde está Garcilaso?: La oscilación del sujeto colonial en la formación de un discurso transcultural." *Revista de Crítica Literaria Latinoamericana* 17, no. 34 (2nd semester, 1991).

White, Hayden. "The Historical Text as Literary Artifact." In *Tropics of Discourse: Essays in Cultural Criticism,* by Hayden White. Baltimore: Johns Hopkins University Press, 1978.

Wolf, Eric. *Sons of the Shaking Earth: The People of Mexico and Guatemala—Their Land, History, and Culture.* Chicago: University of Chicago Press, 1959.

Yarbo-Bejarano, Yvonne. "The Female Subject in Chicano Theatre: Sexuality, 'Race,' and Class." In *Performing Feminisms: Feminist Critical Theory and Theatre,* edited by Sue-Ellen Case. Baltimore: Johns Hopkins University Press, 1990.

Yúdice, George. *On Edge: The Crisis of Contemporary Latin American Culture,* edited by Jean Franco and Juan Flores. Minneapolis: University of Minnesota Press, 1992.

Zamora, Lois Parkinson. "The Usable Past: The Idea of History in Modern U.S. and Latin American Fiction." In *Do the Americas Have a Common Literature?,* edited by Gustavo Pérez Firmat. Durham: Duke University Press, 1990.

———. *Writing the Apocalypse: Historical Vision in Contemporary U.S. and Latin American Fiction.* New York: Cambridge University Press, 1989.

Zea, Leopoldo. "Búsqueda de la identidad latinoamericana." *Aztlán* 12, no. 2 (1981).

Zuidema, R. T. "Una interpretacion alterna de la historia Incaica." In *Ideología Mesiánica del mundo andino,* edited by Juan M. Ossio. Lima: Edición de Ignacio Prado Pastor, 1973.

# Index

*Nueva corónica y buen gobierno* (Poma) 91–100, *94–96, 98–99, 126*

Ochún, 18
Oncoymita, 68–69
Ondegardo. *See* Polo de Ondegardo
Ordóñez, Elizabeth, 195n.72
Ortega, Eliana, 192n.10
Ortiz, Fernando, 3–6, 13, 15, 19, 21–22, 27n.44, 56, 177
  and acculturation, 3–4, 26n.7; *Contrapunteo cubano del tabaco y el azúcar,* 3–5, 16, 19, 27n.44; "counterpoint," 5–6, 17; and language, 13; postmodern reading of, 16–20; theory of transculturation, 3–6, 7, 12, 13, 14, 21–22, 26n.7, 27n.33
Otomy Indians, 75n.57

Pachacutec, 133n.23
Pachamama, 69, 82
  conflation with Virgin Mary, 68–69, 75n.57, 82, 112–19; in Cuzco School painting, 112–14
*pachucos,* 203, 214n.25
pagan elements in Christianity, 69, 70, 72n.5, 93–97, 110–11, 122, 124, 136n.64, 136n.66, 137n.100
painting
  colonial, 67, 77, 97, 135n.54 (*see also* Cuzco School; Cuzco School paintings); Inca and pre-Inca, 91
Palestrina, 5
Palm, Erwin, 134n.30
Panaca, Cult of, 119
Pané, Father Ramón, *Relación acerca de las antigue-dades de los indios,* 61
Pánfilo de Narváez, 29, 35
Pannwitz, Rudolf, 176n.101
Paredes, Raymond A., 216n.63
Park, Willard E., 44
Parra, Violeta, 199
Pastor, Beatriz, 39, 51n.3
Paz, Octavio, 24, 180–81, 182, 187–88, 192n.18, 192n.20, 197n.64, 214n.25
  *El laberinto de la soledad,* 180, 187; "Los hijos de la Malinche," 180–81
Pease, Franklin, 73n.32
Peñalosa, Fernando, 204
Pérez de Alessio, Mateo, 80
Pérez Firmat, Gustavo, 12, 13–15, 21–22, 27n.33
  *The Cuban Condition: Translation and Identity in Modern Cuban Literature,* 13, 14; *Do the Americas Have a Common Literature?,* 197

Perú, 1, 7–12, 139–71. *See also* Andes, the; acculturation, in Perú
Philip III, King, 92
Philips, Rachel, 178–79
Pizarro, 106
plantations in Cuba and the Caribbean, 4–5, 13, 16–17, 19
Platin, Christophe, 90
Platt, Tristan, 137n.90
*pochismos* (anglicisms) 203, 204, 206
*Poetics of Translation: History, Theory, Practice, The* (Barnstone), 14
Polo, Marco, 33
Polo de Ondegardo, Juan, 52n.38, 64
  *Informaciones acerca de la religión y gobierno de los Incas,* 62
Poma de Ayala, Felipe Guamán, 9, 67–68, 73n.13, 75n.47, 91–100, 102, 112, 125, 135n.58, 142
  and language, 91–92; *Nueva corónica y buen gobierno,* 91–100, *94–96, 98–99, 126;* and transculturation, 92
Portuguese Crown, 31
Portuguese language, 10
postmodernism, 16–20
Prida, Dolores, 214n.21
priests. *See* Christianization
Puerto Rican literature, 215n.54
Puga, María Luisa, 188
Pumacahua, Mateo, 102–6, *103*
Pupo-Walker, Enrique, 39, 40
Puquina language, 110

Quechua language, 9, 15
  Arguedas's use of, 140, 150–152, 154–55, 161, 165–68, 170–71, 175n.89, 203; Arriaga's use of, 60, 62, 65; Bocanegra's use of, 59–60, 65, 110; and Christianization, 15, 23, 58, 59–60, 62, 65, 73n.13, 110; in *huaynos,* 150–51; Poma's use of, 92
Quispe Tito, Diego, 80, 81, 89, 106, *107–9,* 133n.12, 138n.111

Rama, Ángel, 1, 9, 10–12, 16, 22, 24, 26n.21, 30, 52n.14, 88, 140, 142, 146, 152, 161, 172n.14, 172n.26, 175n.69
  *Transculturación narrativa en América Latina,* 9
Ramos Gavilán, Alonso, 114
Raphael (archangel), 122–24, *123,* 138n.112
Reagan, Ronald, 207
Réau, Louis, 84, 110, 122, 134n.30, 136n.66
Redfield, 3
Reformation, 124
*Relación acerca de las antiguedades de los indios* (Pané), 61